THE AMERICAN NAVAL REVOLUTION

Walter R. Herrick, Jr.

LOUISIANA STATE UNIVERSITY PRESS § BATON ROUGE

THE AMERICAN
NAVAL REVOLUTION

Copyright © 1966 by
LOUISIANA STATE UNIVERSITY PRESS

Library of Congress Catalog Card Number: 66-25974

Manufactured in the United States of America by
Thos. J. Moran's Sons, Inc., Baton Rouge

Designed by Robert L. Nance

Published with the assistance of a grant from the Ford Foundation.

ACKNOWLEDGMENTS

For the inspiration and constant encouragement that have kept me working on this study over the past four years I have to thank first of all Dean Edward Younger of the Graduate College of Arts and Sciences, University of Virginia. Others who have contributed time and effort include Professors Lionel Summers and Jack Lane of Rollins College; Master Sergeant Leroy Eure, a former member of the Air Force Observer's staff at the Naval War College; and Miss Jean Christy, currently a graduate student at the University of Georgia.

I am grateful to the president and staff of the Naval War College for their gracious cooperation during my quest for information in the college archives. Also deserving of thanks are the staffs of the Naval Historical Foundation, the U. S. Naval Institute, the Alderman Library of the University of Virginia, and the Manuscript Division of the Library of Congress.

Finally, I wish to express my gratitude to Rear Admiral E. M. Eller, USN (Retired), curator for the Navy Department, for supplying the illustrations, to Mr. Charles East and Miss June Wiley of the Louisiana State University Press for their patience and interest; and to my wife Catrina for tolerating my prolonged obsession with this work.

v

227128

CONTENTS

LIST OF ILLUSTRATIONS

following page 118

THE AMERICAN
NAVAL REVOLUTION

INTRODUCTION

"IN ANY OPERATION AND UNDER ALL CIRCUMSTANCES, A DECISIVE naval superiority is to be considered a fundamental principle and the basis upon which every hope of success must ultimately depend."[1] So stated George Washington in 1780, but more than a hundred years were to pass before his compatriots reached a similar conclusion. Although the United States has never won a war without at least temporary command of the sea, the strategic implications of naval warfare had virtually no influence on American policy prior to 1890. That year marked the onset of a revolution in doctrine which transformed the United States Navy from a loosely organized array of small coast defenders and light cruisers into a unified battle fleet of offensive capability. Within a decade, the country advanced from twelfth to sixth place among the world's naval powers. It is the purpose of the present study to examine the rationale of this sharp break from tradition, to isolate its origins, evaluate its results, and analyze the motivation of the men responsible for it.

During the early national period, a number of factors militated against strategically oriented naval expansion. For one thing, Americans had inherited from their colonial forebears a profound distrust of permanent armed forces. For another, a thrifty, isolationist public opposed heavy outlays on military establishments, relying instead on the broad Atlantic

---

1 Washington to the Count de Rochambeau (memorandum), July 15, 1780, cited in French E. Chadwick, *The New American Navy* (New York, 1915), 89.

and the delicate European power balance for safety from aggression. These views fostered confidence in the ability of a hastily improvised fleet, backed by militia, to repel invasion at the threshold.

Given the attitudes of the era, the young nation's indifference to sea power seems reasonable; but its failure to maintain even a moderate degree of preparedness thereafter is more difficult to understand, considering the experience gained in the wars punctuating American history through 1865. In each instance, the strategic initiative belonged to the contender who could, through control of the sea lanes, operate along enemy shores with impunity, form a blockade, and lend his troops the mobility of seaborne transport. Nevertheless, the principle thus demonstrated was ignored. For a quarter of a century after the Civil War, traditional policy limited the Navy's wartime mission to defense of the coast and destruction of enemy commerce, which in contemporary opinion required nothing more fearsome than a flotilla of light-draft gunboats and a squadron of seagoing raiders.

Between wars the Navy Department saved money by placing the wooden gunboats in reduced commission. The raiders were dispatched individually or in pairs to remote cruising grounds in order to show the flag overseas. This practice not only precluded formation of integrated squadrons but had the effect of dispersing what little strength the Navy possessed.[2]

The wisdom of perpetuating a peacetime navy was first questioned at mid-century. With the acquisition of Texas and Oregon in the 1840's and the conquest of California in the Mexican War, the coastline of the United States had nearly doubled in length. This, together with the emergence of the Mississippi Valley as the granary of the entire Atlantic basin, created a demand for more warships. A one-ocean fleet hardly worthy of the name could not protect two long, widely separated seaboards and at the same time patrol the shipping lanes of the Gulf of Mexico.

Venturesome businessmen strengthened the argument for naval expansion as they responded to the disappearance of the land frontier

2 See, especially, Alfred T. Mahan, *Sea Power in Its Relations to the War of 1812* (Boston, 1905), *passim;* Theodore Roosevelt, *The Naval War of 1812* (New York, 1903), *passim;* C. S. Forester, *The Age of Fighting Sail* (Garden City, N.Y., 1956), 248; H. I. Chapelle, *The History of the American Sailing Navy* (New York, 1949), 296ff.; H. F. Kraft and W. B. Norris, *Sea Power in American History* (New York, 1920), 174ff.; Chadwick, *American Navy,* 229.

with ambitious plans for extending their operations to the Far East and Latin America. New markets in these areas would absorb surplus products and, hopefully, sustain the national economy at a high enough level to insure it against the recurrence of depressions. Moreover, they reasoned, the shrinkage of distances between continents occasioned by the recent advent of fast ocean steamers would facilitate the development of overseas commercial outlets.[3]

Between 1842 and 1871, three naval expeditions to the Far East pointed up the significance of sea power to commercial expansion. In this period, Commodores Lawrence Kearney, Matthew Perry, and Robert Shufeldt alternated diplomacy with shows of force to obtain commercial privileges for the United States from the governments of China, Japan, and Korea, respectively.[4]

To capitalize on the opportunities at hand, the nation needed, in addition to a larger fleet, a shorter and safer water route to the Pacific than the tedious passage around Cape Horn. Toward the end of the first half of the century, naval strategists urged the government to build a canal across the narrow Central American isthmus, under the exclusive control and protection of the United States. But isolationist majorities in Congress rejected the proposal repeatedly despite the strategic and commercial advantages offered by such a shortcut and despite Britain's ultimate acceptance of the principle of exclusion.[5]

By 1855 Americans were becoming aware of their country's rapid approach to a position of world power. Foreign trade had reached boom proportions, immigrants were arriving in unprecedented volume, and westward migration continued undiminished while Southerners hatched

3 For recent treatments of continental and commercial expansion, see Walter La Feber, *The New Empire: An Interpretation of American Expansion* (Ithaca, N.Y., 1963), 50; Charles Vevier, "American Continentalism: An Idea of Expansion, 1845–1910," *American Historical Review*, LXV (January, 1960), 323–28, hereinafter cited as *AHR;* Thomas A. Bailey, "America's Emergence as a World Power: The Myth and the Verity," *Pacific Historical Review*, XXX (February, 1961), 8, hereinafter cited as *PHR.*

4 La Feber, *New Empire*, 5, 383; E. B. Potter and Chester Nimitz (eds.), *Sea Power: A Naval History* (Englewood Cliffs, N.J., 1961), 238ff.

5 Among the numerous accounts of early American interest in an isthmian canal are Vevier, "American Continentalism," 328; J. W. Pratt, "The Ideology of American Expansion," in Avery Craven (ed.), *Essays in Honor of William E. Dodd* (Chicago, 1935); A. T. Mahan, *The Interest of America in Sea Power, Present and Future* (Boston, 1897), *passim;* La Feber, *New Empire*, 50. For the diplomatic aspect of the project, see S. F. Bemis, *A Diplomatic History of the United States* (New York, 1965), 244–52.

schemes for founding slave states in Latin American territory which they hoped to persuade the federal government to annex.[6] The informed segment of the public, however, had reason to question the nation's ability to maintain the prestige commensurate with great-power rank. National prestige required the enforcement of positive policy by a strong naval force, the like of which the United States did not at the time possess.

The government's failure to protest British and French intervention in Latin American affairs between 1833 and 1841 had prompted misgivings about the status of the Monroe Doctrine. If, for want of adequate sea power, the United States had tolerated defiance of this fundamental element of policy in the past, it might be compelled to do so in the future with consequent loss of face. At a later date, the assurance of British friendship gave the question a different—and more humiliating—emphasis, as there arose in Washington a feeling of dependence on the Royal Navy for help in policing the Caribbean. The situation called for a reappraisal, not only of the Monroe Doctrine but also of the policy that denied the United States Navy the strength to enforce it unaided.[7]

Meanwhile, the transition in marine technology, which had originated in the last years of the Napoleonic Wars, was altering the evolution of naval design. Up to mid-century, the United States led the field in the application of new technology by introducing to naval usage the steam engine and screw propeller; at the same time the British Admiralty seemed content to allow private shipowners the costly privilege of testing such novelties. The United States fell behind after 1850, as Britain and the continental powers converted their warships to screw-driven steamers and embarked on construction programs embodying the latest materials and weapons for war at sea.

The pace of transition quickened in 1854 with the outbreak of war in the Crimea between Russia on one side and the Ottoman Empire, assisted by Anglo-French forces, on the other. In the course of the struggle, Russian shell-guns and French armor served to forecast the demise of wooden naval construction. After the war ended in 1856, European admiralties played a game of measure versus countermeasure, which the British won handily by producing the world's most efficient

6 Harold and Margaret Sprout, *The Rise of American Naval Power* (Princeton, N.J., 1946), 139–40; hereinafter cited as Sprout, *Naval Power*.
7 Kraft and Norris, *Sea Power in American History*, 175ff. Dexter Perkins, *A History of the Monroe Doctrine* (Boston, 1955), 93ff.; A. K. Weinberg, *Manifest Destiny: A Study of National Expansion* (Baltimore, 1935), 70–130, *passim*.

shell-rifle and first all iron battleship, H.M.S. *Warrior*, the heaviest and best-armed man-of-war in history.[8] By contrast, Congress limited America's growth for this period to seven wooden, unarmored gunboats.[9]

Unlike the Crimean conflict, the American Civil War acted as a deterrent on postwar naval progress in the United States, owing to the national habit of forgetting the lessons learned in war. This accounts in large measure for the failure of the policy revolution of 1890, on which this study is focused, to materialize earlier in response to the dramatic development of European fleets in the late 1850's.

Fortunately for the Union, President Lincoln's secretary of the navy, Gideon Welles, proved unexpectedly competent as director of combat operations at sea. When the war started in 1861, the Navy Department had neither a strategic plan nor the ships and men required to execute one. To overcome these deficiencies, Welles and his naval advisers hastily devised a strategy of "cautious constriction," while initiating a drive for recruits and a vast program of new construction and ship procurement.

The first phase of this plan envisaged a close blockade of the Southern ports on the Atlantic and the Gulf. Mastery of these areas would deny the Confederacy essential imports from Europe, prevent its staples from reaching their markets overseas, and deter foreign intervention. To attain the second strategic goal—occupation of the enemy's inland waters —Welles assigned small craft to patrol the sounds and inlets dotting the coast from Norfolk to Key West and formed river squadrons for duty on Midwestern streams.[10]

---

8 Sprout, *Naval Power*, 111–26; Potter and Nimitz (eds.), *Sea Power*, 232–40. The standard work for the transition in naval design is James P. Baxter, *Introduction of the Ironclad Warship* (Cambridge, Mass., 1933). See also, Michael Lewis, *History of the British Navy* (Harmondsworth, Essex, 1957), 255ff.

9 Sprout, *Naval Power*, 148. For the influence of slavery politics on President Franklin Pierce's naval policy, see Sprout, *Naval Power*, 140–48; and Pierce's messages in James D. Richardson (comp.), *A Compilation of the Messages and Papers of the Presidents, 1782–1902* (Washington, 1904), V, 198–99; hereinafter cited as *Messages and Papers*.

10 The implementation of Union naval strategy during the war may be traced in the Navy Department's *Annual Reports of the Secretaries of the Navy*, 1861–65; hereinafter cited as Navy Dept., *Annual Report(s)*. Other sources of interest include Gideon Welles, *The Diary of Gideon Welles, Secretary of the Navy under Lincoln and Johnson*, ed. J. T. Morse (New York, 1911); Alfred T. Mahan, *The Gulf and Inland Waters* (New York, 1883); *Official Records of the Union and Confederate Navies in the War of the Rebellion* (Washington, 1880–1901), hereinafter cited as *Official Records, Navies*.

Besides enlisting hundreds of raw recruits in the course of the war, Welles built up a war fleet around the tiny nucleus of twenty-six wooden steamers and sixteen tactically useless sailing craft on the Navy List of 1861. The impressment of some four hundred merchantmen, in addition to the two hundred new warships he ordered, reaffirmed the durability of the traditional reliance on improvisation in emergencies. Although this dubious custom persisted to a degree through World War II, it diminished in importance as a result of the abrupt transition to offensive doctrine in 1890. Eight years thereafter, as the nation yielded to the jingoes and the Navy prepared to engage supposedly potent Spanish forces, the department supplemented its combat-ready fleet with 128 private vessels, less than half the number procured by Secretary Welles to cope with the navy-less Confederacy![11]

The Union strategy of constriction, though sound in theory, proved difficult to sustain. In April, 1861, Lincoln's proclamation of a formal blockade, two years before the Navy had the ships to enforce it, implicitly endowed the South with belligerent rights. Hampered by the technicalities of international law thus invoked, as well by its own inadequacy, the blockade advanced slowly from port to port, unable at first to seal off more than a fraction of the enemy's coast.[12]

No sooner had the Navy mustered sufficient strength to enforce a legal blockade of the entire enemy coast than gaps appeared in the line owing to breakdowns and secondary demands on its units. Political pressure obliged Welles to detach blockaders frequently for the purpose of ferrying Unionist refugees to safety, supporting coastal military operations, or pursuing Confederate raiders, whose destruction of Union shipping had given rise to panic along the seaboard.[13] These dispersals in violation of strategic law unquestionably prolonged the conflict.

---

11 Welles, *Diary*, I, *passim*. For details about merchantmen on active naval service during the war with Spain, see F. E. Chadwick, *The Relations of the United States and Spain: The Spanish War* (New York, 1911), I, Appendix A, 404–407; hereinafter cited as *Spanish War*. The results of Welles's policy are indicated in J. R. Soley, *The Blockade and the Cruisers* (New York, 1883), 241–43; Sprout, *Naval Power*, 153–54; and Navy Dept., *Annual Reports*, 1863–65.

12 John B. Moore, *Principles of American Diplomacy* (New York, 1918), 53, 60–61. Cf. Richard S. West, Jr., *Mr. Lincoln's Navy* (New York, 1957), 57–58.

13 The effects of dispersing strength are interpreted in Alfred T. Mahan, *The Influence of Sea Power upon History* (Boston, 1890), 43–44; Welles, *Diary*, I, 134, 333, 342, 497; II, 39, 102–19. *House Executive Documents*, 39th Cong., 2nd Sess., No. 1, pp. 159–77. R. S. West, Jr., *Gideon Welles: Lincoln's Navy Department* (New York, 1943), 102ff.

Wartime testing advanced numerous weapons to, or near to, operational status, including the revolving turret, marine mine, ram, torpedo, submarine, and iron armor. Of all such innovations, the ironclad steam monitor attracted the greatest attention.[14] Perhaps overcome with enthusiasm for the capacity of these small craft for absorbing gunfire at close range, observers of actions like the historic drawn battle between the C.S.S. *Virginia* and U.S.S. *Monitor* in March, 1862, neglected to mention the conditions governing them. In every instance, the contestants fought in sheltered waters where shoal depths and close quarters favored their limited capabilities. But, as postwar maneuvers offshore indicated, the monitors' low freeboard, light draft, and lack of power reduced to zero their efficiency at sea.[15]

Inevitably, the myth of monitor invincibility and the inflated reputation of Southern raiders substantiated the traditional interpretation of the naval mission. With the return of peace, therefore, the monitors assumed the task of patrolling the shoreline, while wooden cruisers resumed their flag-showing function overseas. Although the war had revealed the ineffectiveness of these types when unsupported by a strategic force, they continued to symbolize American naval doctrine until Congress authorized construction of the country's first steel warships in 1883.[16]

In the interim, the decline of national sea power, which began with

14 *Official Records, Navies*, Ser. II, Vol. II, 67–70; Joseph T. Durkin, *Stephen R. Mallory, Confederate Navy Chief* (Chapel Hill, N.C., 1954), 3–140, *passim*. Mallory instituted the first ironclad building program of the war after his study of the Crimean War convinced him that ironclads might offset the Union's overwhelming naval superiority. For other technical developments in the period, see *Official Records, Navies*, Ser. II, Vol. I, 740–43; Navy Dept., *Annual Reports*, 1861–65; David Ammen, *The Atlantic Coast* (New York, 1889), 160ff.

15 The *Virginia* was converted to an ironclad from the hulk of the U.S.S. *Merrimac*, which had fallen into Confederate hands upon the surrender of the Norfolk Navy Yard. Defects in the *Monitor* design began to show up before the war ended; see, for instance, C. E. Macartney, *Mr. Lincoln's Admirals* (New York, 1956), 122–30; Ammen, *The Atlantic Coast*, 160–68, citing "Memoir of Admiral Dahlgren" (n.d.), 436, 552.

16 John D. Long, *The New American Navy* (New York, 1903), I, Chap. 1, *passim*. See also, Sprout, *Naval Power*, 162, 164. Long, who became William McKinley's secretary of the navy in 1897, pointed out that Gideon Welles's policy of impressing merchant vessels into naval service had reduced the size of the American merchant marine far more drastically than had the attacks of Confederate raiders. For the resumption of prewar operations, see Navy Dept., *Annual Reports*, 1866–69.

the rapid demobilization of the war fleet, continued unchecked as the government strove to adjust to reunion and industrialization. Following Welles's retirement in 1869, a succession of apathetic secretaries allowed the fleet to deteriorate as they exploited shore installations for political advantage. Nor did Congress act to replace obsolete, worn-out warships and weapons, let alone provide funds for further development of the products of Civil War technology.

These circumstances influenced the department's decision to subordinate steam power to sail and to resist the efforts of forward-looking designers to armor the cruisers with iron plate. Indeed, steam engineers found themselves downgraded by their conservative seniors of the line, who welcomed the reversion to sail and wooden hulls.

Paradoxically, the postwar period of regression marked the birth of professionalism in the service. It produced a new breed of officers inspired by the progressive ideas of Commodore Stephen B. Luce and Captain Alfred T. Mahan, whose promotion of the Naval War College fostered the study of naval warfare as a science. Founded by Luce in 1884 at Newport, Rhode Island, this institution—the first of its kind anywhere—barely survived the attacks aimed at it in infancy by anti-intellectual senior officers but ultimately won recognition as an essential naval facility.

The founding of the War College coincided with a revival of activity in the department, whose leadership had passed into competent hands as the decade opened. The three men in charge from 1880 to 1889, though neglectful of the strategic aspect of naval expansion, contributed handsomely, if haphazardly, to the enlargement and improvement of the fleet. Morever, in belated acknowledgment of the nation's growing prestige and responsibilities, Congress registered its commitment to naval rehabilitation in 1883 by providing for the construction of three steel cruisers and a dispatch vessel.

By March, 1889, when Benjamin Harrison's Republican administration took office, relatively powerful steel cruisers were replacing the iron monitors and wooden cruisers of Civil War vintage. Sail gradually yielded to steam, and at last the breech-loading steel rifle became a standard feature of shipboard armament. Despite these hopeful signs, which were reinforced by the rise of professionalism and the consequent opening of the War College, the requisites of strategy exerted no more influence on construction and design than they had a century earlier. As then, the Navy retained its defensive character as an instrument of coast defense and commerce destruction.

During the next four years, amid the crises fomented by Harrisonian imperialism in the Pacific and Caribbean, the Navy experienced an administrative revolution that discarded the entrenched ideas of the past in favor of a bold new policy grounded on strategic principles. For the first time in a period of peace, the service assumed an offensive stance.

The man directly responsible for this abrupt departure from the peace-navy tradition was Harrison's imperialist secretary of the navy, Benjamin Franklin Tracy. In appreciation of the decisive nature of Tracy's role in the development of the modern United States fleet, what may seem a disproportionately large part of this study is devoted to his steward-ship of the department.

In the fall of 1890, the secretary proposed a construction plan based on the belief he shared with Captain Mahan that a strong battle fleet, capable of destroying an enemy's main force in mid-ocean, represented the surest means of defending the coast against foreign aggression. Tracy's promotion of this theory, tempered by his own acute sense of political reality, won congressional approval of a first-rate battleship building program, without precedent in American history. Before he retired in March, 1893, Tracy not only secured funds for four capital ships designed to match the best of their type in the world, but also arranged for the practical and theoretical education required of the officers and men who would man them.

As the chapters dealing with the five years leading to the Spanish–American War suggest, Tracy's actions conditioned the process of naval expansion long after his retirement. The dictates of strategy continued to dominate warship design and professional education under the guid-ance of his successor, Hilary Abner Herbert, secretary of the navy in Cleveland's second administration. A recent convert to the doctrine of Mahan, Herbert prevailed on President Cleveland, who had moved far from the isolationist position of his first term, to endorse a battleship program. Between 1893 and 1897, Congress appropriated the where-withal for building a total of five additional capital ships—the last vessels of their type to be authorized prior to the declaration of war on Spain in late April, 1898.

The administration of William McKinley called a halt to further heavy construction as soon as he assumed the presidency in March, 1897. This decision derived from the conviction, in which his secretary, John Davis Long, concurred, that the Navy had grown strong enough to satisfy the requirements of national security. Although Long's assistant in the department, Theodore Roosevelt, did his energetic best to revive the battleship program, it remained dormant until after the war began. Roosevelt, Tracy's friend and fellow imperialist, dedicated his time and talents to preparing the Asiatic and North Atlantic Squadrons for the conflict he felt sure would come. Detractors to the contrary, Roosevelt's efforts on behalf of the Asiatic force made possible Commodore George Dewey's triumph at Manila.

The outbreak of the Spanish-American War found United States naval units deployed and ready as never before for action against enemy squadrons. And, although some of the mistakes made in the Civil War —especially the strategic error of dispersion—were repeated in the western Atlantic zone of operations, the new American Navy passed its initial test of strength by defeating a reputedly powerful Spanish fleet with remarkable ease.

At last the country possessed the strength at sea to enforce the principles of its foreign policy, as the lopsided victories at Manila and Santiago so clearly illustrated. The outcome of the "splendid little war," which served to fulfill America's new Manifest Destiny, vindicated beyond doubt the naval revolution of 1890 and attested to the accuracy of Washington's evaluation of sea power a hundred years before.

I

FROM DRIFT TO DIRECTION

With the coming of peace in 1865, after four years of civil strife, Americans turned their attention to the central topics of the day: reconstruction, industrialization, and continental expansion. As the postwar era began, therefore, such a peripheral matter as naval progress held little popular appeal.

True, the general preoccupation with internal affairs did not deter Secretary of State William Seward from negotiating the purchase of Alaska, raising the Stars and Stripes over Midway, and concluding a treaty of reciprocity with Hawaii—all in a period of less than twelve months.[1] But, in a sense, Seward's imperialist actions proved premature; America was not yet ready for empire-building or for acquiring its primary instrument—superior strength at sea.

For a number of reasons, apart from the domestic problems attending the process of reunion, sea power seemed less important than it once had. The shrinkage of the merchant marine, occasioned by Gideon Welles's impressment of four hundred vessels for wartime service, lessened the demand for protection of seaborne commerce; and the extinction of Southern hopes of annexing Latin American territory deprived the navalists of a second element of support. These circumstances, in addition to the prevailing war-weariness, changed the outlook of many former big-navy enthusiasts and drove them into the isolationist camp.

---

1 An analytical account of Seward's imperialistic transactions appears in La Feber, *New Empire*, 24–32.

Moreover, between 1865 and 1869 the postwar reaction against all things military hastened the demobilization of the existing fleet.

Consequently, the last four years of his term found Secretary Welles presiding over the dissolution of the force he had worked so hard to create. By March, 1869, when he retired, the Navy had reverted to prewar practices which negated most of the technological gains made under combat conditions.[2]

When the Navy Department returned to a peace footing, Gustavus Vasa Fox, who had served as Welles's assistant since 1861, devised a system of defense that contradicted the lessons of the Civil War. Recommending the construction of fast wooden commerce-destroyers for offshore operations, to be complemented by a flotilla of light-draft monitors on inshore patrols, Fox's plan amounted to an updated version of the policy that had limited American naval growth from the beginning. Nevertheless, the department acquiesced, heedless of the lack of high-powered ordnance on which the success of the program would depend.[3]

In the execution of Fox's ideas, the department turned the clock back further. Bowing to the opinion of professional advisers, Secretary Welles again violated the cardinal law of naval strategy by spreading the best of his units thin among widely separated stations overseas.[4] As a result, the Navy could neither concentrate the striking power required of an effective fighting force nor provide its personnel with essential training in tactical doctrine for squadron evolutions.[5]

The resumption of the flag-showing mission encouraged Old Navy seniors to press for the retention of sail as the main motive power on ships so assigned. Since this duty consisted largely of lengthy cruises in foreign waters, argued the conservatives, wooden vessels under canvas could discharge it just as competently and more economically than costly, coal-eating iron steamers. Sail power alone would furnish the cruising range necessary to American men-of-war on extensive voyages in areas where there were no facilities for refueling them. Besides, concluded

2 Navy Dept., *Annual Report*, 1865, 1869. By the latter year, only fifty warships remained in commission, most of them obsolete.

3 *Ibid.*, 1866–68; Ammen, *Atlantic Coast*, 160ff.; *Army and Navy Journal* (New York), December 7, 1889. For arguments favoring Fox's formula, see the remarks of Senator James G. Blaine in *Congressional Record*, 45th Cong., 3rd Sess., 627–29; and others of Representative H. Clymer in *ibid.*, 2nd Sess., 1, 956.

4 Navy Dept., *Annual Report*, 1865, 1866; *Naval Power*, 166ff.

5 A. T. Mahan, *From Sail to Steam: Recollections of Naval Life* (New York, 1908), I, 270.

the older officers, steam engines had yet to prove themselves dependable enough on sustained runs to be used for anything other than auxiliary purposes, despite their successful recent performance under fire.[6]

Reactionary as the step back to sail appears in retrospect, it appealed to the service hierarchy at a time when the United States stood in no danger of an attack from abroad and when neither Congress nor the public wished to invest in the questionable luxury of a battle fleet. From this standpoint, the return to sail seemed logical.

On the other hand, the renewed reliance on full canvas rigs not only subordinated steam power but also produced harmful side effects which progressives feared might delay indefinitely the modernization of the Navy. Gun stations, for instance, had to be modified in such fashion as to be kept clear of booms and rigging; otherwise such paraphernalia would hamper the servicing of guns. In another move to insure the primacy of sail, the department ordered hulls and propellers tailored to specifications which would permit higher speed under canvas. Finally, the bureau chiefs dealt engineers a mortal blow when they reduced the capacity of boilers for the sake of increasing storage space, at the expense of tactical mobility under steam power.[7]

The conservative men of the Old Navy found a temporary champion in Vice-Admiral David D. Porter, who took charge of the department in 1869 at the behest of his former comrade-in-arms, President Ulysses S. Grant. Desiring to reward Adolph E. Borie, an elderly Philadelphia merchant, for his contribution to the Union League, Grant appointed Borie to relieve Welles and informed the merchant that Porter would have actual control of naval affairs. As Borie confided to a friend, "The Department is managed by Porter; I am only a figurehead." [8]

To the gratification of veterans of marlinespike seamanship, Porter set out at once to remove from the department certain key men bent on the elimination of sailing rigs from warships. The first to go was naval architect John Lenthall, for seventeen years chief of the Bureau of Construction. Once a student of master designer Samuel Humphreys, Lenthall had drafted the plans for the wooden steamers that maintained

6 *Ibid.*; Navy Dept., *Annual Report*, 1869.

7 For further discussion of these modifications and their effects, see Sprout, *Naval Power*, 167–68; Walter Millis, *Arms and Men* (New York, 1956), 133–34.

8 Quoted in G. S. Boutwell, *Reminiscences of Sixty Years in Public Affairs* (New York, 1902), II, 212. A sketch of Borie's life appears in *Dictionary of American Biography*, II, 464; hereinafter cited as *DAB*.

the Union blockade. Porter then detached Benjamin F. Isherwood from
to Bureau of Steam Engineering.[9] During his ten-year tenure as chief
engineer, this former railroader had completed a book which revolu-
tionized steam theory and which—like Captain Mahan's masterpiece—
was translated into six languages. Isherwood, too, had figured promi-
nently in the Union's wartime construction program. Toward the end
of the Civil War, the chief engineer had initiated tests of swift hulls
driven by high-powered steam engines in which Porter and his colleagues had no confidence. Consequently, when Isherwood announced
in 1868 the readiness of the first of his experimental sloops-of-war for
acceptance trials, her rejection was foreordained.[10] This craft, the U.S.S.
Wampanoag, sustained a speed of 16.6 knots throughout her trial and
reached a maximum rate of 17.7 on one leg of the run—a record previously unequalled by any steamer, naval or merchant. Nevertheless, the
trial board, headed by Rear Admiral L. M. Goldsborough, disapproved
the sloop.

The conservative attitude, as applied to the rejection of the *Wampanoag*, not to mention the dismissal of Lenthall and Isherwood, must—
like the reversion to sail—be judged in terms of contemporary opinion.
The condemnation of the *Wampanoag* by the Goldsborough Board was
not so absurd as hindsight renders it. Members of the board felt obliged
to save money wherever possible; and though a few may have vetoed
the sloop to prolong the age of sail, the majority undoubtedly acted on
the conviction that the national situation did not justify the costly maintenance of such a powerful vessel.

Similarly, Admiral Porter's dismissal of the department's two outstanding technicians did not appear exceptional at a time when the life
of the entire engineering corps was endangered by the postwar reduction
in personnel and the coincidental downgrading of steam engines.[11] He
singled out Lenthall and Isherwood for detachment because he considered them visionaries, whose imaginative theory of coast defense by
means of an armada of iron-hulled, steam battleships might, if given free
rein, prove both divisive and expensive.[12]

9 Sprout, *Naval Power*, 178; F. M. Bennett, *The Steam Navy of the United
States* (Pittsburgh, 1896), 608. Biographical sketches of Lenthall and Isherwood are
included in *DAB*, XI, 173, and IX, 515, respectively.

10 Navy Dept., *Annual Report*, 1868; Bennett, *Steam Navy*, Chap. 29.

11 *House Executive Documents*, 41st Cong., 2nd Sess., No. 1, p. 145; Navy Dept.,
Annual Report, 1869. For insight into Porter's character, see J. R. Soley, *Admiral
Porter* (New York, 1913), 460ff.

12 Navy Dept., *Memorandum to the Secretary*, March 17, 1892.

Porter's campaign to weed out opposition to sail did not stop with his purge of the bureaus. Conforming to the congressional program of military retrenchment, the admiral revised regulations to the effect of requiring warship commanders to log in red ink every ton of coal consumed and to pay fines for incurring unauthorized fuel bills! [13] The naval economy drive also accounted in large measure for the revival of interest in wooden construction. Officers, who believed as Fox did that well-armed wooden raiders of high speed could attack enemy shipping at long range and evade hostile ironclads, saw no necessity for costly iron hulls. Their reasoning implied a reliance on modern ordnance and machinery not yet available to the Navy. Although European fleets were converting to long-range, breech-loading rifles, American men-of-war still mounted short-range smoothbores.[14] As for evasive action at high speed, the fate of the *Wampanoag* had ruled out the powerful engines essential for the execution of the tactic.

The department's reluctance to test innovations in naval design, equipment, and material stemmed partly from congressional parsimony and partly from the advice of American observers in Europe to play a waiting game. In view of the rapid obsolescence of warships, they thought it wiser for the time being to let foreign powers take the initiative and foot the bill for experimentation. The money thus saved could be banked against the day when the nation felt ready to build a battle fleet—a suggestion which appealed to both isolationists and other economy-minded politicians.

Neither the politicians nor the conservative sailormen had any cause for alarm in June, 1869, when President Grant named George M. Robeson to replace Borie as secretary of the navy. This action, which ended Porter's personal control of the department but not his influence on it, marked the onset of eleven dark years for the Navy—a period in which the service would stagnate for want of competent direction.[15]

The affable Robeson, a Republican politico and lobbyist, neglected naval business for his own affairs and was quick to make political capital out of the navy yards. Determined to provide jobs for the party's faithful, the new secretary contrived a method of financing the reconditioning of useless hulks by diverting funds earmarked for legitimate repairs. This questionable practice, which kept the yards filled with

13 Navy Dept., *Regulations for the Government of the Navy*, 1870, pp. 24–40.
14 See D. W. Mitchell, *History of the Modern American Navy* (New York, 1946), 9; hereinafter cited as Mitchell, *Modern Navy*.
15 See sketch of Robeson in *DAB*, XVI, 31.

Republican workmen, culminated in a congressional investigation.[16]

Throughout his long tour in the department, Robeson expressed satisfaction with the condition of the Navy. As soon as the hitherto conservative Porter, who succeeded David G. Farragut as senior admiral in December, 1870, realized that the secretary was either unable or unwilling to face the truth and attempt to remedy the deterioration of the fleet, he assumed the role of a relatively progressive reformer. Whatever the primary cause of the waning of Porter's conservatism, his association with Commodore Luce certainly hastened it. Luce and the admiral were old friends; they had cruised as shipmates and served together at the Naval Academy, the former as Commandant of Midshipmen, the latter as Superintendent. The influence of Luce, who converted Porter first to the ironclad persuasion and later to the cause of the Naval War College, counted heavily in the admiral's transformation.[17]

In 1871, Porter handed a report to Secretary Robeson which indicated the alarmingly weak position of the United States among the world's maritime powers. The Navy List for that year, stated the admiral, showed only twenty-nine serviceable warships, as against twenty-two in 1829 and forty-six in 1853. The nation ranked eighth in ironclad strength, after Brazil and Holland. France led with sixty-nine, Britain placed second with sixty-three, while Robeson's fleet boasted fourteen overage monitors. As to personnel, Porter praised American officers but deplored the inferior quality of enlisted men, many of whom were foreign born and ignorant of English. Declaring that "an officer can hardly take pride in commanding a ship manned by such cosmopolitans," he proposed the formation of a pool of American boys for furnishing seamen in the future.[18]

The admiral's warning failed to ruffle Robeson. Although the secretary admitted in his final report that the Navy could not compare "in number or character of vessels with the expensive establishments" of

16 *House Miscellaneous Documents*, 44th Cong., 1st Sess., No. 170; Long, *New Navy*, I, Chap. 1. Robeson had found it impossible to secure funds for new construction from a House dominated by Democrats.

17 Albert Gleaves, *The Life and Letters of Rear Admiral Stephen B. Luce* (New York, 1925), 137.

18 *Ibid.;* Navy Dept., "Report of the Admiral of the Navy," *Annual Report*, 1871. See also, Luce-Porter correspondence in the Naval Historical Foundation Collection, Division of Manuscripts, Library of Congress; hereinafter cited as NHF. The idea of creating such a pool of boys originated in the fertile mind of Commodore Luce.

Europe, he judged the existing fleet adequate to the defense of "a peaceful people . . . separated from warlike naval powers" by 3,000 miles of ocean.[19] Indeed, when Robeson retired in 1877, the prospect of peace in Europe seemed bright enough to preclude naval expansion. Napoleon III, heeding President Grant's warning not to compound his violation of the Monroe Doctrine, had withdrawn French troops from Mexico a decade earlier. And since 1871, the problems of paying an indemnity to Prussia and creating the Third Republic had fully absorbed France. The danger of an Anglo-American clash had subsided with the peaceful arbitration of the *Alabama* claims in 1872, and the threat of German and Japanese naval might had yet to materialize.[20]

On the other hand, the same period produced a series of events in the western hemisphere tending to revive interest in upgrading American sea power. In 1873, a Spanish warship intercepted the steamer *Virginius*, which was falsely flying the Stars and Stripes and carrying a company of Cuban filibusters. The consequences of the ship's seizure gave rise to a crisis of such gravity as to compel the department to concentrate a fleet, with Admiral Porter in command, at Key West. The amicable settlement of the matter by Secretary of State Hamilton Fish came as a great relief to naval officers facing the suicidal alternative of engaging modern Spanish cruisers with oboslete monitors.[21] Six years thereafter the War of the Pacific broke out, with Chile contesting the combined arms of Peru and Bolivia. American observers, taking note of the warships involved in the struggle, informed the department that three recently designed Chilean cruisers outclassed the most effective United States man-of-war afloat.[22]

Meanwhile, the operations in Colombia of Ferdinand de Lesseps, builder of the Suez Canal, implied completion of his plan to construct an interocean waterway across the Panamanian Isthmus. Disregarding the terms of the Clayton-Bulwer Treaty of 1850, President Rutherford Hayes reacted to the inference of French domination of a transisthmian canal by reasserting the principle of sole American control of any project of this nature and by pressing the Colombian government for

19 Navy Dept., *Annual Report*, 1877.
20 Long, *New Navy*, Chap. 1.
21 Potter and Nimitz (eds.), *Sea Power*, 343; J. R. Soley, *Porter*, 466.
22 Navy Dept., "Report of the Admiral," *Annual Report*, 1871; D. E. Worcester, "Naval Strategy in the War of the Pacific," *Journal of Inter-American Studies*, V (January, 1963), 37.

cooperation. But, though Hayes stationed warships of the Pacific Squadron in the area between Panama and the prospective site of an American canal in Nicaragua, Colombia refused to comply.[23]

The man in charge of naval administration while these developments were pointing up the country's weakness on the sea was Colonel Richard W. Thompson, who had succeeded Secretary Robeson in 1877. Hayes's choice of the colonel was apparently dictated entirely by political expediency and is considered the only bad appointment he made.[24] Even Thompson's sympathetic biographer, who credits him with eliminating Robeson's extravagances, admits that his man was obsessed with private business and out of touch with naval affairs.[25]

In the opinion of Finley Peter Dunne, better known as Mr. Dooley, the first qualification of a secretary of the navy was that he must never have seen salt water outside of a pork barrel.[26] Thompson met this standard; his ignorance of all things nautical added the problem of semantics to intradepartmental communications. Besides, his lobbying activities on behalf of railroad companies left him little time for learning about the Navy. In spite of the implications of the alarms in Latin America, the combination of a secretary with "no taste for executive work" and a divided Congress trying to cope with a depression raised the odds against naval expansion in the immediate future.[27]

Following the settlement of the *Virginius* incident in 1873, Admiral Porter relinquished his command at Key West and returned to the department where he was appointed head of the Board of Inspection. From this point of vantage, the admiral submitted a report of naval conditions in 1878. He advised Thompson of the worsening plight of the fleet, warning him that only thirty-three cruisers, thirteen monitors, and two gunboats were capable of active service. Repeating the warning two years later, Porter notified the secretary that the United States had by then dropped to twelfth rank in ironclad strength—below China and Chile.[28]

These statistics made no impression on Thompson, who preferred

23 *Messages and Papers*, VII, 585–86; Potter and Nimitz (eds.), *Sea Power*, 343; La Feber, *New Empire*, 43.
24 Charles Roll, *Colonel Dick Thompson* (Indianapolis, 1948), 1–3, 11–12; E. P. Oberholtzer, *History of the United States since the Civil War* (New York, 1919–37), IV, Chap. 25, *passim*.
25 Roll, *Thompson*, 240–41.
26 Sprout, *Naval Power*, 181n.
27 *Ibid.*, 181; Roll, *Thompson*, 250.
28 Navy Dept., "Report of the Admiral," *Annual Report*, 1880; J. R. Soley, *Porter*, 463.

restoring the merchant marine to emulating European admiralties by building battleships whose effectiveness in combat he doubted.[29] Furthermore, the colonel announced to Hayes toward the end of 1880 that he had accepted the chairmanship of De Lesseps' Panama Canal Company, apparently unaware of the inherent conflict of interest with his naval post, not to mention his country's canal policy. In December Hayes made his official comment on the secretary's decision, whereupon Thompson resigned from the cabinet.[30]

Despite the inertia that characterized the eleven-year period of naval development after 1869, there were a few instances of forward movement. Luce and a group of progressive colleagues took the first step in promoting professional *expertise* in 1873 by founding the Naval Institute, whose *Proceedings* have ever since provided a medium for the airing and exchange of ideas submitted by naval writers.[31] Articles in the early issues set forth the attitudes of officers discouraged by the sad state of the Navy. As a lieutenant wrote in 1878: "For many years we have . . . remained . . . idle because the art of building ships was making such rapid strides that it was out of the question for us, with our small appropriations, to keep pace with European nations, and because we felt that it was just as well to save our money and remain observers. . . ."[32] Another junior dwelt on the nation's dependence on improvisation: "The public has become . . . possessed of the idea that it will always be possible to improvise a navy when war threatens. In times of peace hardly anything more is necessary than a few officers keep alive the germs of naval knowledge, much as monks did of letters in the Middle Ages."[33]

Most officers of the era felt the Navy should be strengthened but, as their writings suggest, they differed not only on the proper purpose, size, and organization of an enlarged fleet, but even on the features and dimensions of its components. Conflict was inevitable owing to the speed of the European naval transition, which these men had to watch from the sidelines; but it worked against the creation of congressional sympathy for naval projects.[34]

One of the liveliest exchanges of the decade followed the maneuvers

29 Navy Dept., "Report of the Admiral," *Annual Report,* 1878.
30 Roll, *Thompson,* 256.
31 U.S. Naval Institute *Proceedings,* I (1874), 1–16; hereinafter cited as *NIP.* George T. Davis, *A Navy Second to None* (New York, 1940), 16–18.
32 Lt. J. C. Soley, "On a Proposed Type of Cruiser," *NIP,* IV, Pt. 2 (1878), 126.
33 Lt. Frederick Collins, "Naval Affairs," *NIP,* V (1879), 166.
34 See related titles appearing in *NIP,* 1874–80.

of the "United Fleets" held off Key West in 1874 under the supervision of Rear Admiral A. L. Case and his chief of staff, Commodore Foxhall Parker. The exercises removed all doubt as to the tactical ignorance of American officers and the unfitness of their ships for offensive operations. As Parker lamented: "The vessels . . . were in no respect worthy of a great nation . . . for what could be more painful . . . than to see a fleet armed with smooth-bore guns, requiring close quarters for their development, moving at . . . four-and-a-half knots? What inferior force could it overtake or what superior one escape from. . . ?"[35] Subsequently, Parker presented his prescription for a suitable fleet. He proposed a balanced, seagoing force of medium size, made up of rams, torpedo-boats, commerce raiders, and "artillery vessels" equipped with high-powered engines and auxiliary sailing rigs. Above all, declared the commodore prophetically, the whole must be "a unit of force acting under one head."[36]

In the same year, a senior ordnance officer urged the department to adopt breech-loading rifles. Rifled barrels furnished higher velocity and deeper target penetration than smoothbores could, while guns equipped for loading at the breech required less space than the old muzzle-loaders, which had to be run back until their mouths lay even with the ship's rail. Also, slower powder could be used in rifles, making them safer to handle.[37]

The department was not wholly deaf to the suggestions of officers groping, however obliquely, for solutions to the Navy's problems, nor did it ignore technological advances in Europe. The Bureau of Navigation sent Chief Engineer J. W. King abroad in 1875 to assess the changes taking place in foreign fleets. On his return, King urged experimentation at any cost, especially with compound steam engines which he felt should replace single-cylinder plants for greater efficiency.[38]

But the funds to pay for experiments lay no nearer at hand than did the appropriations for building replacements needed to stem the decline of American sea power. Only once since the end of the Civil

35 Commodore F. A. Parker, "Our Fleet Maneuvers in the Bay of Florida, and the Navy of the Future," *NIP*, I (1874), 169.

36 *Ibid.*, 174. The department formed the Navy's first "squadron of evolution" fifteen years after Parker made this proposal.

37 Capt. W. N. Jeffers, "The Armament of Our Ships of War," *NIP*, I (1874), 119–20.

38 Navy Dept., *Annual Report*, 1876; Davis, *Second to None*, 18. King's report appeared in book form in 1877, titled *Warships and Navies of the World* (Washington, D.C.).

War had Congress authorized new construction. In 1873, to offset the publicity given the Navy's plight by the investigation of Robeson, congressmen had voted to build four wooden cruisers, three monitors, and one iron-hulled cruiser, the *Trenton*.

Commissioned in 1879, the 3,900-ton *Trenton* mounted thirteen 8-inch converted rifles and two Gatling guns, and had one compound steam engine designed to deliver a top speed of 14 knots. Rigged as a full brig and fitted with a ram bow, the cruiser resembled an unarmored commerce raider. Though rated the strongest warship in American service, the *Trenton* was no match in speed or firepower for her counterparts in foreign fleets, not to mention their battleships.[39]

As the decade ended, even the conservatives were beginning to see the urgency of acquiring a battle force which could engage, with some chance of success, armored squadrons of the type currently operating under the ensigns of Britain, France, and Russia. With this change of heart came fresh complaints of the defects in monitor design. When the department adopted Parker's tactical doctrine, Commodore Luce pointed out that monitors could not carry out the new line-of-battle evolution, which necessitated rapid maneuvering from a line abreast to steaming in column or echelon.[40]

By 1881, therefore, experienced seamen had taken traditional policy under fire. None of their ideas were as advanced as those of Lenthall and Isherwood, nor had any of them presented a comprehensive program of expansion along strategic lines. The spirit was willing, nevertheless; and professional determination to build up the fleet added to the pressure on Congress for larger appropriations. By dramatizing the *Virginius* affair, the rise of Chilean sea power, and the prospect of a French-owned canal in Panama, the writings of naval officers in the 1870's had popularized the demand for a battle fleet.

When James Garfield entered the White House in March, 1881, the tide was turning toward naval expansion. The public favored a positive foreign policy and had come to realize that its enforcement required more and better warships. Related to this realization was the growing need for overseas markets created by the 200 per cent increase in the volume of exports over the past decade. Moreover, an international race for commercial supremacy appeared imminent; in naval opinion, this

39 Navy Dept., *Annual Report*, 1873, 1879; Potter and Nimitz (eds.), *Sea Power*, 343; G. W. Baird, "The U.S. Ship Trenton," *NIP*, IV, Pt. 1 (1878), 5–20; J. C. Soley, "Proposed Type of Cruiser," 126ff.
40 Commodore S. B. Luce, "Fleets of the World," *NIP*, III (1877), 20.

competition would surely become a struggle for survival in which sea power would prove decisive.[41]

Political circumstances also supported the navalist cause. With Garfield in the presidency and Republicans dominating Congress, naval expansion became a concrete—and respectable—goal. Leaders of both parties were now committed to the attainment of this objective, and the means of financing it lay in the treasury's surplus of $100,000,000. [42] Use of this money for naval purposes would appeal to protectionists, who opposed reducing an idle surplus by lowering the tariff.[43] Additional arguments for enlarging the Navy were voiced by congressmen eager to rebuild the merchant marine in hopes of securing a greater share of the world's carrying trade.[44]

Although the United States had not yet become fully involved in the burgeoning rivalry among imperialist states for overseas possessions, the recent proclamation of a protectorate over Pago Pago signified the nation's aspirations to power on the Pacific.[45] Not that isolationism was dead; the posture of defense remained so firmly entrenched that most officers continued to think in terms of a peace navy.[46] But American imperialists, though few in number at the time, were winning recruits by linking their ideology to democracy and humanitarianism and by stretching Darwinism to support the thesis that national survival depended wholly on armed might. For this was the era of Bismarckian statecraft, when the ideas of *Blut und Eisen* and *Realpolitik* were enticing the statesmen and militarists of the Western world. Admiral Porter, for instance, spoke of an unarmed America as a "soul-less machine"; and Cleveland's first secretary of the navy, William C. Whitney, observed that lack of armament "denotes the decadence of a country." [47]

The theory of right-through-might was taking hold in the United States when President Garfield posted to the Navy Department a

41 Robert Seager, "Ten Years before Mahan: The Unofficial Case for the New Navy," *Mississippi Valley Historical Review*, XL (December, 1953), 497; hereinafter cited as *MVHR*.

42 Sprout, *Naval Power*, Chap. 12, *passim*.

43 *Journal of the Iron and Steel Institute* (1881), cited in *NIP*, VIII (1882), 269.

44 Henry Hall, "American Shipping," *Atlantic Monthly* (February, 1881), 162.

45 Davis, *Second to None*, 33. For the Shufeldt story, see Russell Smith, "Robert W. Shufeldt" (M.A. thesis, University of Virginia, 1956), *passim*.

46 The durability of this conception is indicated by the number of pertinent articles written for *NIP* from 1880 to 1889.

47 Navy Dept., *Annual Report*, 1887, especially "Report of the Admiral" therein.

former associate judge of the federal court of claims, William Henry
Hunt of New Orleans.[48] Appointed to give the South representation
in the cabinet, Hunt acted swiftly to prevent further naval degenera-
tion. At Admiral Porter's suggestion, he formed the first Advisory Board
"under no authority granted by Congress" to acquaint him with the
needs of the Navy, which Porter likened to a Chinese fort on which
"dragons were painted to frighten the enemy away." [49] With the help
of his "naval assistants," as Porter referred to the members of the board,
Hunt started a drive for the promotion of new construction. Shortly
after Garfield's assassination, he informed President Chester Arthur of
the paucity and obsolescence of existing warships. Arthur conveyed the
information to Congress in a message which he concluded by declaring:
"Every condition of national safety, economy, and honor demands a
thorough rehabilitation of the Navy." [50]

Thus prompted, Congress appointed Admiral John Rodgers head of
a statutory advisory board of fifteen line officers and constructors with
instructions to determine the size and composition of a suitable fleet
and to recommend equipment and hull material for its units. Cooperating
with the Rodgers board to the extent of his authority, Hunt went before
the House Naval Committee to plead for endorsement of the forthcoming proposals.[51]

At length Commander Robley Evans, secretary of the board, submitted a report of its findings which reflected the ambivalence of
officers trapped between rapid technological progress on the one hand
and the frugality of Congress on the other. Most of the members concurred in a proposal to add eighteen unarmored steel cruisers, twenty
wooden cruisers, ten torpedo-boats, and five rams—to be built as soon
as possible. For the next eight years, they recommended a phased program calling for a total of ninety-one more cruisers—twenty-one of them
armored—and twenty-five additional torpedo-boats.[52]

Although the findings of the Rodgers board by no means represented
a departure from peace-navy policy, it was certainly the most compre-

48 Thomas Hunt, *The Life of William H. Hunt* (Brattleboro, Vt., 1922), 250ff.;
see also, sketch of White in *DAB*, IX, 369.
49 Livingston Hunt, "Founder of the New Navy," *NIP*, XXXI (1905), 173-99;
Navy Dept., *Annual Report*, 1881, especially "Report of the Advisory Board" and
"Report of the Admiral."
50 *Messages and Papers*, IX, 463.
51 Long, *New Navy*, I, 16.
52 Navy Dept., *Annual Report*, 1881. Interpretations of the report of the Rodgers
board may be found in Sprout, *Naval Power*, 199; and Mitchell, *Modern Navy*, 11.

hensive plan yet to appear. One of its provisions especially—the choice of steel for some hulls and wood for others—perplexed many officers at first. John Davis Long, who later served as secretary in William McKinley's administration during the war with Spain, attributed the board's decision in this instance to the majority's desire to foster the growth of the domestic steel industry. Considering the industry's promising production figures for 1881, Long's interpretation is questionable. American plants produced 29 per cent of the world's total steel output for that year and led the British in the production of Bessemer steel.[53] The relatively small amount required for the ships proposed by the board would have affected the steel industry hardly at all.

For some time before the board convened, naval designers had shown interest in steel. As Chief Engineer E. D. Robie pointed out, though steel cost 20 per cent more than iron, it weighed that much less. He rejected the argument that domestic plants lacked the facilities and techniques to supply the Navy with steel of high quality by drawing attention to the million or more tons of steel rail they had turned out in the preceding year. American mills, declared Robie, would be able to furnish steel up to naval specifications as soon as the demand for it existed. And, since steel executives were encouraging the application of their product to shipbuilding, that day was approaching.[54]

Referring to the wholesale use of steel in British yards, Robie predicted that the department could soon buy steel as cheaply as iron. The successful trials of Argentina's armored corvette *Almirante Brown*, history's first all steel man-of-war, had demonstrated the fitness of that metal for naval construction. Furthermore, concluded Robie, the rewarding experience of the Cunard line with steel-hulled passenger ships had long since proved that steel was not only stronger and more buoyant than iron, but less liable to fouling as well.[55]

The omission of armored vessels in the first phase of the Rodgers board's program had no bearing on the iron-versus-steel issue since domestic mills for producing steel armor were not in operation prior to 1890. Besides, recent British tests had confirmed the utility of iron

53 Long, *New Navy*, I, 20–47; Bureau of the Census, *Historical Statistics of the United States, 1789–1945* (Washington, 1946), 187; E. C. Kirkland, *Industry Comes of Age* (New York, 1961), 280–86.
54 *Journal of the Iron and Steel Institute* (1881); E. D. Robie, "Discussion of Iron and Steel in the Construction of Vessels of War," *NIP*, VIII (1882), 168.
55 Robie, "Discussion of Iron and Steel," 162.

plate when placed at an angle. As the board's critics stated, the cruisers could be armored with angled iron plate, if desired.[56]

According to one member of the board, Lieutenant E. W. Very, the majority adhered to the traditional policy of using monitors for coast defense and unarmored cruisers for commerce destruction, while the minority, led by Lenthall and Isherwood, dissented on the grounds that these types were inadequate to the missions contemplated. Unarmored raiders could not be "considered as fighting machines" because they would be forced to "fly the presence of all foreign ironclads." [57] This opinion appeared in an appendix to the report, which recognized the necessity of armored warships "in the future" but explained that they had been left out of the first stage of the plan in deference to an economy-minded Congress.[58] Thus it seems that the decision of the majority denoted something more than blind loyalty to the peace-navy tradition.

Chairman Benjamin Harris of the House Naval Committee, after reading the report, "interrogated members individually" and "examined the ship-builders . . . and many naval officers." [59] His inquiries led him to conclude that the board's recommendations were both extravagant and politically explosive. In addition, Harris inferred from them a tacit censure of Congress for failing to enlarge the Navy beforehand.[60]

The House Committee reduced the array of warships proposed to six cruisers and a ram. Subsequently, owing to "a political difference between two committees of the House," this number was cut to two steel cruisers, which Congress authorized in August, 1882, without appropriating funds for building them.[61]

The Act of 1882 also established a second statutory advisory board composed of a president, five officers, and two civilian experts, only one of whom had served on the Rodgers board. To preside, Congress

56 *Army and Navy Journal* (October 29, 1881); "Discussion," *NIP*, VIII (1882), 454–55.
57 E. W. Very, "Prize Essay Discussion," *NIP*, VIII (1882), 454.
58 Navy Dept., "Report of the Naval Advisory Board," *Annual Report*, 1882.
59 F. T. Bowles, "Our New Cruisers," *NIP*, IX (1883), 596. Bowles was at the time an assistant naval constructor.
60 Sprout, *Naval Power*, 195.
61 Bowles, "Our New Cruisers," 596–97. The author was assisting Evans with the board's secretarial work. See also, Navy Dept., *Annual Report*, 1882; Russell Smith, "Shufeldt," 41.

selected Commodore Robert W. Shufeldt, who in the preceding year had concluded the agreement that opened Korean seaports to American shipping. Organized in November, the Shufeldt board applied the art of the possible to its deliberations and submitted a modest request for four steel cruisers and a dispatch vessel. Congress eliminated one of the cruisers, and the request became law in 1883. [62]

Meanwhile, Secretary Hunt's tenure in the department had ended abruptly. During his brief career as secretary, he had accomplished a number of improvements besides creating, on his own initiative, the board which began the work of modernizing the Navy. Second in importance was his successful move to harmonize the relations of the department with Congress, as well as those of the bureau chiefs with their civilian superior. Hunt had the foresight to found the Office of Naval Intelligence and to station naval attachés at American legations in principal capital cities the world over. He deserves credit also for redefining in specific terms the jurisdiction of each of the department's eight bureaus.

Despite Hunt's substantial record of achievement as secretary, President Arthur removed him from office on April 7, 1882, and assigned him to a diplomatic post in St. Petersburg, Russia. Although Arthur had consistently endorsed his secretary's actions and engineered his transfer to Russia for political reasons only, Hunt regarded it as a dismissal which he resented for the rest of his life.[63]

As Congress was beginning to debate the proposals of the Shufeldt board, William Eaton Chandler, a prominent New Hampshire Republican, replaced Hunt. A controversial figure, Chandler has been variously described as "the father of the modern Navy," the "stormy petrel of politics," and a "hack politician." Professor E. P. Oberholtzer, an authority on politics of the Gilded Age of American history, judges him "a not unfitting successor" to George Robeson, whose "amenability had made him incompetent to hold a great office of trust. Chandler, on the other hand, was a stirring, intelligent, and cunning leader." [64]

The new secretary, who had served as Lincoln's advocate of the navy and later as Andrew Johnson's secretary of the treasury, won his party's esteem for counseling the Florida electors in the disputed election of 1876. Four years thereafter, he became James G. Blaine's floor manager

62 Russell Smith, "Shufeldt," 42ff.; Navy Dept., *Annual Report*, 1884.
63 Navy Dept., *Annual Report*, 1882; T. Hunt, *Hunt*, 218–40; G. F. Howe, *Chester A. Arthur* (New York, 1934), 232ff; *Messages and Papers*, VIII, 51–52.
64 Oberholtzer, *U.S. since the Civil War*, IV, 346.

at the Republican national convention where, with Blaine's consent, he shifted his support at the last minute to James Garfield. President Arthur, wishing to acknowledge his gratitude to Blaine, placed Chandler in the cabinet.[65]

The aforementioned Navy Act of 1883, for which Chandler was largely responsible, gave birth to the nation's first steel warships: the protected cruisers *Atlanta, Boston,* and *Chicago,* and the dispatch boat *Dolphin.*[66] Popularly known as the "ABCD's," these ships formed the nucleus of the White Squadron. Numerous obstacles hindered their construction. Never before had an American mill rolled steel for hull plates, nor had a vessel ever been built of domestic steel.[67] Shipbuilders lacked skill in the application of the material, and foundries were unused to forging steel for heavy guns.[68] Needless to say, bureaucratic jealousies did not help matters.

Consequently, the secretary faced a difficult task in providing for the construction of the ABCD's and furnishing them with the latest products of technology. At the time, few United States men-of-war boasted compound engines; and even fewer carried modern steel rifles. Until the *Chicago* was launched in 1885, naval armament consisted of antique Parrott or Dahlgren smoothbores, crudely converted to rifles by the insertion of rifled, iron tubes in their barrels. All shipboard guns, save certain lighter pieces, were muzzle-loaders.

This state of affairs could have been remedied earlier if the department had possessed the funds for testing such inventions as those of ordnance pioneers John Ericsson and Benjamin Hotchkiss. But the scarcity of funds compelled the Bureau of Ordnance to decline such weapons, and they often found a warm welcome in the naval ministries of Europe.[69]

To build the ABCD's, Chandler bypassed the navy yards and advertised for bids from private contractors. Of the sixteen he received for the four contracts, the lowest for each came from his friend John Roach, whose yards were in Chester, Pennsylvania. Roach's bids totalled $2,-

65 L. B. Richardson, *William E. Chandler, Republican* (New York, 1940), 283ff.
66 Protected cruisers carried thick belts of armor lengthwise along their sides; armored cruisers had armor plates on decks, turrets, and other vulnerable spaces.
67 Rear Adm. Edward Simpson, "The United States Navy in Transition," *Harper's Magazine,* LXXIII (June, 1886), 4.
68 *Congressional Record,* 48th Cong., 1st Sess., 2317, 2759–64.
69 Navy Dept., *Annual Report,* 1884; Mitchell, *Modern Navy,* 13. Ericsson had developed a heavy steel rifle, and Hotchkiss the rapid-fire cannon which the British Navy used successfully for many years.

440,000, or $315,000 less than the next lowest figure and $774,000 below the Shufeldt board's estimate. The wide range of bids betrayed the builders' uncertainty as to the cost of producing mild steel of the high grade specified in the contracts.[70]

The secretary infuriated the higher bidders by awarding all four contracts to Roach. The losers considered the awards outrageous and made no bones about it, accusing Chandler of favoring Roach unfairly because of the improper political *liaison* existing between the two.[71] The press picked up the story and embroidered it, and historians have since made much of the "contract scandal" as a prime example of corruption in an era noted for political turpitude. Allan Nevins describes Roach as an "illiterate, elderly, infirm ironmaster," employing skulduggery to win naval contracts, and Chandler as a political hack sufficiently immoral to cheat the government for the sake of rewarding a campaign contributor. Although the characterizations are overdrawn, the secretary's association with Roach did blacken his record and furnish his Democratic successor with a ready-made scapegoat.

John Roach had donated money to Chandler's war chest and, on occasion, made him personal gifts of sums up to $1,000; that much is sure. As a result, the secretary left himself open to criticism when he awarded his henchman the ABCD contracts, even though Roach had submitted the lowest bids.[72] Aside from his alleged misconduct in the contract scandal, however, Chandler displayed a courageous disregard for personal considerations where the welfare of the service was concerned. He risked his political future first by rejecting requests of Republican chieftains to reinstate officers who had been dismissed for good reason and again by attempting, in vain, to deprive the families of influential naval seniors of free government transportation to foreign duty stations.[73]

Finally, by braving the wrath of conservative opponents in authorizing the establishment of the Naval War College in October, 1884, Chandler

---

70 Bowles, "Our New Cruisers," 596–600.

71 For contrasting interpretations of the Roach contract scandal, see L. B. Richardson, *Chandler*, 356–80; Allan Nevins, *Grover Cleveland: A Study in Courage* (New York, 1941), 218–19; and Mark D. Hirsch, *William C. Whitney, Modern Warwick* (New York, 1938), Chap. 10, *passim*.

72 Nevins, *Cleveland*, 218–19; L. B. Richardson, *Chandler*, 356–62; Hirsch, *Whitney*, Chap. 10. For further contract details see Bowles, "Our New Cruisers," 595–610. Bowles served on both the Rodgers and Shufeldt boards, the only member to do so.

73 Navy Dept., *Annual Report*, 1884.

made a lasting contribution to the Navy which stood second in importance only to his sponsorship of the ABCD's. To allow the College, which was to provide "an advanced course of professional study," the chance to develop as independently as possible, he placed it under the general supervision of the Bureau of Navigation and wisely selected the institution's progenitor, Commodore Luce, to preside directly over it.[74]

In the course of a conference in early January, 1865, with General William T. Sherman of the Union Army, Luce had conceived the idea of founding a postgraduate school for naval officers. As captain of the monitor *Pontiac*, then on leave from the South Atlantic Blockading Station to provide cover from the Savannah River for Sherman's troops on their march north, Luce reported to the general for instructions. Outlining his plan to take Charleston which, he insisted, the Navy could have accomplished long since but for the absence of coordination with land forces, Sherman declared: "I will cut her communications and Charleston will fall into your hands like a ripe pear." He convinced Luce that certain fundamental principles "of general application on land or sea" governed warfare and inspired him with determination to institute a program for educating officers in military as well as naval science.[75]

To obtain expert advice on his project, Luce decided in March, 1876, to consult Brigadier General Emory Upton, whose report on military establishments in Europe and Asia had attracted his attention a year earlier. The commodore visited Upton at Fortress Monroe, where he had charge of the Artillery School of Practice, the country's sole postgraduate military school. Seeing in Luce the spirit of professionalism with which he hoped to imbue the Army, General Upton encouraged him to translate his idea into action. Accordingly, in the next year, the commodore conveyed his plan to Secretary Thompson, who received it noncommittally. There the matter rested for seven years.[76]

Arriving in Newport, Rhode Island, in the fall of 1884 with Chandler's authorization in his pocket, Luce drew up a list of nominees for

---

74 Copy of secretary's General Order No. 325, October 6, 1884, Naval War College Library, Newport, R.I.; hereinafter cited as NWC.

75 Gleaves, *Luce*, 99–101.

76 Stephen E. Ambrose, *Upton and the Army* (Baton Rouge, 1964), 85–96; Upton to Luce, October 16, 1877, in NWC; Luce to secretary of the navy, August 8, 1877, enclosing a copy of the Artillery School's "Programme of Instruction," in NWC. See also, Luce, "Department of Military Art and Science," *NIP*, IX (1883), 647. For an excellent treatment of professional expertise, see S. P. Huntington, *The Soldier and the State* (New York, 1964), Chap. 9, *passim.*

the War College faculty. The two key men he selected were Captain
A. T. Mahan, as head of the "Naval Branch," and Professor James
R. Soley of the Naval Academy, as lecturer in international law. Mindful
of the advice of Sherman and Upton, the commodore startled the department by asking for an Army officer to take charge of the "Military
Branch" of the curriculum. But the bureau chiefs balked at first at
the notion of a soldier instructing sailors in land warfare and withheld
their consent.[77]

Having conferred with Adjutant General R. C. Drum in the meantime, Luce had chosen Lieutenant Tasker H. Bliss of the 1st Artillery
for the post in question.[78] The commodore informed Chandler of his
choice and asked him to persuade the chiefs to reconsider, which the
secretary with difficulty managed to do.[79] In August, 1885, General
Drum assigned Bliss to duty at the War College.[80]

In a sense, the College was the product of Luce's philosophy of war.
A militant Social Darwinist, he considered war a historical imperative,
the frequency of which could be reduced only through the deterrent
presented by the most destructive weapons available in the hands of
highly professionalized servicemen.[81] The commodore hoped, by applying this theory to the College, to overcome "the crass ignorance of
naval officers . . . and the imbecility of our Navy department as a
director of . . . operations during war." [82]

Apart from the theoretical aspect of naval affairs, the Navy made
considerable headway in technological development before Chandler retired, largely because of the impetus generated by the ABCD program.
An unwonted feeling of pride infused Navy men as they watched the
installation of newly devised electric lighting circuits and the Washington Gun Factory's first output of high-velocity, breech-loading rifles
on the unfinished hulls.[83] By 1885, furthermore, many engineers were

77 Luce to Chandler, October 28, 1884, in NWC.
78 R. C. Drum to Luce, October 13, 1884, in NWC.
79 Luce to Chandler, October 28, 1884, in NWC.
80 Extract from adjutant general's Special Order No. 195, August 26, 1885, in
NWC.
81 S. B. Luce, "Benefits of War," *Literary Digest*, IV (December 26, 1891),
6–7; S. B. Luce, "War Schools," *NIP*, IX (1883), 658.
82 Luce to Mahan, July 15, 1907, NWC. See also, Sgt. Leroy Eure, U.S.A.F.,
"History of Military Colleges" (typescript, NWC, 1961). Attached to the War
College's Permanent Air Force Observer's staff, Eure was acting in 1961 as the
library's unofficial curator.
83 E. W. Very, "Development of Armor for Naval Use," *NIP*, IX (1883), 421–22;
Bowles, "Our New Cruisers," 596–608.

urging the adoption of liquid fuel as a part-time substitute for coal. Although the space required for tanks rendered full replacement impractical as yet, oil could be used for short runs at flank speed since it burned faster and thus delivered more power—and saved coal in the process. But the Department deferred a decision on the proposal for some time after Chandler's term ended.[84]

As he prepared to relinquish his office in March, 1885, Chandler could not help sensing the change in atmosphere over the past four years. Apathy had given way to enthusiasm and drift to direction. The Navy was moving forward now, despite the inattention of its leaders to strategic requisites.

When the Democrats came to power with the inauguration of Grover Cleveland, William C. Whitney of Concord, Massachusetts, became secretary of the navy. Unlike Chandler, the new secretary had inherited a puritan streak which occasionally inhibited his behavior as Democracy's "kingmaker." During the Civil War, Whitney had attended Yale College and Harvard Law School and was thereafter admitted to the New York bar. His practice of corporation law and his marriage to Standard Oil heiress Flora Payne had brought him a fortune and close ties with prominent industrialists. A "natural supporter" of Cleveland, Whitney had been summoned to Washington to clean up the Navy Department.

Whitney's first move was to tighten the disbursing system and increase the accountability of property custodians. Then he undertook a survey of the navy yards where he found solid evidence of political knavery. For years, he reported, "the yards have been nests to hold lazy heelers . . . of the Republican party. . . ."[85] Though dormant much of the time, they became beehives of activity around election day when scores of hastily hired workmen were marched to the polls by local party bosses. The secretary attempted with little success to stop this practice by directing yard commandants to rid their commands of political hirelings.

Turning to departmental organization, Whitney deplored the absence of an agency for informing him of the Navy's military requirements, such as the preparation of war plans and the employment and distribution of naval vessels. The separate, technical responsibilities of the bureau

84 Navy Dept., *Annual Report*, 1884; N. B. Clark, "Petroleum for Warships," *NIP*, IX (1883), 798–99.
85 Hirsch, *Whitney*, Chaps. 1-9, *passim*; Nevins, *Cleveland*, 217–19; Navy Dept., *Annual Report*, 1887.

chiefs, he pointed out, prevented them from assuming an overall advisory role in military matters. He improved the situation somewhat by reorganizing the department into three major divisions, which resulted in greater coordination of bureau activities and closer contact between the chiefs and himself.

In the spring of 1886, Whitney took inventory of equipment stored in naval depots. Here he found more than $1,000,000 worth of rotting clothes and enough canvas to rig out the British fleet! [86] Appalled by the waste revealed in the course of his search, the secretary instituted that summer the new supply policy recommended by the Gun Foundry Board, which Congress had created in 1883 to gather data relative to the establishment of a domestic armament industry.[87] The task facing the members of this board was not merely a technical one; they were expected to propose either private or public ownership for the industry, and, for several reasons, neither appealed to them. Private contractors of the day were not noted for their ethics, and government ownership smacked of socialism and inefficiency. Influenced by their observations of the European armament complex, the board submitted a compromise plan. The government must offer private firms contracts attractive enough to induce them to produce basic forgings for delivery to public facilities, such as navy yards and gun factories, where the material would be tested. If acceptable, the forgings would then be used in the fabrication of guns and other heavy equipment. Congress endorsed the proposals of the board in 1885, and thereby ushered in the American armament industry.[88]

In the following year, therefore, Secretary Whitney circulated a single advertisement for bids among domestic steelmakers with a full statement of the Navy's needs and a clause allowing the supplier thirty months for delivery. The Bethlehem Steel Company responded with the winning bid and a promise to build a special mill for rolling steel hull plates. In this case, navy yards would play the part of government shipbuilder as soon as the material arrived.[89]

Congress had appointed in 1885 a second board to study the question

---

86 Huntington, *Soldier and State*, 248; Oberholtzer, *U.S. since the Civil War*, IV, 341–43. Congress had not appropriated funds for uniforms since 1875.

87 *House Executive Documents*, 48th Cong., 1st Sess., "Report of the Gun Foundry Board," No. 77; Millis, *Arms and Men*, 150–51.

88 *Ibid.*

89 Navy Dept., *Annual Report*, 1886; Nevins, Cleveland, 217–22; Millis, *Arms and Men*, 151. Whitney predicted in 1886 that Bethlehem would soon furnish the Navy with steel "second to none."

of coast defense. Headed by Secretary of War William Endicott, this board at length submitted a report which called for a vast network of coastal fortifications and a fleet of monitors to supplement them. The influence of two naval members, Captains William T. Sampson and Charles F. Goodrich, doubtless saved the report from becoming a mere restatement of outmoded ideas. In final form, the board's program included the assumption that in the future the Navy would possess numerous heavy ironclads able "to act offensively and not be confined to the defense of ports." [90]

All the while, Secretary Whitney worked effectively to obtain additional warships, exposing current weaknesses as well as past extravagances. "In March, 1885," he announced, "the United States had no vessel . . . which could have kept the sea for one week as against any first-rate power." Yet, since 1868 the Navy had squandered some $75,000,000 on useless hulls. The old *Omaha* had been rebuilt at about half the cost of a small steel cruiser, while the 900-ton *Mohican* had absorbed $908,000 worth of futile repairs, or $233,000 more than the contract price of the *Atlanta*.[91] In response to Whitney's disclosures, Congress limited expenditures on wooden ships to 20 per cent of their original cost and, at the same time, displayed unaccustomed liberality in advancing funds for steel replacements.[92]

As for new construction, the secretary found much to criticize in Roach's work on the ABCD's and did not hesitate to say so in press interviews. Owing to the notoriety given the alleged structural defects of the cruisers and the *Dolphin* in the releases Whitney approved for publication, Roach's health and business declined so far that the department had to complete the four ships in his yards.[93]

Whether, as Secretary Whitney's biographer suggests, all blame for defective construction belongs to the contractor is open to debate. Another school of thought indicts the department for inefficiency and inept supervision, and a third imputes Whitney's harsh treatment of Roach to political malice. In any event, the secretary's concern for the cruisers proved groundless in the long run: all three surpassed expectations during

---

90 *House Executive Documents*, 49th Cong., 1st Sess., "Report of the Endicott Board," No. 49. See also, Sprout, *Naval Power*, 199–200; and Millis, *Arms and Men*, 151–52.
91 Navy Dept., *Annual Report*, 1886.
92 Oberholtzer, *U.S. since the Civil War*, IV, 341–44; Hirsch, *Whitney*, 256.
93 Navy Dept., *Annual Report*, 1886, especially, "Report of the *Dolphin* Trial Board"; Sprout, *Naval Power*, 190–98.

trials. Even the *Dolphin*, which failed her initial test at sea, ultimately performed well.[94]

The ABCD's, though much admired in the United States, were puny by foreign standards. Battleships of leading European powers displaced from 6,000 to 15,000 tons, steamed at 17 knots, and carried rifles of up to 17 inches in caliber. Second in popularity abroad were fast armored cruisers which, while smaller and less heavily armed than the capital ships, had twice the tonnage and firepower of the largest of the ABCD's, the U.S.S. *Chicago*. This vessel displaced only 4,500 tons and mounted four modern 8-inch steel rifled guns in her main battery. Driven by twin screws, the *Chicago* had four two-cycle, compound engines which generated 5,000 horsepower for a top speed of 18 knots. Measuring 325 feet overall, she was rigged as a barkentine. Her brig-rigged, lighter sisters had less speed and fewer guns; and the 1,500-ton *Dolphin* carried but one 6-inch rifle as her main armament. Resembling the first three cruisers in most respects were the *Newark* and *Charleston*, both authorized late in Chandler's term and nearing completion in 1886.

The character of the new ships revealed the contradictions inherent in Whitney's building program. For example, the *Chicago's* twin screws assured exceptional maneuverability, but her boilers lay atop old-fashioned brick furnaces unable to build up steam rapidly.[95] Similarly, though all the cruisers mounted modern armament, none had the protection of armor or the freedom to service guns swiftly, unimpaired by sailing gear. The thirty ships added by Whitney reflected the haphazard planning of officers who grasped the tactical significance of mobility and firepower, but failed to appreciate the strategic advantage inherent in a unified battle force of sufficient strength and endurance to destroy an enemy fleet a thousand miles offshore.[96]

Certain features of two warships in Whitney's program, the cruisers *Maine* and *Texas*, implied that technology had outrun policy. Authorized in 1886, they were designed to displace more than 6,000 tons, to attain

---

94 Differing accounts of the matter appear in Oberholtzer, *U.S. since the Civil War*, IV, 345; Long, *New Navy*, I, Chap. 2; Nevins, *Cleveland*, 219–22; Hirsch, *Whitney*, Chap. 10.

95 Navy Dept., *Annual Report*, 1883, 1886. The 1886 report describes the cruisers' trials. ABCD specifications are detailed in Bowles, "Our New Cruisers," 596–608. See also, Sprout, *Naval Power*, 188; Mitchell, *Modern Navy*, 15–16.

96 See, especially, Edward Simpson, "The Navy and Its Prospects of Rehabilitation," *NIP*, XII (1886), 1–39; W. B. Hoff, "A View of Our Naval Policy," *NIP*, XII (1886), 126–39.

speeds up to 18.5 knots, and to carry the heaviest guns yet approved for American men-of-war. Their coats of armor and 10-inch rifles, while appearing to indicate a shift to offensive doctrine, actually represented nothing more than technological progress.[97] Concurrently, work proceeded on the protected cruiser *Baltimore*, whose 20-knot speed rendered her superior to the *Chicago* which in other details she resembled.[98]

During 1887, Congress authorized construction of seven more warships, of which the most memorable was the 8,000-ton armored cruiser *New York*. The heaviest man-of-war laid down in America before 1890, this vessel equalled the *Baltimore* in speed and surpassed her in firepower. Other ships of the lot included the small cruisers *Raleigh* and *Cincinnati* and the 6,000-ton protected cruiser *Olympia*. Destined to share glory with the *New York* in the victory over Spain, the *Olympia* had a top speed of 22 knots and a main battery of four 8-inch rifles. Three additional *Charleston*-class cruisers completed the list of authorizations for the year.[99]

As expansion continued, eventful changes occurred. First, the *Charleston* dealt the Old Navy a lethal blow by shedding her canvas, a precedent quickly followed by her sisters. Then, inventor Arthur Whitehead produced the "automobile torpedo," which had equally important consequences. Prior to the advance of the torpedo to operational status, the ram bow had temporarily replaced the heavy gun as the Navy's primary weapon, occasioning the relocation of gun stations so as to concentrate maximum firepower dead ahead. But, by deterring warships from closing to ram, the torpedo forced designers to shift turrets back to the center line, fore and aft, in order to permit firing over a wide arc from broadside to broadside.[100]

Meanwhile, the War College had experienced travail. In June, 1886, on the departure of Luce to assume command of the North Atlantic Squadron, Captain Mahan—whom Whitney disliked—became presi-

---

97 The *Maine* mounted four 10-inch rifles, while the *Texas*, which was the last American warship of European design, carried two guns of the same caliber. Prior to the destruction of the *Maine* in 1898, both ships—originally designated second-rate battleships—were reclassified as armored cruisers. The *Texas* was subsequently renamed *San Marcos*.
98 Navy Dept., *Annual Report*, 1886.
99 *Ibid.* Several small craft authorized by the Act of 1877 have not been mentioned.
100 Millis, *Arms and Men*, 154.

dent.[101] Two months later, for reasons unclear, the secretary decided to remove the College from the benign supervision of Rear Admiral John G. Walker, chief of the Bureau of Navigation, and give it a new home at the Torpedo Station on Goat Island, across Narragansett Bay from Coaster's Harbor.

Captain Charles Goodrich, commandant of the Torpedo Station, tried to rescue the College's independent status by persuading Whitney to secure funds for housing it separately from his command. The secretary complied, as he explained: "I am doing this because Goodrich wants it . . . but why he wants it, I'm blessed if I know!" [102] Though appreciative of Goodrich's good will, neither Mahan nor Luce liked this plan. The latter, who had brought his squadron to Newport for the College session, attempted in vain to undermine the transfer by informing Army friends of Whitney's desire to erect a naval facility at Goat Island, on land belonging to the War Department. As 1888 came to a close, the secretary moved the College to the island and assigned Mahan duty in Puget Sound.[103]

The secretary's action pleased many of Mahan's superiors who, believing naval warfare could best be studied at sea, disdained his bookish ways and condemned the College as an intellectual frill. As one admiral commented: "Teach the art of war! Well, I'll be damned! You have Cooper's *Naval History* and Parker's *Fleet Tactics;* what more do you want?" [104] The experience of Old Navy men perhaps justified their attitude; but Whitney's opposition to the College is hard to understand, especially in view of his demand for an agency to supply the secretary with essential military data. This function suited the War College and was subsequently assumed by it.

William C. Whitney devoted his term to administrative reform and fleet expansion with great success. On the other hand, perhaps because of the conservative influences around him, he ignored strategy and left naval policy basically as it had been in the days of Thomas Jefferson.

101 See various items of Luce-Mahan correspondence, 1889–1903, in NHF; W. D. Puleston, *The Life and Works of Captain Alfred Thayer Mahan, U.S.N.* (New Haven, 1939), 92; A. T. Mahan, "Reminiscences" (unpublished typescript), March 24, 1908, in NWC; R. S. West, Jr., *Admirals of American Empire* (Indianapolis, 1948), 149.
102 Goodrich to Captain C. S. Sperry, March 5, 1906, in NWC, Luce Collection, quoting Whitney.
103 Luce to General Schofield, March 8, 1888, in NWC, Luce Collection. See also, Puleston, *Mahan*, 85–87.
104 Gleaves, *Luce*, 176–78. For the low opinion Mahan's superiors had of him as a deck officer, see their reports of his fitness, 1885–88, in Mahan Papers, Puleston Collection, in the Division of Manuscripts, Library of Congress.

II

TRACY TAKES THE HELM

ON THE MORNING OF MARCH 5, 1889, THE FIRST WORKING DAY of Benjamin Harrison's administration, an erect, gray-haired figure strode briskly into the outer office of the Navy Department. As he did so, the entire staff, from white-belted messengers to gold-braided bureau chiefs, maneuvered for a glimpse of their new civilian boss. They beheld a handsome man of athletic build in his late fifties whose firm chin sported a Van Dyke beard. On further acquaintance, they found him courteous, perceptive, and willing to listen.[1]

Harrison's secretary of the navy, Benjamin Franklin Tracy, had the experience and personality required of an outstanding administrator. Tracy was born in 1830 of middle-class farming-stock in Tioga County, New York. His success in law and politics had won him statewide recognition before he accepted the summons to Washington. Not that anything in his background suggested special interest or competence in naval affairs; even his avocation as a breeder of trotting horses—for which he was nationally known—was as far removed from the sea as any hobby imaginable.[2]

Unlike Secretary Whitney, Tracy decided to forego college after

1 W. R. Herrick, Jr., "General Tracy's Navy" (Ph.D. dissertation, University of Virginia, 1962), 72, citing, E. G. Dunnell, "Secretary B. F. Tracy," *The Epoch* (New York, June 7, 1889), 285-86; author's interview with Tracy's granddaughter, Mrs. Frederic Coudert, January, 1961, New York, N.Y.
2 Herrick, "Tracy's Navy," Chap. 2, *passim.*

graduating from high school and received his legal training in an upstate attorney's office. Admitted to the New York bar at the age of twenty-one, he became Tioga County's district attorney within three years, the youngest man elected to such office in the history of the state. After serving two terms, Tracy retired to take up private practice, which brought him substantial fees until 1861, when his district sent him to the state assembly in Albany.[3]

The Civil War cut short Tracy's term in Albany. As colonel of the 109th New York Volunteers, he led his troops with distinction in the Wilderness campaign until disabled in action at Spotsylvania. In 1864, he recovered sufficiently to assume command of the Union's prisoner-of-war camp at Elmira, New York. Prior to his discharge in the following year, Tracy was rewarded for bravery at Spotsylvania with the rank of brevet brigadier general and, in the course of time, with the Congressional Medal of Honor.[4]

His military duty completed, the general moved with his wife, Delinda Catlin Tracy, and their three children to Brooklyn, where he resumed the practice of law. His rapid rise to prominence at the metropolitan bar attracted the attention of President Grant, who appointed him United States district attorney for the eastern district of New York— a position Tracy retained for eight years. Thereafter, he went back to an increasingly lucrative private practice, which he interrupted again in 1881 to run in vain for mayor of Brooklyn against a strong candidate backed by Tammany Hall. Probably to compensate him for running a hopeless race for mayor that year, Governor Alonzo Cornell named Tracy associate justice of the state court of appeal and within a few months promoted him to Chief Justice of this court, whose record of achievement gained it high esteem in New York's "Golden Age of jurisprudence and scholarship."[5]

In December, 1882, ill health forced the general into retirement for nearly three years. On his recovery, he became senior partner of the

3 *Ibid.* See also, W. B. Gay (comp.), *Historical Gazetteer of Tioga County, New York: 1785–1888* (Syracuse, N.Y., 1888), 351–52; C. E. Fitch, *Encyclopedia of Biography of New York* (New York, 1916), 278.

4 *The War of the Rebellion: A Compilation of the Official Records of the Union and Confederate Armies* (Washington, 1880–1901), Ser. I, Vol. LI, 882; XXXVI, 113; XLIII, 907; hereinafter cited as *Official Records*. For details of the medal award, see Secretary of War D. S. Lamont to General Isaac Catlin, June 15, 1895, in B. F. Tracy Papers, Division of Manuscripts, Library of Congress. Catlin was Tracy's brother-in-law.

5 Frank Platt, *Memorial to B. F. Tracy*, in New York County Lawyers' Association *Year Book* (May, 1916), 52–56.

newly formed law firm of Tracy, Boardman, and Platt, where he specialized in the profitable field of estate management until the President selected him to head the Navy Department.[6]

Throughout this period of his life, Tracy played an active role in local politics, first upstate and later in Brooklyn. His interest in political affairs dated back to high school days at Owego Academy where he had become friendly with Thomas Collier Platt, a schoolmate destined for leadership of New York's Republican organization. The general's close association with Platt over the years had a profound effect on his political fortune. In all his campaigns for public office, Tracy enjoyed Platt's support and doubtless would not have attained a cabinet post in 1889 without his friend's assistance.[7] Well ahead of the call to Washington, therefore, the general had distinguished himself not only as a lawyer and jurist, but also as a skillful lieutenant of Boss Platt's state Republican machine, in which capacity he dominated party activities in Brooklyn. For his mastery of both pursuits, he had his own ambition and intellect to thank, as well as Platt.

To understand how this henchman of a political boss, whose unsavory tactics were as well-known in his time as they are today, could win a term as secretary of the navy and make a phenomenal success of it, necessitates knowledge of the man's character. Energy, willpower, and an almost naïve sense of loyalty personified Tracy. The third of these traits conditioned his subjective attitudes and actions, revealing his consistent fidelity to country, party, and friends—in that order. This quality, which contrasted sharply with his sophisticated approach to legal and political problems, explains the development in an honest, intelligent individual of more than a trace of jingoism, of a tendency to identify the nation's welfare with that of his party, and of a lasting friendship with a machiavellian political leader. The general's conservative frame of reference, moreover, induced in him a dedication to the established order of things and facilitated his conversion to the ideology of imperialism.

Tracy learned early in life to shade his native idealism with expediency —within certain limits. By utilizing the resulting blend of morality and pragmatism, he was able to square with his conscience any compromises he made for the sake of his party. Despite his devotion to Republicanism,

---

6 Miscellaneous legal correspondence, Box IV (1889), in Tracy Papers.

7 H. F. Gosnell, *Boss Platt and His New York Political Machine* (New York, 1924), 67ff.

the general's principles precluded blind allegiance to Platt's faction; on many occasions he proved his readiness to break with party policy whenever his convictions demanded. Tracy's record rejects the traditional image of the organization lieutenant as a shady manipulator; on the contrary, it represents him as that rarity—an honest machine politician. Tempered as they were by tact and humor, the general's character traits suited him well for the part of a first-rate statesman of the second rank.[8]

Tom Platt proposed Tracy for a place in the cabinet in January, 1889, following a bitter quarrel with the President-elect. For years, Platt had nursed an ambition to preside over the Treasury Department; and, when he heard from national committeeman Stephen B. Elkins that Harrison was considering him for the position, he thought his dream had come true. On learning that such was not the case, Platt became furious and threatened to break permanently from the administration. To placate the New York boss, Harrison offered to include in his cabinet any acceptable representative of Platt's machine. Since Tracy had the backing of both the Stalwart and Half-Breed factions in New York, as well as an excellent personal reputation, Harrison appointed him gladly.[9]

Thus, one of the Navy's most dynamic civilian chiefs was given his office in the interest of party solidarity. In terms of the present, it may seem difficult to reconcile Tracy's fitness for the post with his membership in Platt's organization, yet such a zealous reformer as Theodore Roosevelt explained the apparent paradox with ease: "In the country districts especially, there were many places where Platt's machine included the majority of the best citizens. . . . Some of the strongest and most efficient lieutenants were disinterested men of high character." [10] Harrison's secretary of the navy was one of these men.

General Tracy's enthusiasm for the Navy mounted as soon as he crossed the threshold of his new office. For four years, burdened with heavy strain, political strife, and family tragedy, Tracy directed his energies to the accomplishment of realistic progress on behalf of a service too long bound up in anachronistic policies. When he replaced Whitney, the Navy remained as before an unintegrated collection of

---

8 Herrick, "Tracy's Navy," Chap. 2, *passim.*

9 D. S. Alexander, *Four Famous New Yorkers* (New York, 1923), 133ff. See also, Tracy to Benjamin Harrison, January 2, 1889, in Benjamin Harrison Papers, Division of Manuscripts, Library of Congress. For press reaction to Tracy's appointment, see for example, New York *Times,* March 4, 1889, and Brooklyn *Daily Times,* March 6, 1889.

10 Theodore Roosevelt, *An Autobiography* (New York, 1913), 321.

warships which, for the most part, were better equipped for peace than for war.

The years from 1889 to 1893 witnessed a revolution in naval development. For the first time in American history, strategy superseded tradition as the determinant of policy. With Tracy at the helm, strategic principles governed not only new construction, but also professional education and administrative organization.

The ideas behind this radical departure did not originate in the general's mind; he knew nothing of naval problems when he took office. But he listened to men who appreciated the Navy's needs and understood the implications of sea power. As he listened, he learned, and soon formed opinions of his own as to the size and makeup of the fleet of the future, a subject which a few months earlier would have been incomprehensible to him. In the last analysis, the independent decisions made by this landlocked horse breeder inspired the most revolutionary changes in doctrine ever experienced by the Navy Department.

On a number of occasions during the summer of 1889, Tracy consulted Captain Mahan, from which contact a consequential friendship arose. At the time, Mahan was preparing for publication the manuscript which would appear within a year as a book entitled *The Influence of Sea Power upon History*. After reading the manuscript, the General became convinced of the validity of Mahan's capital-ship theory and decided to incorporate it in his own program of naval expansion, which he planned to announce in November. He made his decision in awareness of the stiff opposition that such a radical policy would encounter from conservative officers, let alone isolationist congressmen.[11]

Tracy's disposition stood him in good stead as he settled into his job. His new associates found him polite and attentive but not given to the backslapping affability affected by certain of his cabinet-mates. He could not "let himself down to the picnic level and become one of a party of noisy merrymakers on the lawn," but he was "otherwise democratic and an understanding listener." [12]

Journalists generally commented favorably on Harrison's secretary, one factor of whose appeal to them was the financial sacrifice he had suffered in accepting the appointment. In the year before he came to

11 West, *Admirals of American Empire*, 149ff., citing A. T. Mahan to S. B. Luce, September 3, 1901.

12 For descriptions of Tracy which tally in general with Mrs. Coudert's recollection of her grandfather, see Dunnell, "Secretary Tracy," 285–86; and H. T. Peck, "Twenty Years of the Republic," in *The Bookman*, XXI (April, 1905), 143.

Washington, Tracy's income had amounted to $22,000 in legal fees and stock dividends. In order to pay for a suitable house for his family and for the elaborate entertainment expected of a cabinet member, he was forced to dispose of most of his securities, not to mention his beloved trotters. What few investments he could afford to retain added only $2,500 to his federal salary of $8,000.[13]

Some observers expressed surprise when the President posted Tracy to the Navy, rather than to the Department of Justice where they thought his talent would show to better advantage, and hinted that a change might be in the offing. But as one editor stated bluntly, the general had already demonstrated the wisdom of Harrison's assignment.

No doubt General Tracy, as Attorney-General, would have been an unspeakable improvement on his predecessor, but there is no reason for moving him. Gen. Tracy is the strongest man in the cabinet . . . and is doing about the only work that reflects much credit on the administration. He is the first thoroughly honest and . . . capable Republican Secretary of the Navy since the end of the Civil War.[14]

It was not long before Tracy was echoing Whitney's complaints about working conditions in the department. Outside the secretary's door, naval officers of all grades crowded together with enlisted messengers and civilian clerks and typists in the narrow confines of the eight bureaus, whose staffs had outgrown their quarters. His personal crew, which consisted of one clerk, a stenographer, and three seamen acting as messengers, had to help him cope with the endless details of departmental, and frequently political, business.[15]

The relationship of the bureau chiefs to the secretary struck Tracy as especially galling. It seemed to him a matter of matching eight professional leaders of an entrenched bureaucracy against a lone civilian, who usually lacked the knowledge to question their conduct of naval business. Not that these senior officers always stood united—far from it; each exercised direct control over matters within his jurisdiction aboard ships and at shore installations of all kinds. As often as not, they pursued contradictory objectives and occasionally, out of jealousy, duplicated

13 Various financial statements (1889) in Tracy Papers. An account of the sale of the trotters appears in New York *Sun*, March 21, 1889. Salary is given in Navy Dept., *Annual Report*, 1889.

14 New York *Sun*, editorial, October 30, 1889. See also, S. B. Elkins to Henry Davis, October 30, 1889, in S. B. Elkins Papers, Library of the University of West Virginia, for further comments.

15 Hirsch, *Whitney*, 264. For administrative relations in the Navy Department, see Leonard White, *The Republican Era, 1869–1901* (New York, 1958), 167.

each other's efforts.[16] The chaotic operations of these uncoordinated commands dismayed the general. In no wise did the lore of the bureaucrats demand their loyalty, or even obedience, to the secretary. On the contrary, the chiefs' attacks on Tracy's policy compelled him to appear repeatedly before one or the other of the congressional naval committees to defend his judgment.[17]

That the bureau chiefs went so far as to challenge the general openly indicates their inability to influence him. It had been the custom of these usually conservative seniors to try to pocket incoming secretaries at the outset. Mindful of the chiefs' domination of Whitney, the redoubtable Admiral Porter voiced his fear of Tracy's falling prey to them as the new administration began.

Whitney . . . was completely hoodwinked by the bureaus and never had his own way at any time when he imagined himself master of the situation. Mr. Tracy is an old gentleman . . . who is very accessible and will do nothing in a hurry. He listens quietly and doesn't commit himself.

From certain questions he asked me about the Bureau of Equipment, I imagine that Whitney left the chief . . . to Mr. Tracy to aid the latter in the task of running the Navy, hoping his successor would fail as egregiously as Whitney himself. Whitney and Tracy having been friends, the latter may well fall into that trap.[18]

Porter need not have concerned himself; the general had too much experience with intrigue to be taken in as the admiral feared.

At first, most of the mail addressed to Tracy consisted of congratulatory notes, the contents of which ranged from the sublime to the ridiculous. One well-wisher wrote admiringly, "I little thought that your name would so soon become a household word in our country," while another predicted that the general would surpass Whitney, "who wanted to know when he went in where they got the red and green oil for the signal lamps." [19]

16 White, *Republican Era*, 167ff.
17 *House Reports*, 52nd Cong., 1st Sess., No. 1677, p. 9.
18 D. D. Porter to Luce, March 14, 1889, NHF. See W. S. Schley, *Forty-Five Years under the Flag* (New York, 1904), 190–92; Schley was the bureau chief Porter mentioned. Tracy ordered him to command of the *Baltimore* in April, 1889, and appointed Captain George Dewey chief of the Bureau of Equipment in Schley's place. Another version of the transfer appears in Captain Oliver Selfridge to W. E. Chandler, January 28, 1890, in W. E. Chandler Papers, Division of Manuscripts, Library of Congress. Selfridge implies that Tracy ousted Schley from the bureau because Porter advised the change.
19 W. White to Tracy, March 6, 1889, and C. Requa to Tracy, March 10, 1889, in Tracy Papers.

Far less welcome was the flood of politically inspired correspondence that followed. Letters from congressmen asked favors for friends or relatives in the service or sought the fruits of patronage on behalf of their supporters. Heedless of possible repercussions, Tracy gave such requests short shrift. For instance, when House Speaker Thomas B. Reed of Maine pleaded with him to retain a troublesome engineer at the navy yard in Kittery, the general politely refused. The chairman of the Senate Naval Affairs Committee, James D. Cameron, received a similar response to his appeal for clemency in the case of a lieutenant commander's absence without leave from his ship. Again, when Pennsylvania's formidable political boss, Matthew Quay, suggested extending a lieutenant's assignment at the Brooklyn Navy Yard "for social reasons," Tracy braved the Senator's wrath and sent the officer to sea.[20] On the other hand, the secretary was ready to lend a hand whenever a situation involved genuine hardship, as Cardinal Gibbons' clerk acknowledged in a note thanking him for helping a crew member of a warship based at Baltimore.[21]

Party leaders encouraged the general to permit the hiring of faithful Republicans for work in the navy yards, a persistent custom that had defied former attempts to abolish it. Tom Platt, Henry Cabot Lodge, and Judge Robert D. Benedict, among others, implored him to populate the yards with "sustainers of our party." [22] Admiral Porter assured the secretary that the practice of politics in the naval establishment had been treated as a matter of course by his predecessors—Democratic as well as Republican. In a memorandum on the subject, Porter declared, "I have given Secretary Tracy an idea of how that virtuous Mr. Whitney diverted the funds on the eve of election from building ships to large contracts for clothing." [23]

Tracy appreciated the political advantage of dispensing patronage *en masse* by filling the numerous navy yard jobs with Republican hirelings; and for the time being, he allowed commandants to keep them on

20 Correspondence between M. P. Wentworth and Thomas Reed, April 23 and May 2, 1889; J. D. Cameron to Tracy, April 8, 1889; M. S. Quay to Tracy, May 3, 1889; and Tracy's endorsements thereon; all in Tracy Papers. See also, J. A. Smith to Chandler, December 30, 1889, in Chandler Papers, protesting Tracy's refusal to allow political considerations to influence officers' assignments.
21 V. Hogan to Tracy, November 1, 1889, in Tracy Papers.
22 See the Tracy Papers for various letters from these and other prominent party leaders. The quotation is from R. D. Benedict to Tracy, August 5, 1889. V. D. Groner expressed similar feelings in his letter to S. B. Elkins, March 19, 1889, in Elkins Papers.
23 Porter to Luce, March 21, 1889, in NHF.

the payroll. But before the year was out, he came to the conclusion that employing civilian workmen by the single criterion of political affiliation was not in the best interest of the Navy; and for that reason he resolved to rid the yards of spoilsmen as soon as he could. The general's obstinacy in this connection drew heavy fire from party chiefs and henchmen at various levels. In September, an outraged Brooklyn ward captain wrote Tracy, demanding to know if "it is possible you are so thick in the head as to suppose the 800 or 900 Democrats you retain in the yards will vote the Republican ticket? You are either approaching your dotage or you are a fraud on the Party." [24]

Of such stuff was the unpleasant fringe of Tracy's routine made. Setting it aside, he turned his attention to a reorganization of the administrative system in hopes of increasing the efficiency of the department. Mindful of the need for coordinated planning and execution on the part of those bureaus which would be responsible for the design and construction of the fleet he intended to forge, Tracy created—by virtue of General Order 372—a board of five bureau chiefs to supervise all phases of his forthcoming building program. He sought to obtain thereby the joint cooperation of the Bureaus of Steam Engineering, Construction and Repair, Ordnance, Yards and Docks, and Equipment and Recruiting. If the consolidation succeeded, the secretary would be able henceforth to count on a consensus and to enjoy relative freedom from parochial jurisdictional disputes. Extending his reorganization to the Bureau of Navigation and the Bureau of Provisions and Clothing, Tracy assigned the former full direction of ship and personnel movements and the latter management of all business related to supplies and accounts.[25]

This accomplished, the general prepared to rescue the Naval War College from limbo. Determined to preserve the institution's independent character in accordance with the aims of its founder, he planned to move it from Goat Island back to its original home at Coaster's Harbor. Although he was unable to effect the transfer for almost a year, he managed during the interim to keep the College alive and separate from the Torpedo Station.[26]

The general's masterful defense of the War College placed him squarely in the progressive camp and tended to repudiate the attitude

24 Charles Brandle to Tracy, September 5, 1889, in Tracy Papers.
25 Navy Dept., *Annual Report*, 1889. The Bureau of Provisions and Clothing became the Bureau of Supplies and Accounts in 1892.
26 Luce-Mahan correspondence, 1889–1903, in NHF; Mahan, *Sail to Steam*, I, 221; Puleston, *Mahan*, 92.

of Whitney who, in Mahan's words, "had absolutely no appreciation for the systematic study of naval warfare." [27] Neither had Tracy at first, but once he had made up his mind to apply the capital-ship theory to his expansion program for 1890, he realized that only the War College could furnish the advanced education essential to officers expected to operate the battleships he contemplated. Besides, the general had the foresight to regard the institution as a potential sounding board for the exchange of ideas among men versed in the various aspects of naval and military operations. This function alone would, in Tracy's opinion, justify the existence of the College. As the source and disseminator of information relative to modern naval warfare, it would afford his program the strategic guidance so conspicuously absent in the past.[28]

The general's first act on behalf of the College, pending its removal from Goat Island, was to recall Mahan from Puget Sound and reinstate him as president. Returning to Newport in August, 1889, Captain Mahan resumed his scholarly duties with misgivings. Conscious of his unpopularity with authoritative superiors, he decided to cast about for a ranking ally on whom he could count for assistance in the struggle against the school's detractors. Stephen Luce was not available for this purpose; he had been promoted to rear admiral and would remain at sea until relieved of his squadron command toward the end of the year by Rear Admiral Bancroft Gherardi.[29] After much thought, Mahan selected Admiral Porter as a likely substitute.

Porter was well-situated to help Mahan. Not only had his defection from the conservative hierarchy left him a lonely figure in the department, but his high rank and position as chief of the Board of Inspection gave him easy access to the secretary. Also, the admiral's conversion to the new creed of professionalism, which had begun earlier in his association with Luce, was by now complete, owing to the knowledge he had acquired in the summers of 1886 and 1887.[30] In these years, Porter owned a cottage in Jamestown, Rhode Island, a short sail across Narragansett Bay from Newport, where he spent his free time in order to be near his daughter, the wife of Lieutenant J. C. Logan, aide to Luce and Mahan, successively. In the course of frequent visits to the Logans'

---

27 Mahan, "Reminiscences," 6. See also, West, *Admirals of American Empire*, 149.
28 Mahan, "Reminiscences," 2–7, in which Mahan predicted Tracy's support of the College. See also, S. B. Luce, "The U.S. Naval War College," *NIP*, XXXVI (1911), 671. Here Luce acknowledged the College's debt to Tracy.
29 *Navy Register*, 1886, 1889.
30 Luce-Porter correspondence, 1889, in NHF; J. R. Soley, *Porter*, 465ff.; Huntington, *Soldier and State*, 237–41.

quarters, Admiral Porter became familiar with the objectives of the College and, after Luce left for sea duty, with the ideas of Mahan.

Consequently, Porter responded eagerly to the captain's distress signal. He had urged first Chandler, and later Whitney, to sustain the College while Luce was president; and he proved more than willing to try his hand with Tracy on Mahan's account. In the process, the admiral provided the *liaison* between Mahan and Tracy that led the latter to depend on the captain during the next three years for advice on the strategic element of naval policy. As middleman, Porter influenced the secretary's acceptance of Mahan's definition of sea power.[31]

Prior to the captain's first assignment as president of the War College in 1886, he had followed the usual career of a naval officer. The previous year had found him in Peruvian waters as commander of the U.S.S. *Wachusett*. During this tour of duty, he devoted his leisure hours to study ashore, particularly at the library of the English Club in Lima where he absorbed the works of Mommsen, Napier, and Jomini on military science. Guided by his reading, Mahan gradually shaped his own theory of the role of naval power in national defense.[32]

In the interval between his arrival at the War College and Luce's departure, the captain presented his ideas to student officers in a series of lectures embodying his research at Lima and elsewhere. The lectures impressed Luce so favorably that he encouraged Mahan to apply his findings to naval warfare and publish the results as soon as possible. Thus persuaded, the captain put his material into manuscript form and added a searching analysis of sea power in action.[33] The thesis of Mahan's manuscript had two principal parts which set forth his justification of a battle fleet's existence in peace as well as war. The first dealt with the strategic mission of a fleet in wartime. Stated briefly, it asserted the author's conviction that victory depended on control of the sea which, in turn, required the maintenance of a permanent force of capital ships under unified command. Possession of such a force, declared Mahan, must be considered the primary requisite of a maritime nation's security.[34] This conception was not new. The British Navy had operated on the capital-ship principle for two hundred years, and strategists of continental

31 J. R. Soley, *Porter*, 465-67; Mahan-Porter correspondence, 1886–89, in NHF; *Navy Register*, 1885. When Mahan became president of the College, his staff consisted of Logan and Bliss, now a captain. Subsequently, Bliss helped establish the Army War College. Huntington, *Soldier and State*, Chap. 9, *passim*.
32 Mahan, "Reminiscences," 2–7; Luce to Mahan, July 15, 1907, in NWC.
33 Mahan, *Sail to Steam*, I, 280–300; Puleston, *Mahan*, 81–90.
34 Mahan, *Influence*, 26–139, *passim*.

powers had pronounced it valid long before Mahan put pen to paper. But by acting on Luce's suggestion and by making use of his own extensive research and literary skill, Captain Mahan produced the first systematic codification of the implications of sea power ever published.

The second part of the captain's theory, which presented the rationale for keeping a navy at full strength in peacetime, attracted even more attention. A permanent battle fleet, reasoned Mahan, would necessitate the acquisition of overseas bases to support its far-ranging operations. Colonies planted around these bases would benefit commercial interests as well by serving as sources of raw material and markets for surplus products. Another corollary of naval and territorial expansion, an enlarged merchant marine under constant naval protection, would not only bring merchants a greater share in the carrying trade, but also furnish the additional manpower and vessels needed by a navy at war.[35]

Mahan's ideas fell together neatly in a manner reminiscent of the old mercantile system. His cogent arguments for maintaining a high state of preparedness at sea under all circumstances captivated navalists everywhere and filled an embarrassing void in the public relations of admiralties from Berlin to Tokyo.[36] Since Tracy's patriotism had already assumed imperialist overtones, the ideas expressed in the captain's manuscript were especially appealing to him. He knew that the American public must be conditioned to accept the positive policy he had in mind and to understand why he considered it necessary. To educate the nation in the needs of the Navy, therefore, and to promote certain related objectives of common interest to him and Mahan, the secretary promised to do all he could to give the captain the opportunity to continue his writing and teaching.[37]

In the fall of 1889, having already conveyed Luce's opinions on policy and introduced Mahan to the secretary, Admiral Porter brought Professor James R. Soley to Tracy's attention. During his tenure at the Naval Academy, Soley had distinguished himself as a scholar with his *Report on Foreign Systems of Naval Education* which, published as a government document, enriched professional knowledge in the United States. The report, together with his naval monograph on the

35 *Ibid.*
36 For example, Kaiser Wilhelm II ordered a copy of Mahan's work for every German naval library. It is said also that, though the book was translated into Japanese, midshipmen of Japan's navy were required to read Mahan in the original as a primer in English!
37 Puleston, *Mahan*, 115.

Civil War, *The Blockade and the Cruisers*, appearing in 1883, won him his appointment to the War College three years later.[38]

Porter's friendship with the professor began in Washington at the Office of Naval Records where the latter was working, between sessions of the College, as compiler and editor of the records of the Civil War navies[39] and where the admiral was engaged in research for his own naval history of the war.[40] Perceiving in the scholar a high dedication to the Navy and an unusual depth of understanding of its strategic mission, Porter presented him to Tracy.

Three men—Luce, Mahan, and Soley—supplied the theoretical component of Tracy's new policy with Porter standing by as adviser and communicator. Drawing on his legal and political experience, the general couched their ideas in businesslike language which, he hoped, even the isolationist wing of Congress would find hard to resist.

To Luce goes the credit for initiating the study of naval warfare as a science. It was he who persuaded Mahan to teach naval officers the strategic doctrine governing both military and naval warfare and the true relation of one to the other. By delineating in his *magnum opus* the historical implications of sea power, Mahan became the prophet of the policy revolution taking shape in 1889. The third member of this eventful team, Professor Soley, a reliable source of all manner of naval *data*, emerges as the scholarly workhorse of the revolution.

Porter continued to provide the linkage between the trio and the secretary's office until, in the winter of 1889–90, he fell seriously ill, whereupon Captain Mahan replaced him as Tracy's chief consultant.[41] By then, the general had almost completed the policy statement he planned to make in the following November.

Mahan's situation at Newport worsened in the winter months. True, his recently inherited position of influence in the secretary's councils offset the loss of his ally Porter, but he still faced the problem of administering the curriculum and nonacademic affairs of the College while attempting at the same time to cope with its foes. To compound the dilemma, Rear Admiral Walker, who had constantly supported the War College, was relieved of his command by Rear Admiral Francis

38 J. R. Soley, *Porter*, 465ff.; "Soley, James Russell," in *DAB*, XVII, 392; *Navy Register*, 1889.
39 Formally entitled *Official Records of the Union and Confederate Navies in the War of the Rebellion.*
40 Porter's *Naval History of the Civil War*, is based largely on personal recollections and is considered inaccurate.
41 Various letters, Porter to Luce, 1889, in NHF; Soley, *Porter*, 466–70.

M. Ramsay, an equally consistent opponent of the institution. As superintendent of the Naval Academy in 1884, when Luce founded the College, Ramsay had condemned it on the premise that any postgraduate naval school should be designated an extension of the Academy and be placed under the authority of the superintendent. Thereafter, he attempted to thwart Luce's endeavors by dissuading officers from enrolling in the College.[42] But now, as head of the bureau in control not only of the College but also of the detailing of its staff, Ramsay could, if he chose, relegate the institution and its instructors to oblivion. There was good reason, moreover, to believe that he would single out Mahan for exile since the captain's record as a deck officer, in Ramsay's opinion, left much to be desired. With this powerful adversary in a position to detach him at will, Mahan felt his days ashore were numbered.[43]

Sure enough, just as Tracy's proposal to return the War College to Coaster's Harbor came up for consideration in Congress, Mahan learned that Ramsay was preparing to send him back to sea. At the captain's request, General Tracy intervened. First, he prevailed on Admiral Ramsay to defer Mahan's transfer indefinitely by emphasizing the beneficial effects of his writing on public relations. Then, he removed the College and its faculty from the jurisdiction of the Bureau of Navigation and brought it under the supervision of the secretary's office—a drastic action which Tracy considered advisable under the circumstances. For the time being at least, the College retained its independence and Mahan was allowed to work in peace.[44]

No sooner had the general arranged this reprieve for the captain than another problem arose. Having prepared the final draft of his manuscript, Captain Mahan discovered that lack of funds, coupled with the indifference of publishers to naval histories, might postpone its appearance for some time. Aware of Soley's experience in such matters, he turned to him for help. By dint of considerable persuasion, the professor finally convinced the Boston firm of Little, Brown and Company that the manuscript was worth publishing.[45] As a result, the summer of 1890

42 Mahan to Luce, May 7, 1890, in NHF. See also, Puleston, *Mahan*, citing Luce to Tracy, March 14, 1889.
43 Numerous fitness reports on Mahan, 1878–80, Puleston Collection of Mahan papers, Division of Manuscripts, Library of Congress. See also, Mahan, *Sail to Steam*, I, 280–300.
44 Eure, "Military Colleges"; Mahan to Luce, May 7, 1890, in NHF.
45 Puleston, *Mahan*, 90, citing Luce to Tracy, March 14, 1889; Mahan to Soley (undated memorandum) in NWC. For an interesting sidelight of Mahan's financial problem, see Mahan to Luce, September 21, 1889, in NHF. Here Mahan wrote: "Mr. J. Pierrepont Morgan . . . said he would contribute $200 of the remainder of the sum."

witnessed the publication of *The Influence of Sea Power upon History*, a book which brought its author acclaim as the world's foremost naval theoretician.

In time, the captain's renown overshadowed General Tracy's service to the Navy and gave rise to the belief that Mahan deserved the lion's share of credit for shaping the development of America's first battle fleet. The fallacy of this contention is clearly revealed in the captain's correspondence; he attributes to Luce the philosophy underlying the achievement and to Tracy the insight, willpower and political skill to bring it to pass.

Although the general allowed himself to be influenced by Luce and Mahan, he never forgot that he alone had final responsibility for naval policy. Even Mahan found Tracy impossible to budge in any given situation until he had analyzed it carefully and reached his own conclusions, many of which did not coincide with the captain's judgment.[46] General Tracy's independent mind prevented him from toadying to Mahan or anyone else, as his subsequent actions made clear.

46 West, *Admirals of American Empire*, 149ff., citing Mahan to Luce, September 3, 1901. This letter suggests that Tracy had developed strong opinions of his own by the end of 1889, and that Mahan was not always happy at his chief's intransigence thereafter.

III

THE REVOLUTION TAKES SHAPE

In the summer and fall of 1889 General Tracy embarked on a carefully phased program designed to create a receptive atmosphere for the policy he had formulated in collaboration with Mahan. In mid-July he organized a policy board for the purpose of obtaining the best technical advice available concerning the projected battle fleet. Ten weeks thereafter, he ordered the chief of the Bureau of Navigation to form the Navy's first "squadron of evolution" in order to give practical application to the strategic and tactical principles under study at the War College and to provide professionalized training at sea.

To make up this squadron, Tracy selected the cruisers *Atlanta, Boston,* and *Chicago,* and the recently commissioned gunboat *Yorktown.* The ships were to operate together, undertaking tactical evolutions as an integrated force, under an independent, unified command. Small as it was, the group would in time become the nucleus of a permanent American fleet.[1]

In November the secretary submitted his initial report to the President; in it he introduced his policy and the reasons behind it in terms that reflected the intellectualism of Luce and Mahan, combined with his own appreciation of political reality.[2] This document, one of the more forceful in the history of naval policy, lashed out at the weakness of the

1 Navy Dept., *Annual Report,* 1889.
2 Sprout, *Naval Power,* 207.

54

nation's first line of defense and prescribed radical remedies for correcting the situation.[3]

General Tracy, in his report, ranked the United States twelfth among the world's naval powers. The American fleet then consisted of three armored cruisers, eight smaller armored vessels, and thirty-one unarmored ships, built or being built. The United Kingdom, on the other hand, had in service an array of 367 warships, of which 76 were armored. Lesser maritime powers Tracy rated after Britain in order of strength: France, Russia, Germany, Holland, Spain, Italy, Turkey, China, Norway-Sweden, and Austria-Hungary. All had larger total numbers than the United States, and all save China boasted more armored men-of-war. On the basis of this comparison, declared the general, "with all the additions authorized by the legislation of the last seven years, the country will . . . be absolutely at the mercy of states having less than one-tenth of its population, one-thirtieth of its wealth, and one-hundredth of its area."

Tracy warned Harrison that any one of the powers listed could raid the seaboard and levy enough tribute in a single attack to pay the cost of a naval war and pointed out that half of this amount would purchase sufficient sea power to provide the country with a "guaranty of perpetual peace." Deploring the tendency of the previous administration to expand the fleet by building unarmored steel cruisers as false economy, Tracy insisted that the United States must construct armored battleships which could defend the coast by destroying an enemy fleet of capital ships at sea.

We must have the force to raise blockades. . . . We must have a fleet of battleships that will beat off the enemy's fleet on its approach, for it is not to be tolerated that the United States . . . is to submit to an attack on the threshold of its harbors. Finally, we must be able to divert an enemy's force from our coast by threatening his own, for a war, though defensive in principle, may be conducted most effectively by being offensive in its operations.

The secretary considered the posture of offense a "practical business question of insuring our property and our trade" and of fundamental concern to Americans in the interior as well as on the seaboard. He cited in particular the necessity of protecting American interests in the Gulf

3 Navy Dept., *Annual Report*, 1889.

of Mexico and the Pacific, where the occurrence of crises affected national development and prosperity too profoundly to be ignored.

As to the cost of such insurance in the form of an enlarged, reconstituted fleet, the general felt it a small price to pay for national survival, especially in view of the beneficial side effects accruing to both business and labor in the construction process. In conclusion, he urged haste:

> Naval wars in the future will be short and sharp. It is morally certain that they will be fought out to the end with the force available at the beginning. The nation that is ready to strike the first blow will gain an advantage which its antagonist can never offset, and inflict an injury from which he can never recover.

Estimating that the ships he had in mind would require about fifteen years to complete under existing conditions, the secretary called for an immediate start in construction.

The foregoing represented a preamble in justification of the specific proposals that followed as to the types and number of warships the general deemed essential to meet the demands of the country's strategic situation. To establish the minimum striking power he thought commensurate with this situation, Tracy recommended the creation of two fleets of seagoing, armored battleships: twelve for duty in the Atlantic, and eight for the Pacific. These vessels, he emphasized, must be the best of their type anywhere with respect to structural strength, armor, firepower, and speed.

As a gesture to isolationists, the secretary included a proposal to build twenty coast-defense ships. Inasmuch as such craft had no place in an offensive fleet, he undoubtedly intended to use them as bait for catching the votes of congressmen otherwise apt to oppose his plan as too warlike.[4] In addition, Tracy requested authorization to build twenty-nine cruisers to complement those already in service or under construction and a number of torpedo-boats. Underlining again the need for speed in completing the capital ships, he suggested delaying the building of the proposed monitors and cruisers and starting work on eight of the twenty battleships at once, in view of the inability of domestic shipyards to take on the whole program at one time.

For the immense task of building the capital ships, Tracy stated his preference for private contractors. Not only did he consider the navy yards unreliable, but he saw the advantage of encouraging private industry to participate in naval expansion.

4 *Ibid.;* Sprout, *Naval Power,* 205–210.

The general had several secondary proposals. In the absence of a well-trained naval reserve, he urged the government to stimulate the development of the naval militia units then being formed in certain states. Pending the establishment of a national reserve, he maintained, such units, if properly led, would serve the Navy well in time of emergency. In direct contradiction to Whitney's policy, the general recommended the transfer of the War College to an independent command and expressed hope that it would be returned to Coaster's Harbor in the near future. "The War College," he said, "is unquestionably one of the most important institutions connected with the Navy."

Like many of his predecessors, the general suggested—to no avail—that the Revenue Marine, parent of the Coast Guard, be merged with the Navy. But revenue cutters continued as before to operate as instruments of the Treasury Department except in wartime, when they were placed under the command of the Bureau of Navigation.

In his statement of the Navy Department's financial condition, the secretary announced his intention to reduce expenditures by discontinuing all repair work on obsolete vessels. His estimate for the fiscal year 1889–90 amounted to $25,599,253.79, about $1,000,000 less than the sum spent by Whitney in the preceding year.

Toward the end of his report, Tracy voiced his imperialist leanings by plumping openly for the acquisition of bases to service the Atlantic and Pacific fleets he had proposed. Referring specifically to the Samoan Islands, he observed that "the necessity of establishing foreign coaling stations, and the commercial importance of these islands, render it desirable to place this station as soon as possible on a permanent basis." [5]

It happened that the secretary was in a position to dramatize the importance of a Samoan base to the United States owing to certain occurrences in the islands during the previous year. Well aware of its probable impact on Congress and the public, he told the story in full. Prior to Harrison's inauguration, a crisis had arisen in Samoa over the conflicting interests of the controlling powers—the United States, Great Britain, and Germany. Inasmuch as American aspirations here centered on the establishment of a coaling station, the Navy was immediately involved. Early in March, 1889, a false rumor of a skirmish between German and American naval units reached Washington, provoking a spate of belligerent outcries and drawing attention to the weakness of American sea power in the Pacific, as compared to that of Germany. Within a few days of the alleged fighting at Apia, Tracy received a dispatch from

5 Navy Dept., *Annual Report*, 1889.

Rear Admiral L. A. Kimberly reporting the devastation caused by a savage hurricane that had just swept the islands. High winds and heavy seas had taken their toll of the warships anchored in the harbor at Apia, sinking the German gunboats *Eber* and *Adler* and forcing the crew of the *Olga* to beach their ship. The American contingent fared no better; at the height of the storm, the *Trenton* and *Vandalia* had "settled to their gundecks," while the U.S.S. *Nipsic* had run aground after a severe battering. H.M.S. *Calliope*, however, had sufficient power to pitch and pound her way to the safety of the open sea, being "roundly cheered as she crept by the doomed American vessels . . ." [6]

Presenting Kimberly's account of the storm in his report, General Tracy pointed up its significance in his own words. Not only had the brilliant performance of Britain's *Calliope* served to reveal the deficiency of the underpowered American squadron but, when the storm had cleared, the United States had "almost no . . . warships worthy of the name in the Pacific Ocean." [7] Because of the impetus the news of this disaster might lend his construction program, the secretary saw to it that the story received considerable attention in the newspapers.

The White House released the substance of Tracy's recommendations to the press in late November, 1889. Lead articles and editorials gave his ideas full play. As the secretary expected, the reaction was mixed. A Midwestern editor opposed the battleship program on the ground that "taxing the country's plows and hammers to build large navies is poor economy." [8] In an article extolling the monitor-raider system of defense endorsed by Gustavus Fox, the *Army and Navy Journal* predicted confidently: "We have never had . . . a Secretary . . . of more natural ability than Mr. Tracy. When his experience equals his ability, he will come to the same conclusions as Captain Fox." [9]

These samplings represented the minority editorial opinion. The editor of New York's leading newspaper heartily welcomed Tracy's pragmatic approach to the question of naval expansion, declaring, "Secretary Tracy states the principles of national policy with the clearness and force of a business proposition." [10] A lengthy article in *Leslie's Newspaper* ex-

---

6 Rear Adm. L. A. Kimberly, "Report on the Samoan Hurricane," March 19, 1889, Navy Dept., *Annual Report*, 1889. For further details, see D. W. Knox, *History of the United States Navy* (New York, 1936), 326ff.; New York *Herald*, March 9, 1889.

7 Tracy is quoted in New York *Herald*, March 9, 1889.

8 St. Louis *Republic*, December 3, 1889.

9 *Army and Navy Journal* (New York), December 7, 1889.

10 New York *Times*, December 5, 1889.

emplified the sentiment of the majority, particularly in its emphatic conclusion: "Until the United States has a fleet of twenty battleships, with . . . cruisers and torpedo-boats in suitable proportion . . . this country can never consider that it possesses a navy, and a navy it cannot afford to be without." [11]

In his inaugural address, President Harrison had left no doubt of his determination to build up the Navy along the lines dictated by strategic necessity. On that occasion he had stated, "The construction of a sufficient number of modern warships . . . should progress as rapidly as is consistent with care and perfection in plans and workmanship." Then, revealing his imperialist colors, Harrison called for the acquisition of "convenient" bases for the general maintenance of the fleet in foreign seas.[12] The President followed up these proposals with a more specific recommendation after he had digested the content of Tracy's report. In his first annual message, Harrison urged Congress to authorize eight battleships immediately and to initiate a survey of merchantmen for the purpose of determining their adaptability to naval service in wartime.[13] Thus, the President gave his tacit endorsement to Mahan's theory as well as to Tracy's requests.

Indirect support for naval expansion came from another important figure in the administration, Secretary of State James G. Blaine. Although Blaine apparently kept his thoughts to himself on this score in 1889, his desire to achieve hemispheric solidarity and his perception of the implications of the Samoan situation certainly imply an appreciation of the importance of sea power. Statesmen of the day relied on naval strength to reinforce aggressive diplomacy, and Blaine is remembered in part for his assertion of American rights in various quarters of the world.[14]

The presence of numerous Navy buffs in Congress gave Tracy his most valid reason for optimism. For the first time since 1875, the Re-

11 *Frank Leslie's Illustrated Newspaper* (New York), March 9, 1890. For additional favorable comment on Tracy's program, see Louisville *Courier-Journal*, San Francisco *Daily Evening Bulletin*, Philadelphia *Press*, December 2, 1889; *The Landmark* (Norfolk), Baltimore *Morning Herald*, Chicago *Tribune*, New York *Daily Tribune*, Brooklyn *Daily Eagle*, December 3, 1889.
12 *Messages and Papers*, IX, 10.
13 *Ibid.*, 44–45.
14 A. T. Volwiler, "Harrison, Blaine and American Foreign Policy," American Philosophical Society *Proceedings*, LXXIX (1938), 637; hereinafter cited as Volwiler, "Harrison, Blaine." See also, Russell Bastert, "James G. Blaine and the First International Conference of American States" (Ph.D. dissertation, Yale University, 1952), 426–40; hereinafter cited as Bastert, "Blaine and Conference."

publicans had clear majorities in both houses, though their margin of control of the lower house was thin.[15] Here Speaker Tom Reed could be counted on to utilize his slim superiority in numbers to the advantage of Tracy's program. Another Maine man, Chairman Charles Boutelle of the House Naval Affairs Committee, who was a friend and correspondent of Admiral Luce, supported Tracy's recommendations enthusiastically. The second ranking member of this committee, Massachusetts' Henry Cabot Lodge, demanded a frankly imperialist policy and the strongest possible naval force. Fortunately for Tracy's cause, Lodge had the tact and eloquence to impress his colleagues with the urgency of the business at hand without unduly alarming them. Although the navalists enjoyed less support on the Democratic side of the house, Hilary Herbert of Alabama and William G. McAdoo of New Jersey, both of whom considered the naval issue nonpartisan, could be relied on to back the battleship construction plan.[16]

Perhaps the most influential spokesman for naval expansion in the Senate was Eugene Hale of Maine, who ranked second on Chairman James Cameron's naval committee. Although Hale proclaimed himself an anti-imperialist and later opposed the expansionist leadership of Theodore Roosevelt, his lengthy correspondence with Secretary Tracy reveals the Senator's interest in upgrading the fleet.[17] Hale's defection from navalist ranks after 1893 is difficult to explain, but his significance in the drama about to unfold cannot be denied. Tracy knew he could depend on the Senator from Maine when Congress prepared to debate his proposals in the spring of 1890. [18]

The favorable attitude taken by congressional leaders and prominent editors gratified the general, but he wished to appeal to a larger audience for support. He and Mahan appreciated the importance of public educa-

15 Harrison was a "minority" president; his party controlled the House by 173 to 156.

16 *Congressional Record*, 51st Cong., 1st Sess., 3167–69, 5227–28. For other observations on congressional alignments during the debates, see A. C. Buell to C. Cramp, September 17, 1891, in Tracy Papers. Also, Sprout, *Naval Power*, 206ff. Herbert and McAdoo had at first favored the traditional monitor-raider policy, but were finally persuaded to side with the battleship supporters in 1890; both served the Navy in Cleveland's second administration, Herbert as secretary and McAdoo as his assistant.

17 Hale to Tracy, various letters, December, 1889, through June, 1890, in Tracy Papers; Boutelle to Luce, March 1, 6, 1890, in NHF, Luce Collection; Martin Meadows, "Eugene Hale and the American Navy," *The American Neptune* (July, 1962), 187–90.

18 *Ibid.*; Sprout, *Naval Power*, 209ff.

tion in naval affairs; to that end they sought the assistance of articulate men capable of popularizing the battleship program. Theodore Roosevelt, a member of the Civil Service Commission, and Charles Dana of the New York *Sun* cooperated with the secretary in publicizing the strategic needs of the Navy. Others soon joined them as leading citizens in government and private life became increasingly aware of their country's rapid approach to great power status and of the significant part the Navy must take in this evolution. Analyzing the contemporary climate of opinion, a New York editor had this to say: "We feel sure we are on the eve of important changes . . . so fraught with enterprises that will have a momentous effect on the future destiny of our country that the cordial support of all true friends of the Union will only be necessary to perfect attainment of other things within our grasp." [19] In the light of subsequent events, the editor's optimism proved premature. Despite substantial agreement in principle on Tracy's recommendations, sharp dissension—even among navalists—developed as to the manner of their execution.

On December 5, 1889, Senator Hale introduced four bills incorporating General Tracy's immediate program. The first proposed the construction of eight battleships displacing from 7,500 to 10,000 tons in addition to two armored monitors, three cruisers, and five torpedo-boats. Following Tracy's suggestion, Hale's second bill instituted the policy of naming battleships after states and cruisers after cities, with the intention of stimulating local interest through identification with the new men-of-war. The Senator's third measure, which was devised to attract superior enlisted recruits, lengthened the term of enlistment and offered bounties for longevity of service. If the bill became law, "thirty-year men" would receive three quarters of their active duty pay after retirement. The fourth of Hale's measures provided for a survey of the nation's merchant ships to determine their worth as naval auxiliaries in wartime.[20]

What degree of success would have attended Hale's legislation if unforeseen developments had not muddied congressional thinking is a matter of speculation. Within a month of the day the Senator introduced his bills on the Senate floor, the recently appointed Naval Policy Board submitted findings that confused the situation and changed the minds of a number of congressmen who had voiced approval of Tracy's brand of naval expansion.

19 *The Seaboard* (New York), December 5, 1889.
20 *Congressional Record*, 51st Cong., 1st Sess., 3163–70; New York *Mail and Express*, December 6, 1889.

The board had begun its deliberations the preceding July in compliance with Tracy's instructions.[21] To preside over its sessions, the secretary had assigned Commodore W. P. McCann, with Captains W. T. Sampson and R. L. Phythian as the Commodore's senior assistants. Four additional officers were subsequently ordered to complete the membership.[22] Contrary to the intentions of the secretary who, as a veteran practitioner of the art of the possible in politics, understood the fallacy of presenting a program too radical for contemporary attitudes, the members of the board attempted to provide for the future as well as the present by recommending the authorization of an unprecedented number of warships. Although the substance of their plan was not out of line with the ideas advanced by Luce and Mahan, the board members failed to anticipate the reaction of a nation not yet ready to stomach a policy which would challenge the world's naval powers.

The board's report opened with an analysis of the country's position and prospects at the time of writing, January 20, 1890. In view of the apparent absence of national interest in acquiring overseas colonies and the high degree of security existing on all frontiers, McCann and his men admitted that the likelihood of war seemed remote for the present. Nevertheless, they perceived certain danger signals in the wind. For one thing, the conflicting commercial aspirations of the maritime states might soon lead to a collision involving the United States. For another, the current American bid for a larger share of the world's cargo trade could lead to a breach of the peace. Thirdly, the creation of an isthmian canal under the sole protection of the United States would invite foreign intervention so long as the nation lacked an adequate deterrent on the sea.[23]

Agreeing with Tracy that the best defense was a good offense, the board recommended a fleet of ten battleships having a 15,000-mile cruising range, to be supplemented by twenty-five short-range capital ships. As a supporting force, the board proposed building twenty-four armored cruisers, fifteen lighter torpedo-cruisers, and more than one hundred small torpedo-boats. A number of rams and miscellaneous small craft completed the armada envisaged by the policy board. The

21 "Report of the Policy Board," *NIP*, XVI (1890), *passim*. The report comprises the whole of this issue of *NIP*.
22 *Ibid.*, Appendix A, 272–73. The four officers were Commander W. M. Folger, Lieutenant Commander W. H. Brownson, Naval Constructor R. Gatewood, members; and Ensign P. R. Alger, recorder. Of these men, at least two—Sampson and Folger—were known supporters of the War College, sympathetic to Tracy's plans.
23 *Ibid.*, 214ff.

members estimated the total cost of construction at $281,550,000. The projected armada would displace an aggregate of 497,000 tons which, added to the tonnage of warships already in service or authorized, would bring the grand total up to 610,000 tons! A glance at displacement statistics of European navies for 1890 indicates the magnitude of the challenge the board was presenting. If its plan took effect and no major change occurred in the size of foreign fleets during the construction process, the United States Navy would rank second to Great Britain in tonnage and well ahead of France.[24]

The publication of this program provoked a storm of protest throughout the country. Even the more extreme expansionist editors condemned it as a product of "naval fanaticism."[25] Senator Hale agreed, declaring that no responsible man in government could support the board's recommendations. In the House, Representative Herbert indignantly called upon Congress to reject the report out of hand, while the general himself washed his hands of the document.[26]

Tracy's disavowal seems inconsistent on the surface, considering his own request for a quantity of battleships; but he had good reason for his repudiation of the board's findings. It had been the general's intention to have the substance of the report kept secret and to use it as a long-range master plan for building up the Navy along strategic lines, piece by piece. The news of its unauthorized, and untimely, publication dismayed him.[27] He realized that the board's program would be interpreted generally as a sign of the administration's agressiveness and that as a result his proposals would surely lose popular support. Senator Hale reacted in much the same way. An officer close to Hale and Tracy reported: "No report of the policy board was to be published. The general feeling here is that it was unwise to make any portion of it public, and it has unquestionably hurt the service as far as this year's appropriations are concerned. Senator Hale has been pretty positive on this point."[28]

During the winter and spring of 1890, Quakers and other pacifist groups showered petitions on Congress, demanding firm action against the proponents of naval expansion. Apparently these groups shared the

24 *Ibid.; Senate Executive Documents*, 51st Cong., 1st Sess., No. 43, pp. 1–2; *Congressional Record*, 59th Cong., 1st Sess., 6398.
25 New York *Herald*, January 31, 1890.
26 *Senate Executive Documents*, 51st Cong., 1st Sess., No. 43, pp. 1–2.
27 Millis, *Arms and Men*, 158.
28 Cmdr. C. M. Chester to Luce, undated, 1890, in NHF, Luce Collection.

conviction that recent trends in Washington implied the rise of an imperialist spirit which, if not broken at once, would send the nation to war.[29] This vigorous reaction, coupled with that of better-informed and more moderate representatives of public opinion, made it plain that the majority of Americans deplored the notion of competing with foreign states in a naval race. It also became clear before summer that Tracy's relatively modest program was in jeopardy.

To make matters worse, Bethlehem Steel's failure to deliver armor plate to the building yards was holding up completion of the new heavy cruisers. The *Maine* was thus affected, and the superintending inspector at Cramps' yard in Philadelphia warned Tracy that the *New York* could not be launched by the contract date unless her armor arrived soon.[30]

At this point, General Tracy decided to investigate. His personal probe of the department's relations with the domestic steel industry led him to examine records of the Chandler era, when the association had first become significant. After considerable research, he realized that Bethlehem's lapse was the indirect product of a series of developments originating with the laying down of the ABCD's.

From what the secretary could ascertain, John Roach had experienced little difficulty in acquiring the steel needed for these ships from three small subcontractors, despite the high quality demanded by his contract. However, the suppliers lost money on the transaction as a result of their efforts to meet naval standards. The construction of the ABCD's, moreover, occasioned the manufacture of the first open-hearth plates and structural shapes ever produced in the United States. These events had formed a pattern, in which the Navy doubled as spur and counselor to the steelmakers.

Adhering to the rigid requirements set by the department, the naval inspectors consistently rejected unacceptable steel while advisers provided by the Navy helped the producers implement improved techniques. Although the industry's executives had no desire to invest in expensive experimentation for the purpose of satisfying what they regarded as unnecessarily stiff requirements, most of them perceived the

29 Sprout, *Naval Power*, 209ff., citing a number of contemporary periodicals and newspapers.
30 Capt. J. W. Philip to Tracy, December 23, 1889, in Tracy Papers. For Tracy's initial attempts to expedite armor deliveries, see various letters, Bethlehem Steel Company to Tracy, Philadelphia and Reading Railroad Company to Tracy, March 2–May 15, 1890, in Tracy Papers.

long-range financial advantage of cooperating with the Navy. The initial reverses arising from such cooperation would soon be more than offset, they believed, because the demand for steel must grow in direct proportion to the expansion of the fleet. The Navy Department, on the other hand, recognized the desirability of dealing with domestic rather than foreign contractors and for this reason took pains to encourage the industry to look to a golden future. Consequently, Tracy concluded, the steel companies would benefit from the enlargement of the Navy, while the Navy stood to gain from the growth of the domestic steel industry.[31]

The general learned that by 1887 Bethlehem had begun casting steel for large structural forms; the fifteen-ton stern section cast for the cruiser *Charleston* set a record for the day. This method had proved equally successful for the fabrication of gun mounts. But intensive testing had demonstrated that castings lacked the strength required of armor plate.[32] The record indicates that when Whitney discovered this, he encouraged three concerns, through personal channels, to bid on high-grade forgings for armor plate. Dismayed at the prospect of a high rejection rate, both Carnegie and the Midvale Iron and Steel Company refused the invitation. Bethlehem was more receptive, however; and in June, 1887, Whitney awarded the company a contract for 14,000 tons of armor plate and a quantity of gun forgings on the condition that Bethlehem promise to build an armor forging plant in the near future at government expense. Then, Tracy found, Whitney had secured a congressional appropriation of $4,500,000 to foot the cost of construction. Nevertheless, to the general's distress, the plant was not producing armor two-and-a-half years after the conclusion of the contract.[33]

The background of the apparent breach of contract was complex, to say the least. Since no facility for forging steel existed in America

---

31 Dean Allard, "The Influence of the U. S. Navy upon the American Steel Industry, 1880–1900" (M.A. thesis, Georgetown University, 1959), 32–34. For a contemporary account, see American Iron and Steel Association, *History of the Manufacture of Armor Plate for the United States Navy* (Philadelphia, 1899), 17–21. Allard cites this work widely. Roach's subcontractors were Norway Iron and Steel Company, South Boston, Mass.; Phoenix Iron and Steel Company, Philadelphia; and Park Brothers and Company, Pittsburgh. Robley Evans was at the time an inspector of plate for the department. See Robley Evans, *A Sailor's Log: Recollections of Forty Years of Naval Life* (New York, 1903), 123.

32 Andrew Carnegie, *The Autobiography of Andrew Carnegie* (New York, 1905), 122; Navy Dept., *Annual Report*, 1888.

33 Long, *New Navy*, I, 47–49; Nevins, *Cleveland*, 122; Allard, "Influence upon Steel Industry," 65ff.

in 1887, Bethlehem had sought the advice and assistance of European armorers. The outcome of this quest was the purchase and transplanting of an entire forging plant from England. Within a year of the plant's installation at Bethlehem, the company was delivering ahead of schedule the gun forgings specified in Whitney's contract, but no armor. According to the correspondence between Bethlehem executives and Tracy, the delay in armor production had resulted from the necessity to replace the hydraulic press used for making the gun forgings with the steam hammers required for forging armor.[34]

Recognizing that the success of his naval program would depend in large measure on an ample supply of the material, the general decided to seek a second contractor. With this in mind, he approached Andrew Carnegie, whose distaste for the Navy's rigorous inspection methods, together with his canny bargaining technique, prolonged the negotiations until the fall of 1890. Meanwhile, the Navy continued to starve for armor.[35]

An equally annoying though less serious cause of delays in construction originated in the schedules followed in the builders' yards. As the policy board had pointed out, heavy warships took from five to six years to complete in the United States, as opposed to two years in Britain. This disparity existed in part because domestic contractors limited work on government orders to slack periods in their private business in hopes of saving money by keeping a fixed number of men constantly at work. Both Whitney and Tracy tried, to no avail, to terminate this practice by inserting penalty clauses in contracts for new construction; but Congress refused to impose the penalties for fear of alienating industrial leaders.[36]

This attitude prompted the general to take a different tack. Acting on the suggestion of Nathaniel McKay, a veteran shipbuilder and close friend, Tracy directed the chief of the Bureau of Navigation to detail a naval engineer to every private yard under contract to the Navy Department. In the future, therefore, he could count on his own men to maintain a careful watch on the progress of naval construction.[37]

---

34 Navy Dept., *Annual Report*, 1886; Allard, "Influence upon Steel Industry," 86–91.

35 *House Executive Documents*, 51st Cong., 2nd Sess., No. 9, p. 19; William E. Livezey, *Mahan on Sea Power* (Norman, Okla., 1947), 179–80.

36 Navy Dept., *Annual Report*, 1889, 1890; Long, *New Navy*, I, 47–48.

37 Navy Dept., circular letter, undated; Stuart L. Woodford to Tracy, April 1, 1889, in Tracy Papers. Woodford, a lawyer in Brooklyn and a local Republican leader with whom Tracy corresponded frequently, became U.S. minister to Spain in 1898.

As the end of General Tracy's first year in the Department was drawing near, a personal tragedy disrupted his life. In mid-February, 1890, fire destroyed his house on I Street, killing his wife and younger daughter. His older daughter saved herself and her child by jumping from a bedroom window, but both were severely injured in the fall. The general himself barely escaped death as a result of the burns he sustained.[38]

Harrison promptly ordered the secretary removed to the White House where he recuperated gradually and in the process formed a warm friendship with his host. The President's kindness and sympathy at this time made a profound impression on Tracy, instilling in him a sense of loyalty to Harrison that never wavered despite the bitterness of Tom Platt and other Stalwarts, who felt "their man" was neglecting them.[39]

During the sad aftermath of the disaster, the general drew some consolation from the progress made by the department in its first year under his management. He had succeeded in upgrading the naval establishment and, to a considerable degree, in erasing the political smear that had defaced its image since 1865. As a prominent New York editor pointed out, "The creation of a navy has been taken entirely out of politics." [40]

Within the year ending on March 5, 1890, the Navy Department accepted delivery of four new men-of-war: the *Baltimore* and *Yorktown* from Cramps' shipyard; the *Charleston* from the Union Iron Works of San Francisco; and the *Petrel* from the Columbian Iron Works in Baltimore.[41] The armored cruiser *Texas* lay abuilding at the Norfolk Navy Yard, while the *Maine* awaited her armor at the navy yard in Brooklyn. Six protected cruisers were nearing completion at other sites in addition to a number of smaller craft. Toward the end of the period, the Herreschoff Company of Bristol, Rhode Island, delivered the torpedo-boat *Cushing* to the Navy for acceptance trials.[42]

The department's achievements during the year included substantial

38 *Harper's Weekly*, (February 15, 1890), 120ff. This article gives a full account of the fire.
39 Reminiscence of Mrs. Frederic Coudert, granddaughter of General Tracy who survived the fire with her mother and grandfather. She recalled recently the kindness of President and Mrs. Harrison during Tracy's prolonged convalescence at the White House. For Platt's attitude, see various letters, Platt to Tracy, spring, 1890, in Tracy Papers.
40 New York *Tribune*, March 5, 1890.
41 The *Baltimore* and *Charleston* were protected cruisers; the *Petrel* and *Yorktown* were gunboats.
42 Navy Dept., *Annual Report*, 1889, 1890; duplicate of receipt for *Cushing*, date obliterated, in Tracy Papers.

headway in ordnance production and development. The Washington Gun Factory turned out heavy steel rifles in volume for the new warships, from guns of 10-inch caliber down; these were the first all steel rifles ever wholly manufactured in the United States and the most powerful. On Tracy's orders, moreover, the department's proving ground at Annapolis had tested smokeless powder, exploding projectiles, fuses for shells, and Gatling guns.[43]

At sea, the Navy's first "squadron of evolution" had performed well on a globe-circling cruise completed before the end of the year. The controversial dispatch-boat *Dolphin* had accompanied the squadron without mishap to the gratification of Nathaniel McKay, who urged Tracy to publish the log of the "much maligned" vessel "in justice to Roach and Chandler." [44]

March 5, 1890, found General Tracy still at the White House recovering from his burns. Now a firm friend and respected adviser of the President, he had proved himself an unusually capable administrator. The nation had yet to discover that he had also paved the way for the creation of an offensive fleet by building his policy around Mahan's theories. If Tracy had his way—and he would have it—America would be prepared for war at sea before the fact, in defiance of tradition. The new era of American sea power had commenced.

43 Navy Dept., *Annual Report*, 1890.
44 *Ibid.*; for quotation, see McKay to Tracy, September 21, 1889, in Tracy Papers.

IV
FORGING A BATTLE FLEET

As the second year of the Harrison administration began, belief in the new Manifest Destiny was taking hold. Popularizers of Darwinism, like publicist John Fiske and Reverend Josiah Strong, accelerated the rise of American imperialism by supplying justification for extraterritorial ventures. Since the United States would soon replace Britain as the standard bearer of Protestant, Anglo-Saxon culture, the nation must assume responsibility for extending Christian and democratic institutions to less privileged peoples across the seas. Furthermore, the Darwinists pointed out, America must prepare to participate in the imminent, worldwide rivalry for commercial and colonial supremacy, which only the fittest would survive.

The militant Darwinism preached by the likes of Fiske and Strong, which would receive fresh support within a year from the writings of Captain Mahan, appealed strongly to a nation whose rapid physical growth since the Civil War had opened new horizons. The land frontier had disappeared, settlement of the West was all but complete, and both farmers and industrialists were seeking additional outlets for disposal of their surplus products. Finally, the public's awareness of America's emergence as a world power, which the tremendous rise of industry and the naval building program tended to substantiate, generated national confidence and with it a desire to expand.

By March, 1890, General Tracy had established himself not only as the administration's leading expansionist after the President but also as a highly competent public servant. His efficient management of naval affairs over the past twelve months set him apart from his cabinet-mates, most of whom were considered mediocrities. Harry Thurston Peck, scholarly editor of the literary monthly *The Bookman*, made plain his opinion of Harrison's official family: "The new cabinet is one of no very marked distinction or ability, with two exceptions . . . Mr. Blaine and Mr. Tracy." [1]

In the course of the general's second year in office, President Harrison relied increasingly on him for advice on numerous matters, some of which had no bearing on the Navy Department. Discounting the intimacy that had developed between them while Tracy was convalescing, Harrison's dependence on him is not surprising in view of the many interests the two had in common. Both were successful lawyers and skilled machine politicians, capable of disinterested service to their country. Both had seen action in the Union Army and had been rewarded with high rank. And both were dedicated imperialists. [2]

Besides, the President's distrust of Secretary of State Blaine led him to seek counsel from another source. Prior to his inauguration, Harrison had made no secret of his suspicion that Blaine's political prominence might tempt him to usurp presidential prerogatives. Indeed, the President-elect had warned the incoming secretary of state of his determination to control all aspects of the administration. [3]

On his part, the general perceived in Harrison a warmth which people outside the latter's personal circle found lacking. Often caricatured as a "pouter pigeon . . . cold as ice," the President displeased many of his contemporaries who considered him reticent and hard to approach. [4] Tracy, on the other hand, attributed Harrison's apparent aloofness to military training and saw a more attractive side of his personality. [5]

1 Peck, "Twenty Years of the Republic," 144ff. For interpretative comment on the ideas promoted by Fiske and Strong, see Ernest R. May, *Imperial Democracy* (New York, 1961) 8–9. A summary of physical conditions favoring the rise of imperialism appears in F. R. Dulles, *America's Rise to World Power* (New York, 1954), 21–22.

2 Volwiler, "Harrison, Blaine," 637.

3 Albert T. Volwiler (ed.), *The Correspondence between Benjamin Harrison and James G. Blaine* (Philadelphia, 1940), 50–51; *Philadelphia Bulletin*, March 25, 1889; D. S. Muzzey, *James Gillespie Blaine* (New York, 1934), 455–66.

4 Peck, "Twenty Years of the Republic," 144; T. C. Platt, *The Autobiography of Thomas Collier Platt* (New York, 1910), 132.

5 Harrison's biographer agrees with this opinion. See Harry Sievers, *Benjamin Harrison: Hoosier Statesman* (Chicago, 1952), 355. The author's view of Harrison was clarified considerably during an interview with Father Sievers, December 29, 1961, Washington, D.C.

The first fruits of the naval policy initiated by General Tracy, with the endorsement of the President, began to ripen in June when Congress passed the Navy Act of 1890. This measure, guided by staunch expansionists through both houses of Congress, represented the longest single stride yet taken on the road to the new Manifest Destiny. Though the act seemed on the surface to be a compromise between the friends and foes of offensive warships, its passage by implication spelled a decisive victory for the supporters of Mahan's doctrine.

Congressional debates on the Navy reflected broad acceptance of the idea of continuing the quantitative expansion of the fleet, but they also pointed up the confusion rife among professionals and amateurs alike over the composition of the battle force of the future. Tracy felt sure Congress would vote funds for new warships; what concerned him was the type of construction it would authorize. As he knew, many congressmen still regarded the monitor and commerce-raider as the dual symbol of the country's naval tradition, notwithstanding the abundant evidence of their strategic ineffectiveness in wartime. The enthusiastic response evoked in Congress by the *Army and Navy Journal's* endorsement of Gustavus Fox's theories as late as December, 1889, demonstrated the durability of this misconception.[6]

To complicate matters further, the policy board's recommendation of a large, offensive naval force drove many a fence-sitter back to the monitor camp. While the House Naval Affairs Committee was studying Tracy's proposals, no less an authority than Senator William E. Chandler, progenitor of the ABCD's, announced his opposition to battleships on the ground that monitors could provide equally adequate and far less costly protection of the seaboard.[7] Criticisms of this kind drew loud applause from the thrift-minded isolationist bloc, which had strong Midwestern support.

Thus the battleship-versus-monitor controversy became the primary issue facing Congress before the measure came to a vote. General Tracy was convinced that he could count on the votes of east coast congressmen and was gratified by the editorial position of most of the region's newspapers. One eastern editor's statement of the situation pleased him especially:

It is desired to build . . . battleships which can go to sea and stay there; can fight an enemy at all times and wherever . . . encountered; can prevent

6 See *Army and Navy Journal* (New York), December 7, 1889.
7 Chandler to Tracy, January 10, 1890, in Tracy Papers.

a blockade . . . and keep a hostile fleet so far from the coast that it cannot shell our cities. . . . None of these requirements can be met by the low-freeboard monitor. She is a . . . harbor defender but not a coast defender.[8]

Unquestionably, the term "battleship" alarmed many thoughtful Americans because it conjured up visions of imperialist ventures overseas and offensive warfare. Inasmuch as these prospects ran counter to tradition, the cause of the monitor died hard.

In March, Tracy appeared before the House naval committee to plead his case. He urged the members to reconsider carefully that portion of the policy board's report which dealt with battleship characteristics, in hopes of convincing them of the defensive nature of the medium-range vessels recommended. Regarding the cruisers he had proposed, he announced confidently to the press: "They will catch and whip anything afloat or that is likely to float within the next ten years." [9]

Now the lines of battle were drawn—with Tracy's supporters marshaled against those of Chandler. As the debates continued, the primary question of interest to congressmen was whether battleships or monitors should dominate the new fleet. Largely as a result of Tracy's salesmanship, abetted by the indirect pressure applied by Rear Admiral Luce, the House committee adopted the battleship policy.[10]

Perhaps unaware of the liaison existing between Tracy and Luce, Committee Chairman Boutelle had requested the Admiral's opinion of the secretary's proposals. Luce replied that he favored them and hinted at Tracy's real motive in asking for monitors. "The lines laid down in the report seem to be about right. I don't quite understand the object of 20 coast defense ships, but the Department no doubt has substantial reason for including them." [11] Luce agreed with Tracy and Senator Hale, moreover, that work on eight battleships should commence as soon as possible.[12]

For political reasons, however, Boutelle deemed it unwise to call for so many capital ships in the new bill. Considering the strength of isolationist sentiment in Congress, not to mention the harmful effect of the

8 *Frank Leslie's Illustrated Newspaper* (New York), March 1, 1890. The editor of this paper was the President's son, Russell Harrison.

9 Brooklyn *Daily Eagle*, March 26, 1890.

10 Trenton *Daily State Gazette*, March 28, 1890. Cf. Millis, *Arms and Men*, 190.

11 Luce to Boutelle, December 28, 1889, in NHF, Luce Collection. Luce appreciated the necessity of appeasing the monitor advocates in Congress.

12 Boutelle to Luce, March 1, 1890, in NHF, Luce Collection. The admiral knew of Tracy's plan before Boutelle was aware of it.

policy board's report on public opinion, the chairman believed moderation to be the course of wisdom in drafting the measure. Accordingly,
he framed a bill calculated to win enough votes to implement Tracy's
program in principle, if not word for word. Feeling that compromise
was essential to ultimate acceptance of strategic doctrine, Boutelle asked
Congress to authorize the maximum number of battleships he thought
the majority would approve, instead of the eight desired by the Secretary.

In final form, Boutelle's measure specified "three seagoing coastline
battleships . . . to carry the heaviest ordnance upon a displacement of
about 8,500 tons, with a coal endurance of 5,000 knots." [13] This description tallied with the policy board's conception of the medium-
range capital ships needed for the defense of the Eastern Atlantic,
Caribbean, and Western Pacific areas.[14]

Watering down Tracy's original recommendation in order to reassure
the isolationists, Boutelle worded the battleship clause in such fashion
as to emphasize the defensive character of the projected men-of-war,
describing them as "coastline" vessels with limited fuel capacity. He
hoped thereby to comfort the opposition with the knowledge that the
ships in question would perforce operate close to home shores. In
a letter to Luce, the chairman spelled out his intentions: "By building
such ships, we should avoid the popular apprehension of jingoism in naval
matters, while we can develop the full offensive and defensive powers
of construction as completely as in foreign cruising battleships in all
but speed and fuel capacity." [15]

The arguments that followed the introduction of the Navy bill in the
House of Representatives demonstrated Boutelle's sagacity. As expected,
the battleship clause became the principal issue, with Republican Joseph
Cannon of Illinois leading the Populists and other Westerners in opposition to the clause. By mid-April, the Midwesterners, reinforced by a
number of Democrats, seemed on the verge of victory regardless of the
politicking and oratory of Reed, Lodge, and Boutelle on the Republican
side and Hilary Herbert and William McAdoo for the Democrats. The
size and aggressiveness of the anti-battleship bloc dismayed Tracy and
his cohorts and came as a surprise to newsmen, many of whom attributed
the strength of the opposition to the alarm provoked by the "absurdly

13 *Congressional Record*, 51st Cong., 1st Sess., 3169. Five thousand knots, or
nautical miles, equal 5,652 statute land miles.
14 *Ibid.*, 54th Cong., 1st Sess., 3193.
15 Boutelle to Luce, March 6, 1890, in NHF, Luce Collection.

grandiose" report of the policy board.[16] Before long, nevertheless, the political strategy of Speaker Reed and the eloquence of Boutelle and Lodge began to take effect. Reiterating the coastal features of the proposed battleships, Boutelle insisted that they would comprise a purely defensive squadron policing areas of vital interest in close proximity to American seaboards. Lodge took his cue and delivered a soothing, if inaccurate, speech in which he depicted the Navy bill as a mere extension of tried and true national policy.[17]

When the measure came to a vote in the House, the battleship men held a commanding lead; 131 representatives voted for the bill, while 105 opposed it. An analysis of the count reveals the continuing influence on naval affairs of partisan and sectional considerations. A total of 26 Democrats supported the battleship clause and 23 Republicans voted against it; of the latter number, 22 represented electoral districts in the interior.[18]

The Senate acted with greater speed, under the shrewd management of Chairman Cameron of the naval committee. With the able assistance of Senators Hale and Joseph Hawley of Connecticut, Cameron coralled sufficient strength to insure the bill's passage by a comfortable margin In the final roll call, the battleships won by a count of 33 to 18. [19]

On June 30, 1890, the Navy bill became law. It provided for the construction of three battleships, one protected cruiser, one torpedo cruiser, and one light torpedo-boat of the *Cushing* class.[20] The specifications of the capital ships as set forth in the measure actually exceeded Tracy's hopes: each of the new heavy units would displace more than ten thousand tons and mount in her main battery four 13-inch and eight 8-inch rifles. The secondary armament would include numerous rapid-fire guns and four torpedo tubes. Two coal-burning, triple expansion steam engines were to drive each vessel at a speed of about 16 knots. The estimated cost of the three battleships amounted to $18,000,000— a record-breaking sum for the number of warships involved.[21]

16 For example, see New York *Tribune*, April 10, 1890.
17 For the House debates, see *Congressional Record*, 51st Cong., 1st Sess., 3161–71, 3321–23, 3256–71, 3395.
18 *Ibid*. See also, La Feber, *New Empire*, 124–25; Sprout, *Naval Power*, 213ff.
19 *Congressional Record*, 51st Cong., 1st Sess., 5173–82, 5236–38, 5379–80, for the debates and vote in the Senate.
20 Navy Dept., *Annual Report*, 1890.
21 *Navy Yearbook*, 1917, pp. 739, 758, 766; N. L. Stebbins, *The New Navy of the United States* (New York, 1912), *passim*.

Designated *Oregon, Indiana,* and *Massachusetts* to please as many sections as possible, these ships would measure about 320 feet in length, only slightly more than the *Maine* and *Texas*; but the designed tonnage of each was greater—by more than two thousand tons—than any vessel yet built in the United States. Certain features of the nation's first battleships would set the style of domestic naval architecture for years to come.[22] Their low freeboard and huge turrets gave them the appearance of giant monitors, which many citizens believed them to be.[23]

The limited cruising range specified for the *Oregons* supported this illusion, though their builders did not adhere strictly to the five thousand-mile maximum which Boutelle had set in order to relieve the fears of the isolationists.[24] Even if the contractors had construed this restriction literally, however, the offensive characteristics incorporated in the battleships rendered them capable of breaching a blockade, repelling a hostile force headed for the seaboard, and seizing and defending bases in coastal waters from Nova Scotia to Central America.[25]

Whether or not most of the congressmen who voted for the capital ships appreciated the implications of their action, they were responsible for creating American men-of-war equal in strength to the best of their type in existence. The ships of the *Oregon* class compared favorably with the British Navy's formidable *Majestics,* which were rated the most powerful warships in the world at the time. The latter vessels, though "several thousand tons larger and therefore longer-range and slightly faster," than the *Oregons,* "carried lighter armor and smaller main and intermediate calibre guns." [26]

In his report for 1890, Secretary Tracy expressed satisfaction with the offensive and defensive features of the new class. "The battery of the battleships is the heaviest and most effective . . . carried today by any ships afloat or projected. . . ." [27] For defense, they had the protection of a steel armor belt, eighteen inches thick, which ran along most of the length of the hull, in addition to an armored main deck and watertight compartments below.[28] Indeed, declared Tracy, the

22 F. M. Bennett, *The Monitor and the Navy under Steam* (Cambridge, Mass., 1900), 258.
23 *Ibid.;* Sprout, *Naval Power,* 214–16.
24 As witness the *Oregon's* race around Cape Horn in 1898.
25 Potter and Nimitz (eds.), *Sea Power,* 344–45.
26 *Ibid.;* Millis, *Arms and Men,* 190ff.
27 Navy Dept., *Annual Report,* 1890.
28 *Ibid.*

characteristics of the *Oregon* class surpassed his expectations to the extent that he felt twelve such vessels could do the work of the twenty he had originally recommended. This optimistic remark suggests that twenty had been a bargaining figure and that the secretary was pleasantly surprised at the decision of Congress to authorize even as few as three capital ships.

Not only would a dozen *Oregons* guarantee the security of the shoreline, continued Tracy, but they would also relieve monitors of their deep-sea duties and thus free them for tasks better suited to their design with local defense forces. Furthermore, if Congress were to invite the state militia units to furnish crews for monitors on harbor assignments, it would make regular personnel available for ships on more exacting duty. This proposal removes all doubt as to the secretary's low opinion of the monitor type.[29]

Equally pleasing to Tracy were the final plans for the cruiser *Columbia.* Designed to displace 7,375 tons, she would be heavier than either the *Maine* or the *Texas.* For ordnance, the cruiser would carry one 8-inch, two 6-inch, and eight 4-inch rifles. Powerful main engines would drive the *Columbia* at 23 knots, as fast as any naval vessel in service at the time.[30]

Besides the construction clauses in the Act of 1890, certain secondary provisions brightened the Navy's outlook considerably. One, proposed by Senator John W. Daniel of Virginia, scheduled a naval review at Hampton Roads for 1892 with the United States Navy acting as host to foreign men-of-war taking part in the exercises, which were to be held in connection with the Columbian Exposition.

Daniel's proposal pleased Tracy greatly. What better opportunity could be found than a "naval parade" in home waters for showing off new warships to the American people? An impressive performance under such circumstances would do more to enhance public relations than a thousand addresses or press releases. As to the ability of his men and ships to perform well, the secretary had no qualms. "There need be no fear that we will not be creditably represented. The review . . . will have a most wholesome effect on public opinion, because it will bring forcibly before the public the necessity and utility of . . . strong naval equipment." [31]

29 *Ibid.*
30 Mitchell, *Modern Navy,* 29–33.
31 Baltimore *Sun,* May 18, 1890; New York *Times,* March 31, 1890.

A second provision in the Act authorized the return of the War College to its original home at Coasters Harbor, to Tracy's relief. This action assured the development of the institution along the lines established by Luce. Furthermore, it allowed Captain Mahan to remain in charge of the College where he could capitalize on his extended respite from sea duty to continue writing. Finally, the provision meant that Tracy would, for a time at least, be able to call Mahan to Washington on short notice for consultation if the need arose.[32]

The War College clause passed through the House without difficulty, owing to the parliamentary skill of Boutelle and Lodge. When it encountered resistance in the Senate, the disciples of Luce in Congress and the service closed ranks behind Tracy to force passage. Hale, Chandler, and Nelson Aldrich, among others, brought their influence and eloquence to bear.[33] Of Luce's naval allies, Sampson, Folger, and Goodrich in particular added their voices to those of Mahan and Soley on behalf of the College.[34] The strength of the support thus manifested insured the passage of the clause, as drafted by Tracy, through the Senate.

Another provision solved a long-standing problem concerning the distribution of supplies among the bureaus. Ignoring the existence of an adequate, common pool of supplies, each bureau chief had customarily built up a stockpile for his command. In March, 1890, the general had prevailed upon the House naval committee to embody in the bill a prohibition of duplicate purchasing by the bureaus. The result marked the end of a wasteful custom that had plagued administrators ever since the inauguration of the bureau system.[35]

During the arduous transit of the Navy bill through Congress, Tracy was gradually recovering from the effects of the fire. Although his health was mending rapidly by June, the general's physical condition indicated the advisability of lengthy rest periods for an indefinite time in the future. This situation led him to ask Harrison for a civilian assistant, capable of acting as secretary in Tracy's absence. The Presi-

32 Navy Dept., *Annual Report*, 1890; Livezey, *Mahan on Sea Power*, 146–47.
33 Various items of correspondence, 1886–90, in NHF, Luce Collection, especially, Aldrich to Luce, May 17, 1886; Luce to J. F. Meigs, October 29, 1890; Chandler to Luce, February 5, 1890.
34 Tracy's correspondence with Luce and Mahan, January–May, 1890, in Tracy Papers.
35 J. A. Smith to Tracy, May 22, 1889, in Tracy Papers; Navy Dept., *Annual Report*, 1892.

dent endorsed the request and forwarded it to Congress which, for the second time in history, established the position of assistant secretary of the navy.[36]

To find the right man for the new post, Tracy combed through a long list of possibilities. He finally settled on James Soley, who was still lecturing on international law at the War College and who had by then become an ardent convert to Mahan's theory of sea power. Aware of the captain's close association with the secretary, Soley accepted the appointment, even though it meant relinquishing his teaching position.[37]

Known to naval historians primarily for his administration of shore-based civilian personnel while assistant secretary, Soley began his career in the department in a different area of naval affairs. Shortly after assuming office on July 16, he joined Mahan and Folger—then chief of the Bureau of Ordnance—on the secretary's secret strategy committee. The general assigned the trio the task of devising operational plans in the event of war with Spain or certain other powers. It was the committee's duty to size up the direction from which aggression might materialize and the probable points of attack and to set forth appropriate countermeasures to be taken by the Navy. The evidence suggests that the work of the members included planning for offensive as well as defensive operations on the part of American men-of-war.[38]

With Soley on hand to help him, Secretary Tracy turned his attention again to the armor problem. Although Bethlehem's forging plant had begun delivering plate to the building yards by this time, neither the quantity nor the quality of the material delivered proved adequate to the expanding needs of the Navy.[39] While the general continued to press for a commitment from Carnegie to supply the department with armor plate, his dissatisfaction with the quality of the plate furnished

36 Luce to Folger, January 2, 1890, in NHF, Luce Collection; Mahan to Luce, September 3, 1901, in NWC; Livezey, *Mahan on Sea Power*, 146–47. Lincoln created this office for its first occupant, Gustavus Vasa Fox, in hopes of silencing his virulent attack on Seward for diverting the *Powhatan* from the second Sumter relief expedition. For Fox's behavior towards Seward, see various letters in the former's *The Confidential Correspondence of Gustavus Vasa Fox*, ed. Robert M. Thompson (New York, 1918), I and II, *passim*. Following Cleveland's second inauguration in 1893, the new President appointed W. G. McAdoo assistant secretary, whom Theodore Roosevelt succeeded after McKinley took office in 1897. See Roosevelt, *Autobiography*, 245.
37 Livezey, *Mahan on Sea Power*, 147.
38 Luce to Folger, January 2, 1890, in NHF, Luce Collection; Mahan to Luce, September 3, 1901, in NWC.
39 Navy Dept., *Annual Report*, 1890.

by Bethlehem prompted him to seek a substitute for all-steel armor. In May of the preceding year, Tracy had learned of the recent purchase by the British Admiralty of a nickel-steel alloy for experimental purposes.[40] A month later, word had reached him of the successful outcome of the Admiralty's tests, whereupon he ordered samples of armor made of the alloy in France for testing at the Annapolis Proving Grounds. To evaluate the experiment, Tracy appointed a board of ordnance experts headed by Admiral Kimberly, who had recently returned from Samoa.

In September, 1890, the Kimberly board organized a series of competitive tests of French nickel-steel, Bethlehem's all-steel, and British compound steel plates. To the dismay of the manufacturers represented, Tracy insisted on subjecting their samples to bombardment by 8-inch projectiles fired at point-blank range. When the testing demonstrated the greatly superior capacity of nickel-steel for taking such punishment, Tracy resolved to apply the material to naval construction. Since nickel ore was not then available in the United States, and since he could not persuade either Bethlehem or the uncommitted Carnegie to import it from abroad, the general concluded that the government must buy the first lot. Within ten days of the last test at Annapolis, he obtained a congressional appropriation of $1,000,000 for purchasing nickel from an owner of Canadian mines with whom he had corresponded previously. In view of the circumstances, moreover, the general undoubtedly had a hand in the removal of the duty on nickel in the McKinley Tariff Act of October, 1890.[41]

Meanwhile, perhaps because of the declining demand for steel rail for the country's railroad systems and the consequent necessity of diversifying his business, Carnegie reconsidered his refusal to forge armor for the Navy. But, he announced to Tracy, he would under no condition sell the plate for a penny less than the figure stipulated in Whitney's contract with Bethlehem. In vain, the general attempted to bargain with Carnegie, pointing out that his company could benefit from its rival's experience and thus avoid costly initial errors in production. Carnegie

40 W. W. Wellan to Tracy, June 12, 1889, and Charles Cammell and Company of Sheffield, England, to Tracy, May 10, 1889, in Tracy Papers.
41 S. J. Ritchie to Tracy, February 27, 1890; Carnegie to Tracy, September 10, 1890; and Tracy to Ritchie, March 7, 1892, all in Tracy Papers. See also, Navy Dept., *Annual Report*, 1890; L. A. Kimberly, "Report of the Board on the Competitive Trial of Armor Plate," *NIP*, XVI (1890), 629ff.; Allard, "Influence upon Steel Industry," 88–94. S. J. Ritchie of Akron, Ohio, owned the Canadian mines in question.

knew how desperately the secretary wanted armor; he promised to build a forging plant at Homestead which, he predicted, would be in operation within six months. Tracy took the bait and in November awarded Carnegie a formal contract for six thousand tons of nickel-steel armor at the same unit price as Bethlehem's, which was approximately $600.00 a ton. In order to hold the total cost to the government at the level established by Whitney in 1887, the general prevailed on Bethlehem to reduce by six thousand tons the quantity of plate required to satisfy his predecessor's contract.

These arrangements did not solve the armor shortage immediately, of course; not until 1895—three years after the contract dates—did Bethlehem and Carnegie fulfill their obligations. Appreciating the engineering difficulties facing the companies in retooling to forge nickel-steel armor, Secretary Tracy granted two lieutenants extended leaves with the understanding that one would act as a nonofficial adviser to Carnegie and the other would function in the same capacity at the Bethlehem plant.

Subsequently, the general's detractors accused him of favoring Carnegie unduly by awarding the producer a contract without advertising for competitive bids. The truth was that Tracy had done so because no other company—except Bethlehem—was capable of forging naval armor at the time. Other critics of the Navy's transactions with the steel companies protested that Carnegie was in cahoots with Bethlehem, citing as evidence their identical unit prices. This charge proved as false as the one against Tracy; Bethlehem had nothing to say about the figure agreed upon by Carnegie and the general. Carnegie demanded parity with his rival, and Tracy had to comply or forego the armor Homestead would produce in the future.[42]

Having obtained a new source of armor in nickel ore as well as a second supplier in Carnegie, Phipps and Company, Tracy moved again to improve the quality of the plate in domestic production. At the suggestion of his ordnance chief, Commander Folger, the general instituted tests of the recently evolved Harvey process of hardening the face of armor plate. Receiving optimistic reports of the results from the proving grounds, he recommended the application of the Harvey method to the manufacture of nickel-steel plate. Owing to the efforts of Tracy

42 Navy Dept., *Annual Report*, 1890, 1891, 1893, 1895; Davis, *Second to None*, 88; Carnegie to Tracy, August 27 and September 10, 1890, in Tracy Papers; Allard, "Influence upon Steel Industry," 89–108, 406. The lieutenants assigned to advise the steelmakers were C. A. Stone and J. F. Meigs.

and his successor in pioneering such innovations, both Bethlehem and Carnegie were, by 1895, turning out the highest grade armor in the world.

The threat to the construction program posed by the untimely release of the policy board's report and by the alarming scarcity of armor plate represented only one of the serious problems confronting Tracy in 1890. The practice of politics in the navy yards' labor-procurement procedure appalled him—machine man though he was—and he resolved to abolish it at the first opportunity. Adhering to a watch and wait tactic, the secretary issued no blanket condemnation of the procedure; but his decisions in individual cases foreshadowed drastic action in the months ahead. Well in advance of the general shake-up he planned to administer at the opportune time, Tracy began transferring responsibility for hiring workmen from local dispensers of political favors to the hands of the yard commandants.

Although party leaders wished to continue rewarding the faithful with yard jobs, they seemed decidedly reluctant to challenge Tracy's stiffening policy, as a letter from Lodge demonstrates: "If it is your wish that these matters should rest with the Captain of the Yard, I should be glad to know of it, so that I may . . . comply with your wishes." [43] Lodge and other chieftains realized that Tracy's record as a Republican could not be impugned and, therefore, that his attitude towards navy yard politics could be construed only as in the national interest.

In June, the general received a vehement protest from a party lieutenant in Norfolk, condemning his assignment of a Democrat as head of the local yard's steam-engineering department and demanding the man's replacement. Aware of the engineer's political affiliation, Tracy refused to let this bar him from a post for which he was well-qualified.[44]

He saw no harm, on the other hand, in furthering Republican aspirations whenever he could do so without injuring the service. He carried on the custom, common to secretaries of both parties, of scheduling warships for refits at yards where their presence would most benefit local party patronage. For this he drew editorial criticism while winning the plaudits of local Republican chiefs.[45] Called to account by the

---

43 Lodge to Tracy, June 28, 1890, in Tracy Papers.
44 Tracy to Chief Engineer Wilson, June 9, 1890; unidentifiable clipping in "Tracy Scrapbook III" (1890), both in Tracy Papers.
45 Unidentifiable clipping with Norfolk, June 9 dateline, in "Tracy Scrapbook IV" (1890), Tracy Papers.

press when he ordered the *Lancaster* to the Norfolk Navy Yard for an overhaul, he was praised by a grateful Virginian who hailed the arrival of the *Lancaster* as a "boon to the town" and productive of a "Republican gain in the state." [46]

In the sphere of administration, Tracy increased the efficiency of the department by substituting a simple method of individual bureau accounting for Whitney's complex system of consolidated accounts. Although most of the bureau chiefs welcomed the change, the paymaster-general, Commodore William Fulton, took exception to it and indignantly resigned from his post.[47]

On the whole, Tracy enjoyed friendly relations with his professional subordinates, including a number of officers on sea duty whom he seldom saw. In addition to such intimate associates as Mahan, Porter, and Folger, the general counted many prominent naval men among his friends. W. T. Sampson and Robley Evans were frequent callers at his office, for instance, while French Chadwick carried on a lengthy correspondence with Tracy from the *Yorktown*. The secretary had great confidence in Admirals Luce, Gherardi, and Kimberly; somewhat less in Admiral Walker and Commodore Schley.[48]

Captain George Dewey admired the general and visited him on several occasions in the summer of 1890. At lunch one day, Dewey offered him prophetic advice. He suggested concentrating all available warships in two fleets, one to deploy in the North Atlantic, the other in the Central Pacific. The bulk of the Pacific force should remain near the west coast, while the remainder cruised in Asiatic waters. This arrangement, explained the captain, would have the dual advantage of providing adequate coastal defense and insuring the safety of American interests in the Far East.[49]

Dewey was not alone in the conviction that the traditional dispersion of warships on stations extending from the Mediterranean to the China Sea had outlived its usefulness. In the days of sail and "quarterdeck diplomacy," when a naval commander might be America's sole representative in a sensitive area, showing the flag in remote places had merit. But using ships for this purpose seemed impractical by 1890, since

46 William Mahone to Tracy, June 11, 1890, Tracy Papers. Mahone was the powerful contemporary Republican machine leader in Virginia.
47 Navy Dept., *Annual Report*, 1890; St. Louis *Globe-Democrat*, March 15, 1890.
48 Correspondence with officers named, 1890–92, in Tracy Papers, especially Chadwick to Tracy, June–July, 1890. See also, Puleston, *Mahan*, 33.
49 George Dewey, *Autobiography of George Dewey, Admiral of the Navy* (New York, 1913), 291.

high-powered steel warships, equipped with the complex products of modern technology, demanded an unprecedented degree of competence and familiarity from both officers and crew. Moreover, constant exercises in tactical evolutions and gunnery had become essential; and to be effective, these drills had to be executed by unified squadrons rather than individual men-of-war. A number of officers elaborated Dewey's theory by recommending the organization of "flying squadrons" to serve as troubleshooters whenever the occasion arose.[50]

The same summer marked the publication of Mahan's major work on sea power. Although some time would elapse before the book gained popular currency at home, it soon became the navalists' manual in foreign maritime countries. Mahan had set forth the guidelines of naval power in this work; it remained for American expansionists to promote his ideas among their compatriots.

This was also the year of America's emergence as a great international power. The Navy Act of 1890 stands out as the clearest signal for the debut, but not the only one. Other indications included the administration's endorsement of Mahan's doctrine, the recently aroused public awareness of diplomacy and naval policy, and Tracy's rescue of the War College from obscurity. Saluting the general's efforts on behalf of the institution, Admiral Luce declared that if its work could be "carried out . . . it [would] place us in the front rank of the world's navies in the science of naval warfare."[51] Graduates of the College would justify the confidence of its supporters within a decade by virtue of their contribution to the naval victory over Spain.[52]

In November, General Tracy's thirteen-year-old granddaughter, Alys Wilmerding, smashed a bottle of champagne across the bow of the U.S.S. *Maine* and started the largest warship ever launched in the United States down the ways of the Brooklyn Navy Yard. Spectators of the ceremony little realized how tragic a role the new ship would play in the developing drama of the new Manifest Destiny.[53]

Numerous other men-of-war floated clear of their stocks in the crowded months between March, 1889, and November, 1890. Reporting for active duty in this period were the protected steel cruisers *Chicago,*

---

50 For example, see R. C. Smith, "Disposition and Character of the Fleet," *NIP*, XVII (1891), 123–56.
51 Luce to Meigs, October 29, 1888, in NHF, Luce Collection.
52 See Huntington, *Soldier and State*, 241.
53 Recollection of the Maine's christener, Mrs. Coudert, who possessed a plaque with an etching of the ceremony in the Brooklyn Navy Yard.

Charleston, Philadelphia, Baltimore, and *San Francisco*; the gunboats *Petrel* and *Yorktown*; the torpedo-boat *Cushing*; and the experimental dynamite-ship *Vesuvius*. Within a year, the *Maine* and *Texas* would at last receive their armor and become ready for service with the fleet. Contractors were working on the battleships of the *Oregon* class and on Tracy's favorite cruiser, the speedy *Columbia*.[54]

As the fleet increased in size and improved in quality, public pride in the Navy grew with it. The sentiment assumed a highly personal form; because of Tracy's emphasis on good public relations, the department had issued a steady flow of press releases containing progress reports and other items aimed at stimulating the enthusiasm of readers, dating back to the launching of the first of the ABCD's. Furthermore, Americans had begun to identify themselves with individual ships bearing the names of cities or states in which they lived. They manifested their personal interest in different ways; but one custom emerged and remained popular to the present day, the practice of community fundraising for the purpose of buying gifts for crews of naval namesakes at commissioning time.

The proud sense of ownership that developed with the expansion of the fleet led to requests for warships to make courtesy calls at ports along the coast, and Tracy hastened to comply whenever possible. He appreciated the value of such visits, which attracted large crowds who flocked aboard the gleaming new ships to inspect the quarters and equipment.

Coincident with fresh public awareness of the new Navy was the advent of a dynamic conception of the nation as an international power. Prominent imperialists like Henry Cabot Lodge and Theodore Roosevelt found strong support for their cause among people already impressed with the results of naval growth. The imperialist creed equated aggressive diplomacy, backed by sea power, with vigor and manliness. For the benefit of doubters, the would-be empire builders justified their stand on the ground that only progressive, well-armed nations of the world could survive. They pointed out, moreover, that funds lay at hand to pay for the equipment essential to national survival and that more revenue was coming in daily. Not only had the administration decided to liquidate the large treasury surplus for political reasons, but the high-tariff policy to which it was committed would furnish additional money for an indefinite length of time. This was true, in part;

54 Navy Dept., *Annual Report*, 1890.

Harrison wished to expend the surplus as soon as possible, but not entirely on naval expansion. Some of the money made available by the freeing of surplus funds went into warship construction; but more found its way to the pockets of Grand Army veterans in the form of pensions, deserved or not, aimed at bolstering the strength of the Republican party.[55]

In an effort to advance the ideas of imperialism, Mahan furnished a strategic base in a series of articles expanding his original thesis. With Tracy's approval, the captain directed his writing, tailored to popular taste, to the attainment of naval and imperial goals by awakening interest in an American empire created for the purpose of insuring national security and commercial advantage.[56]

Mahan's articles appeared in various periodicals in the years from 1890 to 1898. They summarized his views of the proper position and outlook of the United States in the international race for territorial gain that had already begun. As early as 1890, he predicted the end of American isolation. Like Harrison and Tracy, the captain believed that the nation's destiny lay beyond its coastlines, now that the land frontiers had vanished. He prophesied, too, the development of new interests in the Far East which would necessitate the participation of the United States in the worldwide quest for bases. Since the new objective of national policy was world power, Mahan felt the Navy's mission must be interpreted more broadly than ever before.[57]

The imperialist leaders did their job effectively. By the end of the year, the spirit they sought to instill in their compatriots had become apparent throughout the country. Not even the Democratic upsurge reflected by congressional elections dampened the ardor of the jingoists. Although the Democrats won control of the House and sharply reduced the Republican majority in the Senate, the momentum of imperialism was too great to suffer more than a brief setback.

Thus matters rested as 1890 came to an end. For the first time since the Civil War, the Navy Department was functioning to capacity; and for the first time in history, an offensive American fleet was taking shape in a period of peace. Naval expansion and imperialism were on the move, hand-in-hand.

---

55 Volwiler, "Harrison, Blaine," 637ff.
56 Sprout, *Naval Power*, 213ff.
57 A. T. Mahan, "The United States Looking Outward," *Atlantic Monthly*, LXVI (December, 1890), 152.; J. W. Pratt, *Expansionists of 1898* (New York, 1951), 232.

V

THE QUEST FOR BASES

THE IMPERIALIST SPIRIT GREW WITH THE EXPANSION OF THE nation's sea power. America's "empire days" dawned during the Harrison administration and not, as once believed, in the McKinley era. Indeed, it was the policy launched by Harrison, Tracy, and, to a lesser extent, Blaine, that set the precedent for the diplomacy which led to the acquisition of an overseas empire following the war with Spain.[1]

As previously suggested, conditions at home and abroad invited the formulation of a vigorous foreign policy for the purpose of asserting the claim of the United States to world power in unmistakable language. Domestic tranquility and prosperity in 1889 and 1890 encouraged Americans to look beyond the continental limits for new horizons. The admission of six states[2] to the Union within two years, moreover, called their attention to the advance of the frontier to the Pacific and impelled them to seek fresh fields to conquer. Strategic and commercial considerations added impetus to the thrust of imperialism as navalists and businessmen pointed out the advantages of securing bases and markets in areas of interest to both groups.

These factors, articulated by expansionist leaders, conditioned the pub-

---

1 Volwiler, "Harrison, Blaine," 637ff. Se ealso J. W. Pratt, *A History of United States Foreign Policy* (Englewood Cliffs, N.J., 1955), 372; La. Feber, *New Empire* 111.

2 The new states were Idaho, Montana, Washington, Wyoming, North Dakota, and South Dakota.

lic to the government's newly aggressive attitude toward prospective rivals in the international contest for colonies. Given this climate of opinion, it remained for the imperialist spokesmen of the Harrison administration to translate their ideas into action. Although the aspirations of these leaders—Harrison and Tracy in particular—far exceeded their achievements on this score, they served notice on the powers of Europe of what to expect from America in the future.

Tracy's role in furthering the administration's territorial ambitions ranked second only to that of the President; the evidence leaves no doubt of the general's prominence among the active imperialists of the day. Blaine placed third in importance on this count. Contrary to expectations, which were fully justified by his brief conduct of foreign relations in 1881, Blaine exerted a restraining influence on Harrison and Tracy, though not always decisively. In view of his interest in hemispheric solidarity, which he hoped to build toward in the first Pan-American conference, Blaine took a moderate position on the matter of extraterritorial naval bases. Throughout his second term in the State Department, he attempted to dampen the imperialist ardor of his chief and his energetic naval colleague.[3]

The increasing friction between President Harrison and his secretary of state complicated the situation. Differences of temperament widened the gap between them, which the President's suspicion of Blaine's intentions had opened even before the inauguration. Harrison's reticence and contempt for flattery clashed with Blaine's pretentiousness and love of praise. Furthermore, their opposing attitudes towards incidents affecting national prestige occasioned numerous collisions; Blaine saw such matters through the eyes of a diplomat while Harrison, like Tracy, considered them affronts to the nation's honor.[4] Personal differences separated the two as well. The President's refusal to appoint Blaine's son Walker as first assistant secretary of state, rankled in Blaine's mind for the rest of his life. In addition, the latter took offense at certain articles appearing in *Judge* and *Leslie's Weekly*, magazines managed and owned in part by Russell Harrison, the President's son. Poor health

3 Volwiler (ed.), *Correspondence, passim.* Blaine's notes reveal his fear of Harrison's militancy. See also, S. B. Elkins to L. T. Michener, March 3, 1888, in L. T. Michener Papers, Manuscript Division, Library of Congress, Michener was one of Blaine's political managers during the latter's unsuccessful campaign for the presidency in 1880, while Elkins was a member of the Republican national committee.

4 Volwiler (ed.), *Correspondence,* 1-17.

intensified the secretary of state's discomfiture; frequent bouts of illness interrupted his work, made him careless, and finally forced him to resign from the cabinet in 1892.[5]

The bitterness of this relationship made it easy for Tracy to get the President's ear and to appeal to his militant nationalism on behalf of the Navy. The general took advantage of the circumstances and persuaded Harrison to pursue a course directed at the acquisition of coaling stations and supply depots beyond American territorial limits for the fleet. Although Blaine would not have condoned such policy, the President assured Tracy that a quest for bases would meet with his tacit approval.[6]

Thus encouraged, Secretary Tracy reviewed the history of past diplomatic efforts to maintain America's ill-defined rights in the Samoan Islands, which lay athwart the potentially active lane from California to Australia. In 1878 Secretary of State Evarts had negotiated with the Samoans' Polynesian plenipotentiary their first foreign treaty. It was a treaty of amity, commerce, and quasi-protection and provided for a naval station at Pago Pago for the nonexclusive use of the United States. A year later, however, Samoa made similar agreements with Germany and Great Britain, granting both powers the right to establish exclusive naval bases elsewhere in the islands. Since then, as Tracy realized, Samoa's status had become hazy owing to the conflicting claims asserted by the three interested foreign governments.[7]

Shortly before Harrison succeeded Cleveland in office, Chancellor Otto von Bismarck of Germany had proposed a conference, for which American delegates would be invited to Berlin in hopes of ironing out the Samoan dispute. Cleveland's secretary of state, Thomas Bayard, had accepted the chancellor's invitation but left to his successor the choice of commissioners.

Although the hurricane of 1889 washed away much of the tension that had arisen between German and American agents in the islands,

5 J. W. Foster, *Diplomatic Memoirs* (Boston, 1909), II, 250–51. Foster replaced Blaine in the State Department in 1892.

6 See correspondence with Harrison and other administration leaders, 1891–92, in Tracy Papers; and J. B. Moore, *A Digest of International Law* (New York, 1906), II, 851, 871–76; hereinafter cited as *Digest*. During the Berlin Conference, John Bassett Moore was third assistant secretary of state.

7 Bemis, *A Diplomatic History of the United States*, 455–56; Navy Dept., *Annual Report*, 1889, 1890. Although the Navy Department deposited a shipment of coal at Pago Pago in 1880 to implement the treaty rights, it did not formally establish a naval base there until 1889, after the partition had taken place.

President Harrison decided to send an American delegation to Berlin and selected the men to form it soon after the skies had cleared.[8] Thereupon, Blaine furnished the commissioners with vague instructions to negotiate for an autonomous native government and for equality of influence among the three interested powers. He warned them to adopt a conciliatory attitude towards Herbert Bismarck, the German foreign minister and son of the chancellor.[9]

One member of the commission, John A. Kasson, declined at the outset to conciliate Herbert Bismarck. Sharing Tracy's imperialist ideas, Kasson announced his willingness to partition the islands if such action would bring Pago Pago under full control of the United States.[10] Mindful of Tracy's desire to establish a naval station at this site, President Harrison supported Kasson's position to the extent of ordering Blaine to make direct American ownership of the harbor a third condition of agreement, once the German delegates had concurred in the proposed plan for a native government and tripartite equality.[11]

In May, 1889, the conference produced a settlement which appeared on the surface to favor the stand taken by the American commissioners. The Berlin pact instituted a condominium over Samoa, in which the three governments concerned would have equal influence, and an elective native regime for the administration of the islands' internal affairs. In reality, this arrangement vested full authority in the condominium, allowing the native government to superintend nonsensitive matters of state only.[12]

Observers in Samoa, Europe, and America hailed the treaty with extravagant praise. The commanding officer of the U.S.S. *Adams*, stationed at Apia, informed Tracy by dispatch of the "unanimous approval" given it by the Samoan natives.[13] English and American editors interpreted the Berlin agreement as a major victory of American statesmanship. Even the usually anti-American *London Saturday Review* rejoiced in the accomplishment of Kasson and his colleagues, declaring that "it has been left to the navyless United States to give us a lead in

8 S. F. Bemis (ed.), *American Secretaries of State and Their Diplomacy* (New York, 1927-29), VIII, 122-25.

9 E. E. Younger, *John A. Kasson* (Iowa City, 1955), 152-60, 329.

10 *Messages and Papers*, IX, 10; Navy Dept., *Annual Report*, 1889; Younger, *Kasson*, 152-60.

11 Volwiler (ed.), *Correspondence*, Harrison to Blaine, May 2, 1889.

12 Pratt, *Foreign Policy*, 332. Cf.. Younger, *Kasson*, 159-60; Muzzey, *Blaine*, 395ff.

13 Hunker to Tracy, undated dispatch, Bureau of Navigation Executive Book No. 1, in Records of Navy Branch, National Archives, hereinafter cited as Navy Arch.

the path of duty and honor." The domestic press applauded the skill of Harrison's commissioners with still greater enthusiasm, attributing to them the "first diplomatic reverse" ever handed Chancellor Bismarck.[14]

As events soon proved, this editorial praise was exaggerated. That American diplomacy had succeeded to a degree resulted as much from Bismarck's distaste for overseas colonial ventures as from anything else. Moreover, the pact failed to improve conditions materially in Samoa, and friction among white authorities there continued to thwart Tracy's hope of building a permanent naval facility at Pago Pago.[15]

Hollow as it proved, the "diplomatic victory" over Bismarck did raise American morale. Lengthy press accounts of the negotiations in Berlin awakened the public to its government's participation in world affairs and created a new pride in the country's foreign policy. After all, had not Harrison's commissioners outmatched the most experienced diplomats of Europe in settling the status of a region in the Western Pacific? And would not the rapidly growing United States Navy require bases in other parts of the world, the acquisition of which might involve more adventure than a mere conference?

The contagion of imperialism could not be contained; it was spreading like wildfire to every section of the land. A contemporary American statesman viewed the popular response to the attempt to annex Pago Pago as typical of the spirit of his time. "The old issues were no longer interesting. . . . The desire for a vigorous foreign policy, though it jarred with tradition, had spread and become popular." [16]

General Tracy's interest in naval bases was not confined to Samoa. His frustrated effort to erect a permanent coaling facility at Pago Pago represented only the first of a series of false starts as the administration attempted to grope its way through the atmosphere created by the gospel of Mahan. The corollary of the capital-ship theory, embodying overseas bases and colonies, required a greater departure from tradition than did the fundamental theory, which Tracy had already implemented in part by securing authorization of three battleships from Congress. The bungled diplomacy that marked the administration's quest for bases illustrated the difficulty of America's transition from isolationism to imperialism. It revealed, further more, the *naïveté* of a government long

14 Quotations from Peck, "Twenty Years of the Republic," 153.
15 Pratt, *Foreign Policy*, 332. Cf. Younger, *Kasson*, 160; A. F. Tyler, *The Foreign Policy of James G. Blaine* (Minneapolis, 1927), 249-53.
16 J. B. Moore, *The Cambridge Modern History* (London, 1908), VII, 163

attached to the principles mistakenly attributed to Washington's Farewell Address.

Unquestionably, Blaine's diminishing role in the conduct of foreign policy contributed to the failure of the quest. Regardless of other factors, he was a seasoned statesman; Harrison and Tracy were only amateurs at best. However, even when he had firm control of the State Department, at the beginning of Harrison's term, Blaine moved with caution —and caution was not the watchword of the day. Consequently, the President often seconded Tracy's proposals apropos of sites for bases over the objections of the secretary of state. In the fall of 1891, for instance, Harrison directed Blaine to abandon the policy of isolation and to adopt one which would better serve the needs of expanding naval and commercial operations.[17]

Nevertheless, the secretary of state was able to veto two of General Tracy's recommendations concerning naval stations. The first envisaged the transfer of the Danish islands of St. Thomas and St. John, in the West Indies, to American sovereignty. The United States minister in Copenhagen, Clark E. Carr, informed Blaine late in 1890 of Denmark's inclination to sell the islands.[18] When Carr received no reply from the State Department, he requested Tracy to sound out the President and the Senate. For a time, Harrison shared Tracy's desire to purchase the Danish West Indies; but Blaine finally prevailed on the President to drop the proposition until "by fate we own the larger West Indies." St. Thomas and St. John, declared the secretary of state, "are destined to be ours, but should be among the last West Indies taken." In the light of subsequent developments, it seems likely that both islands would have become American possessions if Carr's message had arrived after Blaine's health declined, when Tracy's influence on the State Department's Caribbean policy loomed almost as large as Harrison's.[19]

In the autumn of 1891, Blaine blocked a second proposal contemplating foreign bases for the Navy. On this occasion, word of the proposition came from the United States minister to France. Whitelaw Reid of the New York *Tribune* had arrived in Paris to assume this post

17 Volwiler (ed.), *Correspondence*, Harrison to Blaine, October 1, 1891.
18 C. C. Tansill, *The Purchase of the Danish West Indies* (Baltimore, 1932), 23ff; Livezey, *Mahan on Sea Power*, 101–102. When Tracy began to exert direct influence on the State Department during Blaine's freqeunt absences in 1891, his actions indicate that he would not have waited for "fate" to bring the Danish islands under American sovereignty.
19 Volwiler (ed.), *Correspondence*, Harrison to Blaine, August 3 and August 10, 1891.

in the spring of 1889, just as the Boulanger affair was yielding space in the French press to the Panama scandal.[20] During Reid's first year in Paris, he was approached by Portugal's finance minister who suggested the possibility of America's sharing Portuguese facilities in the Azores. After a number of conversations with this official, Reid reported the suggestion to Harrison.[21] Discussing the Portuguese minister's offer with the secretary of state, President Harrison spoke favorably of it, though he realized that the prospect of the United States occupying naval bases jointly with Portugal might prove unacceptable both to the American public and to the powers of Europe. Nevertheless, Harrison felt the principals could make "mutually advantageous commercial arrangements" if the naval aspect of the transaction could be concealed from public view.[22]

Predictably, Blaine opposed the scheme. Terming it "entirely inadmissable," he presented Harrison with his own plan of empire which, since he shied away from direct action, seems to have had more form than substance: "I think there are only three places that are of value enough to be taken. . . . Cuba and Porto Rico are not now imminent and will not be for a generation. Hawaii may come up for decision any unexpected hour, and I hope we shall be prepared to decide it in the affirmative." [23] Admitting the impropriety of the Azores project, Whitelaw Reid anticipated Blaine's rejection of it: "I knew of course that the proposition, as sent, could not be entertained." At the same time, however, he requested Harrison's permission to negotiate for a long-term lease of a coaling station in the Azores.[24]

At this Tracy, who had at first favored such a station and later reconsidered his position, intervened in the discussion. Mindful of more immediate naval requisites, he urged the President to review the list of prospective sites in the Caribbean area before granting the permission asked by Reid. Then another dispatch from the minister to France arrived, indicating that the French government might have had a nonofficial hand in Portugal's offer. This clinched the matter; Harrison had no wish to antagonize the British Foreign Office by accepting a proposition inspired by France, nor did he desire to disregard the secretary

20 Royal Cortissoz, *Life of Whitelaw Reid* (New York, 1921), II, 121–30.
21 Reid to Harrison, October 9, 1891, in Whitelaw Reid Papers, Manuscript Division, Library of Congress.
22 Volwiler (ed.), *Correspondence*, Harrison to Blaine, August 31, 1891.
23 *Ibid.*, Blaine to Harrison, August 10, 1891.
24 Reid to Harrison, October 9 and 21, 1891, in Reid Papers.

of the navy's preference for a site in the western hemisphere. Accordingly, the President instructed Reid to discontinue his talks with the Portuguese finance minister.[25]

General Tracy's determination to acquire a foothold in the Caribbean region had two roots—both derived from the doctrine established by Mahan. First, he considered a coaling and supply station in that area essential to the Atlantic component of a far-ranging battle fleet. Second, he appreciated the degree of protection that a well-fortified bastion, situated on the eastern approach to the Central American isthmus, would afford an inter-ocean canal in the future. Continuing this line of argument, the general emphasized repeatedly the importance of building an isthmian canal as soon as possible, on the grounds that it offered the sole practical solution to the problem of defending two extensive seaboards with a one-ocean fleet.[26]

Concurring in Tracy's opinion, Harrison pressed Congress for authority to begin construction of a canal across Nicaragua at once; but Congress refused to comply. The President attributed congressional inaction in this matter to the weak financial state of the Maritime Canal Company, which had been organized in 1887 to build a trans-Nicaraguan waterway. Consequently, he worked with the Senate Foreign Affairs Committee to amend the company's charter in such fashion as to permit strengthening its condition. Harrison expressed satisfaction with the draft amendment which required the government to purchase all company stock and guarantee its bonds, and recommended adoption by the Senate. The latter withheld its consent, however; and the canal had to wait.[27]

The Senate's attitude failed to divert Secretary Tracy from his course. He was sure that the canal would be built in time; and whether construction began immediately or twenty years hence, he was determined to furnish the means of protecting it. Captain Mahan had already selected Hawaii as the logical strongpoint in the Pacific; now he advised Tracy to seek a base in Cuba in order to secure the canal site on the east. Inasmuch as Tracy deemed this impractical for the time being, he discussed other possibilities in the area with the President and the secretary of state.

25 *Ibid.* Cf. La Feber, *New Empire*, 110.
26 Mahan, "U.S. Looking Outward," 816ff.; Navy Dept., *Annual Report*, 1890, 1891.
27 *Senate Reports*, 51st Cong., 2nd Sess., No. 1944. See also, La Feber, *New Empire*, 111; Pratt, *Foreign Policy*, 372–74.

For once, all three agreed on two locations which seemed suited to naval requirements: the Môle St. Nicolas at Port-au-Prince, Haiti, and Santo Domingo's Samaná Bay. Both prospects had the added attractions of weak regimes, lacking in political and economic stability, and of rulers allegedly under obligation to the United States. Without question, the Harrison administration intended to have its way with the island governments.[28]

The complex history of the negotiations for the Môle St. Nicolas began in January, 1889, two months prior to Cleveland's retirement. Blaine made this point clear for the sake of convincing the public that Harrison's policy was no more aggressive than his predecessor's. At that time, President Florvil Hyppolite, of the Provisional Government of Haiti, was waging civil war against the rival faction of François Légitime. Before the end of the month, Hyppolite dispatched an agent, Frederick Elie, to Washington for reasons not yet fully understood.[29]

Rightly or wrongly, Blaine assumed that Secretary of State Bayard and Elie had reached an agreement involving American support of Hyppolite's military campaign. According to Blaine, the agent had committed Hyppolite to certain concessions to the United States, including a lease of the Môle. In return, contended Blaine subsequently, Bayard promised Elie naval assistance in breaking Légitime's coastal blockade and assured the agent that the State Department would not interfere with the export of munitions to Hyppolite's forces.[30]

Certain historians have disputed Blaine's version of the story. Ludwell Montague ascribes it wholly to the secretary of state's talent for imaginative trickery. Montague attempts to support his thesis by arguing that Admiral Luce, while commander of the North Atlantic Squadron, had declared Légitime's blockade ineffective prior to Elie's voyage to America, that national policy governing the export of munitions had long since been fixed, and finally that Elie had not even conferred with Bayard. Scholarly supporters of Blaine, on the other hand, have offered evidence tending to corroborate his interpretation.[31]

In any event, Secretary Blaine took the position that Hyppolite had

---

28 Sumner Welles, *Naboth's Vineyard* (New York, 1928), I, 468–95; Tyler, *Policy of Blaine*, 91–98; Livezey, *Mahan on Sea Power*, 101–103; L. L. Montague, *Haiti and the United States* (Durham, N.C., 1948), 148ff.

29 Montague, *Haiti*, 149, citing dispatches from Haiti, especially Rear Adm. Bancroft Gherardi to Blaine, January 31, 1891.

30 *Ibid.*, 148–50.

31 *Ibid.*, 148–54. For Blaine's version, see Tyler, *Policy of Blaine*, 91–98.

indeed placed himself in debt to the United States; to substantiate this premise he referred to matters of record. American firms had, insisted Blaine, shipped munitions to Hyppolite's army without hindrance; and the vessels carrying the munitions had enjoyed the protection of American escorts while running Légitime's blockade—be it real or paper. That Cleveland had not chosen to take up the option on the Môle was irrelevant; if Harrison wanted the property, Blaine considered negotiations for it in order.[32]

The second phase of the history of the Môle affair is less open to question. It commenced with the arrival of United States Minister Frederick Douglass at Port-au-Prince in October, 1889. A prominent Negro journalist with diplomatic experience, Douglass received the assignment as a reward for the service he had rendered Harrison during the latter's campaign for election.[33]

Regardless of the minister's competence for the post, his appointment was bound to conflict with the plans of the State and Navy Departments. Racially and emotionally attached to the Haitian people, Douglass resented the hard-driving policies of the imperialist camp. Although he saw no disadvantage to Haiti arising from closer ties with the United States, his sympathy for the islanders' sensitivity would surely make him reluctant to negotiate any settlement that might seem to them a violation of their territorial integrity.[34] He had no inkling, moreover, of the administration's intentions concerning the Môle for more than a year after he assumed office.[35]

For that matter, not even Blaine could foresee what the President or Tracy would do next. Actually, the general was playing a double and—it must be admitted—a foolish game. He would cooperate temporarily with the State Department's Haitian policy; then, without warning, he would depart on a tangent of his own devising. Since Harrison seldom if ever objected to the general's maneuvers, he undoubtedly had advance knowledge of them.

Tracy made his first independent move in the fall of 1889. He ordered Rear Admiral Bancroft Gherardi, who had relieved Luce earlier in the

32 For an account of Bayard's alleged dealings with agents of Legitime, see La Feber, New Empire, 127.
33 Montague, Haiti, 148–54. Cf. Gherardi to Tracy, September 2, 1889; Volwiler (ed.), Correspondence, Harrison to Blaine, August 14, 1889, and Blaine to Harrison, August 26, 1889.
34 Douglass to Blaine, December 9, 1889, in Dispatches: Haiti, Diplomatic Branch, National Archives; hereinafter cited as Dip. Arch.
35 Douglass to Blaine, December 9, 1889, in Dispatches: Haiti, Dip. Arch.

year, to detach the U.S.S. *Yantic* from the North Atlantic Squadron
for the purpose of undertaking a survey of the Môle St. Nicolas.[36]

The *Yantic* arrived in the harbor of Port-au-Prince during the first
week of December. As soon as Douglass perceived the nature of the
ship's mission, he dispatched a protest to Blaine. The minister reported
that the activities of the *Yantic's* officers suggested American designs
on the Môle and, therefore, were embarrassing to President Hyppolite,
whose policy on that score had already aroused suspicion among the
people. Having informed Blaine, Douglass hastened to reassure Foreign
Minister Antenor Firmin, explaining that the warship's officers were
making astronomical measurements from the Môle because of its convenient location. This satisfied Firmin for the moment and relieved his
mind; he feared the outbreak of a counterrevolution if Hyppolite gave
the slightest indication of a desire to cede the property.[37]

In his ignorance of the administration's plans, Douglass soon ran
afoul of imperialist and commercial interests. Gherardi regarded the
Negro's appointment to Haiti as a colossal blunder on Blaine's part.
So did William P. Clyde, the influential head of Clyde's Coastwise and
West Indies Lines, who relayed his opinion to Secretary Tracy. Both
the Admiral and Clyde asked Tracy to persuade Blaine of the importance
of replacing Douglass at once, but to no avail. The secretary of state,
Tracy replied, insisted on keeping Douglass at his post for a "decent
interval." [38]

Convinced by Gherardi and Clyde that Blaine's toleration of Douglass
would work against the acquisition of the Môle, Tracy decided to
bypass the State Department again in the winter of 1889–90. To offset
any unfavorable influence that might be exerted by the uninformed,
anti-imperialist minister, the general entrusted to Gherardi the responsibility of guarding the Navy's interests at Port-au-Prince. He had
already made up his mind, moreover, to have Gherardi in charge when
the time came to negotiate officially for the Môle.[39]

In order to open the avenue to such negotiations, Tracy asked Clyde
to approach Hyppolite indirectly. A number of factors prompted this
request. For one thing, Tracy trusted the shipping magnate; Clyde had
traded for him on the floor of the Stock Exchange in the past, to the
general's profit, and had retained the Brooklyn firm of Tracy, Board-

36 Navy Dept., *Annual Report*, 1889; *Navy Register*, 1889.
37 Douglass to Blaine, December 9, 1889, in Dispatches: Haiti, Dip. Arch.
38 Clyde to Tracy, November 19 and December 4, 1889, in Tracy Papers;
Gherardi to Tracy, September 2, 1889, in Tracy Papers.
39 Montague, *Haiti*, 155–57; Volwiler (ed.), *Correspondence*, August 14, 1891.

man, and Platt as legal counsel to his steamship lines.[40] Furthermore, Clyde's influence in Washington and Port-au-Prince qualified him to serve as the Navy's unofficial agent, in Tracy's opinion. The general knew that Clyde's desires would weigh heavily in the councils of Haiti's provisional regime, for Hyppolite owed him money. Ships of the West Indies Lines had carried munitions to the President's army during the recent revolution, a service for which Clyde had not received payment, owing to the wretched financial condition of the Provisional Government.

It had occurred to Secretary Tracy that, considering the unpaid freight bill, Clyde might prevail on Hyppolite to satisfy his debt by granting the shipowner concessions, including a lease of the Môle as a coaling station for his vessels. If accomplished successfully, this transaction could lead to an extension of the concession which would permit men-of-war to coal at the Môle as well without undue embarrassment to President Hyppolite, in view of the purely commercial flavor of the initial arrangement. Clyde agreed with Tracy's reasoning, declaring that "the successful party now know who their friends have been, and if our government will go wisely about it . . . we can secure anything, in my opinion, which we could in decency ask." [41]

At this juncture, Secretary Tracy revealed his hand to Blaine. Then he directed Gherardi to open preliminary discussions with Hyppolite on Clyde's account. Deliberately omitting mention of the Môle, the Admiral won a handsome concession for the West Indies Lines in January, 1890. In August, Clyde followed up Gherardi's opening gambit with a personal call on President Hyppolite.[42] Feigning dissatisfaction with the financial subsidies granted him in January, the shipowner demanded additional recompense in the form of a ninety-nine year lease of the Môle as a coaling station for the exclusive use of American vessels.[43] Much to Clyde's surprise, Hyppolite flatly rejected this demand.[44]

The rebuff caught Tracy off guard, and after conferring with Ghe-

---

40 Clyde to Tracy, December 28, 1889, *et al.*, in Tracy Papers.
41 Clyde to Tracy, September 9, 1892, Tracy Papers, suggests the extent of Clyde's influence in Washington. Quotation from Clyde to Tracy, May 31, 1889, Tracy Papers. See also, Gherardi to Tracy, December 19, 1889, in Navy Arch., Letters Received. Cf. Montague, *Haiti*, 155–60.
42 Gherardi to Tracy, January 22, 1890, in Navy Arch., Letters Received; Clyde to Tracy, April 21, 1891, in Tracy Papers, specifying the amount of subsidy Hyppolite granted Clyde's line—$470,000.
43 Clyde to Tracy (telegram), August 16, 1890, in Tracy Papers.
44 Clyde to Tracy (letter), August 16, 1890, in Tracy Papers.

rardi and Blaine, he decided to let Blaine proceed through normal diplomatic channels once more. Privately, however, he made the reservation that if diplomacy failed he would employ more forceful measures to secure the Môle. As he implied to Admiral Gherardi, a show of naval strength at Port-au-Prince would probably suffice to gain their objective.[45] Meanwhile, Blaine could have his chance.

The secretary of state summoned Douglass, who was then home on leave, to his office and instructed him to negotiate with Firmin and Hyppolite for a lease of the Môle to the United States government.[46] Fully aware of the administration's desires for the first time, Douglass now perceived also the weakness of his position. He had left Haiti for three months in July, 1890, knowing nothing of Gherardi's preliminary talks with Hyppolite. Inasmuch as he had departed a month prior to Clyde's meeting with the Haitian president, he knew nothing of their conversation. His recently acquired knowledge filled him with misgivings; Douglass appreciated the islanders' distate for the mere thought of giving up territory to a foreign power. Moreover, as the minister had informed Blaine, the citizens of Port-au-Prince had become suspicious of the continuing presence of American men-of-war in their harbor. These factors, he felt, would surely nullify any pressure he brought to bear on the Provisional Government.[47]

To add to Douglass' difficulties, Blaine appointed—over his head—a special commissioner to deal with the Haitian officials. The secretary of state, who had rejected Douglass' evaluation of the situation in December, had apparently lost confidence in him. At the same time, Blaine turned to Tracy for assistance in selecting a more aggressive representative to carry out the mission. This curious development gave the general the chance he wanted for placing the negotiations in naval hands. Without hesitation, he recommended that Gherardi take charge at once.

Before the month ended, Blaine named Gherardi his special commissioner to represent the United States in Haiti. He instructed the admiral to convey to Hyppolite the "wish and purpose of President Harrison to acquire a coaling station" at Port-au-Prince and to emphasize the advantage to Haiti of ceding such a naval base to the United States. The cession would not only assure the Haitian regime of adequate protection from seaborne aggression, since American warships seeking coal and

---

45 Gherardi to Blaine, February 7, 1891, in Dispatches: Haiti, Dip. Arch.
46 Douglass to Blaine, January 5, 1891 in Dispatches: Haiti, Dip. Arch.
47 Douglass to Blaine, January 5, 1891, in Dispatches: Haiti, Dip. Arch.

supplies would constantly be in port, but it would also enrich the country with dollars from government contracts and sailors' pockets. Of course, warned Blaine, Gherardi must make it clear that Haiti should under no circumstances grant similar favors to other powers.[48]

The admiral's flagship, the cruiser *Philadelphia*, dropped anchor near the Môle in early January, 1891. Gherardi landed and at once sought out Douglass. The minister, though unhappy at Blaine's lack of faith in him and dubious as to the outcome of the mission, assured the admiral of his wholehearted cooperation and promised to arrange a meeting with Firmin and Hyppolite.[49] At this conference, Gherardi took as his premise the alleged agreement between Bayard and Elie. He pointed out that Hyppolite was obligated to the United States for services rendered during the conflict with Légitime, and reminded him of "certain promises made by . . . the Provisional Government, which it was now the desire of the government at Washington to have fulfilled." As instructed, the admiral garnished his presentation with references to the benefits which would accrue to Haiti if Hyppolite came to terms.[50]

Firmin was not convinced. He expressed his fear of leasing the Môle to the United States, warning his chief that any territorial concession might provoke a popular uprising against the provisional regime. Nevertheless, Hyppolite seemed impressed with Gherardi's reasoning. He agreed to submit the matter to his cabinet and to abide by its decision.[51]

The cabinet deliberated the fate of the Môle for about four months.[52] Toward the mid-point of this period, during which Gherardi and Douglass met frequently with Firmin, Secretary Tracy lost patience with the proceedings and took independent action in an attempt to expedite things. He ordered Admiral Gherardi to schedule target practice for the men-of-war stationed at Port-au-Prince with the intention of providing meaningful background music for the deliberations of the Haitian cabinet.[53]

Annoyed at the inertia manifested by this body, Gherardi recommended more drastic measures in February, undoubtedly at the behest

48 Blaine to Gherardi, January 1, 1891, in Instructions: Haiti, Dip. Arch.
49 Frederick Douglass, "Haiti and the United States," *North American Review*, CLIII (New York, 1891), 342.
50 Blaine to Gherardi, January 1, 1891, in Instructions: Haiti, Dip. Arch.
51 Gherardi to Blaine, January 31, 1891, in Dispatches: Haiti, Dip. Arch.
52 Blaine to Douglass, April 27, 1891, in Instructions: Haiti, Dip. Arch.
53 Gherardi to Blaine, and Douglass to Blaine, February 7, 1891, in Dispatches: Haiti, Dip. Arch.

of Secretary Tracy. Although the record becomes hazy at this point, it seems that the general had decided to move decisively and that he had advised Gherardi to take the initiative and inform Blaine of their plans. In any case, the admiral notified the State Department of his desire to seize the Môle by force. Once this was accomplished, he predicted, "negotiations could then be taken up and carried through successfully, based on the cession of the Môle as a *fait accompli*." [54]

While the admiral was awaiting word of Blaine's reaction to his proposal, Foreign Minister Firmin moved to delay matters further and, at the same time, to weaken the American position. The Provisional Government, he announced, questioned Gherardi's authority to act for the United States; unless the admiral could furnish proof of his status as special commissioner, the current negotiations must be dropped. Gherardi telegraphed Washington immediately, requesting full credentials, which he received within three weeks. [55]

Now it became the Navy's turn to stall for time. While Gherardi delayed the game by concealing the papers issued him by Blaine, Tracy dispatched every available warship to Haiti at full speed. [56] He even diverted the homeward-bound White Squadron from its course for the purpose of building naval strength at Port-au-Prince. [57]

In mid-April, Rear Admiral J. M. Walker's proud white cruisers steamed slowly past the Môle and dropped anchor. [58] From the moment the squadron stood into the harbor, it stirred up anger ashore. The trouble began with a misunderstanding between Walker and Gherardi when the former failed to pay his respects to Admiral Gherardi who, as commander of the North Atlantic Squadron and the senior officer present, was entitled to receive such recognition. [59] Besides touching off a bitter service quarrel, the White Squadron's call at Port-au-Prince provoked popular resentment, as Douglass had foreseen. Sensing the

54 Douglass to Blaine, April 20, 1891, in Dispatches: Haiti, Dip. Arch. Gherardi had attributed this plan to Douglass, which the latter denied in this letter.
55 Gherardi to Blaine, February 16, 1891, in Dispatches: Haiti, Dip. Arch.
56 Chief of the Bureau of Navigation to Gherardi, April 9, 1891, in Cipher Record, Navy Arch; Navy Dept., *Annual Report*, 1891.
57 Clyde to Tracy, April 21, 1891, in Tracy Papers; Navy Dept., *Annual Report*, 1891.
58 Clyde to Tracy, April 21, 1891, in Tracy Papers. Cf. New York *Herald*, May 24, 1891.
59 For the extension of this quarrel, see W. H. Stayton to Walker, September 7, 1891, in Tracy Papers; J. A. Smith to Chandler, December 9, 1889, in Chandler Papers.

hostile reaction of the Haitian public to Tracy's parade of force, the minister warned Blaine that the indignation aroused in the capital by the arrival of additional warships might compel Hyppolite to break off negotiations completely.[60]

Thus advised, Blaine reviewed the situation with Tracy; the secretary of state expressed his concern over the developments in Port-au-Prince, especially in connection with the reaction of the American press to the diversion of the White Squadron. Blaine feared editorial accusations of naval aggression against a defenseless neighbor and wished to anticipate them if possible. Ever conscious of the advantage of friendly relations with the press, Tracy offered to cooperate. The State and Navy Departments promptly released the news of the squadron's whereabouts, explaining that Tracy had sent it to the Haitian capital to help defend the Provisional Government against an insurrection, which the Harrison administration expected might begin momentarily.[61]

This explanation did not, of course, satisfy Haitian officials. Douglass' evaluation had been correct; the Môle negotiations broke down and, on April 22, Firmin informed Gherardi of his government's refusal to lease the property.[62] When news of the decision reached Washington, Blaine's caution prevailed again; he and the President persuaded Tracy to discard his plan for capturing the Môle, and the matter became a dead letter.

With the Môle St. Nicolas out of the question, General Tracy turned his attention to Samaná Bay in Santo Domingo. Despite his publicized concern for the security of Hyppolite's regime, he abruptly denuded Port-au-Prince of American naval protection by means of a terse message to Admiral Gherardi: "Proceed to Samaná Bay with *Philadelphia* . . . make careful inspection with view to coaling station. Walker and White Squadron proceed to Hampton Roads." [63]

Far less dramatic than the Môle affair, the general's attempt to acquire a base in Santo Domingo followed much the same pattern. As early as February, 1890, the State Department had received information which led Blaine to believe that the Dominican government was disposed to cede the bay to the United States under certain conditions. Because of the administration's preoccupation with the Môle St. Nicolas, this pros-

---

60 Douglass to Blaine, April 21 and May 2, 1891, in Dispatches: Haiti, Dip. Arch.
61 Clyde to Tracy, April 21, 1891, in Tracy Papers; New York *Herald*, May 24, 1891.
62 Douglass to Blaine (telegram), April 23, 1891, in Dispatches: Haiti, Dip. Arch.
63 Tracy to Gherardi (signal in plain), April 24, 1891, in Tracy Papers.

pect had not been fully investigated prior to Gherardi's departure from Port-au-Prince at the end of April, 1891, for an inspection of Samaná Bay.[64]

The secretary of state had, however, instructed Harrison's minister to Santo Domingo to keep the proposition alive until it could be explored further. Accordingly, John Durham, the Negro diplomat accredited to the Dominican regime, had attempted to capitalize on its apparently receptive mood. But, as in the case of the Môle, the brash behavior of the American Navy and the press worked against the conclusion of an agreement with Santo Domingo.[65]

In December, the Dominican representative in Washington, Manuel Galvan, offered Secretary Blaine a lease of Samaná Bay. Durham encouraged Blaine to act swiftly and tactfully on the offer, warning him not to give the Dominicans reason to form an inflated estimate of the bay's importance to the United States. This advice came too late; they had already set a high price.[66]

Dictator Ulises Heureaux regarded the proposed lease as a lever with which he might open the door to an offensive-defensive alliance with America. He demanded no rent payment but made the transaction conditional on American support of Santo Domingo in the event his regime embarked on a "just war" against Haiti. To sweeten the arrangement, Heureaux informed Blaine of his intention to seize the Môle St. Nicolas in the course of the war and turn it over to the United States Navy. The secretary of state considered these terms absurd; he rejected them and instructed Durham to press for a less binding agreement.[67]

Again the American press printed inaccurate accounts of the negotiations, and again Tracy proved overeager. The arrival of the *Philadelphia* at Samaná Bay with Admiral Gherardi and a number of correspondents on deck especially antagonized the Dominicans. Tracy's action on this occasion undermined Durham's efforts to persuade Heureaux of the wisdom of lowering his sights. As President Harrison's term ended, the negotiations for Samaná Bay faded into thin air.[68]

The outcome of the quest in Hispaniola compelled Tracy to admit

64 Durham to Blaine, February 11, 1890, in Dispatches: Santo Domingo, Dip. Arch.
65 Durham to J. W. Foster, July 22, 1891, in Dispatches: Santo Domingo, Dip. Arch. During the summer of 1891, Foster often acted as secretary of state owing to Blaine's worsening condition.
66 Durham to Foster, July 22, 1891, in Dispatches: Santo Domingo, Dip. Arch.
67 Durham to Blaine, January 16, 1892, in Dispatches: Santo Domingo, Dip. Arch.
68 S. Welles, *Naboth's Vineyard*, I, 490–95.

defeat in his campaign to establish a base eastward of the projected canal site.[69] It did not, on the other hand, deter him from seeking one in the Pacific. Not only was the status of Pago Pago still in doubt, but Samoa lay too far from the Central American isthmus to serve as a western bastion for the canal. The Hawaiian Islands, however, seemed ideally located for the purpose.

Mahan had already pointed out the advantages of annexing Hawaii in his articles promoting naval expansion. Tracy concurred in the captain's high opinion of the islands as an area which would prove to be of inestimable value to the Pacific Fleet as well as to the defense of the future canal. And, like Mahan, the secretary favored immediate annexation, having read the former's arguments. Dominion over Hawaii, in Mahan's opinion, would establish the western strongpoint of the national defense system. A fortified base in the Hawaiian chain would at once insure the canal against a surprise attack from the Pacific and guarantee additional security to the west coast. Moreover, explained the captain, possession of the chain would operate to the benefit of the nation's expanding trade in the Far East.[70]

Predictably, Captain Mahan's reasoning appealed to leading political and economic imperialists. As usual, he won the support of both Harrison and Tracy, who hastily set in motion the administration's final venture in its ill-fated quest for bases. Perhaps the failures in Hispaniola strengthened their resolve to acquire Hawaii; during their last months in office, events moved rapidly toward this goal. Time alone prevented its attainment.[71]

Even the ailing secretary of state cooperated with the rapid-fire steps taken to complete annexation before Cleveland returned to the White House. On Blaine's recommendation, President Harrison appointed J. L. Stevens United States minister to the Kingdom of Hawaii. Stevens, an old friend of Blaine's and former editor of the *Kennebec Journal*, was a known annexationist.[72]

Within a month of the new minister's arrival in Honolulu, an uprising led by two Hawaiian half-castes took place. In the midst of the

69 Montague, *Haiti*, 162.
70 For these and related ideas of Mahan, see "U.S. Looking Outward," 816ff.; "The Isthmus and Sea Power," *Atlantic Monthly*, LXXII (October, 1893), 471; "Hawaii and Our Future Sea Power," *Forum*, XV (March, 1893), 1ff.; all articles by Mahan.
71 J. W. Pratt, *Expansionists of 1898*, 72.
72 Muzzey, *Blaine*, 393.

disturbance, loyal officials of King Kalakaua permitted Stevens to call on the Navy to provide protection of American lives and property. Although the local militia had matters in hand before the Navy responded, the commanding officer of the U.S.S. *Adams* dispatched a landing party whose "appearance had a favorable effect on the population." [73]

In January, 1891, Queen Liliuokalani succeeded Kalakaua and quickly won recognition of her status from Harrison, who hoped she would cater to the growing American colony in the kingdom. The Queen soon dashed that hope; she opposed American expansion in the islands and refused to curry favor with the leaders of the movement. As a result of her attitude, Judge Sanford Dole and other spokesmen of the American community adopted a revolutionary program—with Steven's knowledge—aimed at deposing the Queen in order to pave the way for annexation.

Dole's revolution materialized in January, 1893. In rapid succession, his provisional government seized control of Honolulu, forced the Queen to abdicate, and asked Stevens to obtain naval assistance for preserving order. The minister acted promptly; he requested Captain G. C. Wiltse, commanding officer of the *Boston*, to send a party of marines ashore as soon as possible.[74]

Wiltse complied, as he reported in a terse message to Secretary Tracy: "At 4:30 P.M. landed force in accordance with the request of the U.S. Minister Plenipotentiary. Tuesday afternoon the Provisional Government was established, the Queen dethroned, without loss of life." [75] Tracy received this dispatch on January 28. Three days thereafter a second message from Wiltse informed him of Stevens' request that the new regime be placed under naval protection although, in Wiltse's opinion, conditions did not appear to warrant such action. In any event, the *Boston's* marines remained ashore.[76]

The imperialist nature of Harrison's Hawaiian policy seems obvious. Nevertheless, his defenders have attempted to absolve the administration of responsibility for the events that colored this segment of Hawaiian

73 Moore, *Digest*, I, 496–98. This abortive revolt was led by Robert Boyd and Robert Wilcox.
74 *Ibid.*
75 Wiltse to Tracy, January 28, 1893, in Bureau of Navigation Executive Book No. 2, Navy Arch.
76 Wiltse to Tracy, February 1, 1893, in Bureau of Navigation Executive Book No. 2, Navy Arch.

history. Likewise, they have held Harrison and his advisors innocent of intrigue in establishing a protectorate as a prelude to annexation.

John W. Foster, who had succeeded Blaine as secretary of state, assumed the burden of defending Harrison, Tracy, and Stevens. Subsequently, Foster drafted an official report of the conduct of American officials during and after the Hawaiian revolution. According to this document, the landing of marines in no way influenced the course of events leading to the conclusion of an annexation agreement between Dole's regime and the Harrison administration. Nor did the presence of the *Boston* at Pearl Harbor, in Foster's view, signify the existence of an imperialist conspiracy. The flagship of the Pacific Squadron was stationed there as a routine, precautionary measure, and for no other reason. Consequently, concluded Foster, Stevens' request for marines had come as a complete surprise to Captain Wiltse and the secretary of the navy alike.[77]

Innocently or not, Harrison obtained his treaty of annexation, short-lived as it was. In the letter of transmittal he submitted with the pact to the Senate in mid-February, the President sharply denied that his administration had intervened on Dole's behalf at any level. The harsh policies of Queen Liliuokalani's government, wrote Harrison, had created the revolution, not the United States. Her reign, he argued, had jeopardized the interests of Americans and other foreigners and had obstructed the peaceful administration of civil affairs in Hawaii.[78]

Opponents of annexation attacked the stand taken by Foster and Harrison. With some justice, they pointed out that Harrison and Tracy, not to mention Stevens, must have known of the extensive, nonofficial American influence at work in the islands prior to the revolution. Moreover, they added, the President's appointment of such a prominent annexationist as Stevens indicated his determination to enlarge the sphere of that influence.

Regarding the landing parties sent ashore, first from the *Adams* and later from the *Boston*, with the knowledge and approval of Secretary Tracy, administration critics questioned Stevens' motive for requesting them. On both occasions, any real threat to American interests had passed by the time the seamen and marines appeared on the scene. In all probability, reasoned the detractors, the minister had called for them

---

77 Moore, *Digest*, I, 496–97.
78 *Ibid.*, 496ff.; Peck, "Twenty Years of the Republic," 370–79. Grover Cleveland withdrew the treaty during his first week in office, in 1893.

as a means of showing the flag in Honolulu and identifying it with the rebellion. Not that Stevens was personally responsible for his actions, observed Harrison's critics; he had simply followed his superior's orders.

The evidence suggests that the administration was indeed guilty of imperialist intent and that many of the accusations leveled at it had substance. But certain pertinent information tends to verify at least that portion of Foster's defense which emphasized the necessity of annexing the islands as rapidly as possible, once the protectorate had been proclaimed. Foster stated that "the situation was very critical, and there was every probability that unless prompt action was taken . . . anarchy might have been created." [79]

Despite the logic of the allegation made by foes of the administration that Harrison's haste could be attributed to a desire to have the treaty raitfied prior to his retirement, there is reason to think that time was not the sole consideration. For instance, a dispatch from the commander of the Pacific Squadron to Tracy in February substantiated Foster's description of current conditions in Honolulu. Rear Admiral J. S. Skerrett had assumed command of the squadron in late January. For a week or more after he had hoisted his flag on the *Boston*, Skerrett studied the political situation ashore, taking careful notes in preparation of an evaluation requested by Tracy. Reaching his own conclusions concerning the caliber of Dole's government, the admiral reported to the secretary that the regime's instability and undemocratic policies rendered it incapable of surviving a popular election. The tone of Skerrett's message recalled the fear of panic expressed by Foster.[80]

A month earlier, the admiral had paid Tracy a courtesy call prior to his departure for Honolulu. The conversation between them on this occasion is interesting, in view of the annexation issue. Skerrett asked the general outright if the administration planned to annex the islands soon. Tracy replied warmly that "the government will be very glad to annex Hawaii." "All right, sir," said the admiral, "I only wanted to know how things were going on, as a casting action." [81]

The Senate's refusal to ratify the Hawaiian Treaty of Annexation

79 Foster, *Diplomatic Memoirs*, II, 168.
80 Skerrett to Tracy, undated dispatch No. 571, in Bureau of Navigation, Dispatches Received, Navy Arch. Skerrett, who had received his orders to take command of the Pacific Squadron in late December, 1892, arrived in Honolulu after the revolution had ended, according to records in Navy Arch.
81 Quoted in J. W. Pratt, *Expansionists of 1898*, 74, citing *U.S. Foreign Relations*, 1894; and in Peck, "Twenty Years of the Republic," 378–79, without documentation.

marked the end of Tracy's tedious search for bases and coaling stations. For the failure of the quest, Tracy had himself to blame in large measure, especially in Hispaniola. His tactless, not to say bullying, direction of the Navy's frequently unilateral maneuvers for Haitian and Dominican territory, undertaken without regard for the probable reaction of the island public or the American press, can only be described as a blunder of the first order. The general's ardent patriotism veered toward chauvinism as soon as Blaine's cautious negotiations appeared to falter.

At a press conference in the fall of 1891, the general stated frankly his imperialist view of America's future: "The sea will be the future seat of empire. And we shall rule it as certainly as the sun doth rise! To a pre-eminent rank among nations, colonies are of the greatest help." [82]

82 New York *World*, November 26, 1891.

VI
TROUBLE WITH CHILE

WAR FEVER ADDED FRESH VIGOR TO HARRISONIAN IMPERIALISM in 1891. For a full year, the jingoists had their say as the administration braced for a fight. In this period of crisis and alarms, General Tracy's positive—and often impulsive—actions in the national interest won him new popularity and prestige. For this, he had a revolution in Chile to thank.

The crisis took shape in January when the president of Chile, J. M. Balmaceda, broke with his congress over a financial issue. Inasmuch as the lawmakers had refused to renew certain appropriations essential to his budget, the president announced that the budgetary measures enacted in 1890 would remain in effect until additional funds were voted. Thereupon, the congress pronounced Balmaceda's conduct unconstitutional and removed him from office.[1]

Civil war erupted on January 7. For a time, most of the land forces supported Balmaceda, who had recently raised the soldiers' pay by 50 per cent. But the bulk of Chile's sea power defected at the outset. The fleet at Valparaiso, which included the fast modern cruiser *Esmeralda* and several ironclads, weighed anchor and steamed north with a number of congressional officials aboard. During the voyage, an insurgent *junta*

---

1 F. B. Pike, *Chile and the United States: 1880–1962* (South Bend, Ind., 1963), 40-46; Bastert, "Blaine and Conference," 433; W. E. Curtis, *From the Andes to the Ocean* (Chicago, 1900), 411ff. Curtis was Harrison's special commissioner for the first Pan-American conference and at one time presided over the Bureau of American Republics, forerunner of the O.A.S.

formed and vested full powers of leadership in Captain Jorge Montt of the Chilean Navy.[2]

At the outbreak of hostilities, the Harrison administration favored the cause of Balmaceda, whose regime, for a Chilean government, had proved unusually friendly to the United States. As the fighting continued, however, the odds on a Balmacedist victory declined. Reporting substantial gains by the congressionalists, American naval observers predicted that if insurgent leaders could procure sufficient arms abroad and recruit troops from the peasantry, victory would be theirs.[3]

In February, Secretary Tracy detached Rear Admiral William P. McCann from the South Atlantic Station and assigned him special duty in Chilean waters. McCann headed his wooden flagship *Pensacola* south, rounded Cape Horn, and ultimately reached Valparaiso where he reported to Rear Admiral George Brown, commander of the South Pacific Squadron. Acting on Tracy's orders, Brown released the new cruisers *Baltimore* and *San Francisco* for service with the *Pensacola*.[4]

McCann's force steamed slowly southward along the coast of Chile, noting the progress of the revolution and drafting evaluations periodically for the Navy Department. In March, the admiral dispatched a report to Tracy: "I have visited Chilean ports to the north. No injury to American citizens or interests. The . . . government forces were defeated at Pazoalmont on March 7. The British commander-in-chief has orders to remain on this station." [5] McCann realized that foreign maritime powers were keeping close watch on developments in the area, as the presence of British, German, and French warships attested. He knew too that their constant patrols, if continued, would tend to hamper the operations of American men-of-war.[6]

While McCann was cruising offshore, the insurgent leaders took steps to provide their troops with arms. From Iquique, the rebel capital, they sent an agent, Ricardo Trumbull, to New York for the purpose of procuring guns and ammunition. There Trumbull, a Chilean-born Yale

2 Pike, *Chile and U.S.*, 44; A. U. Hancock, *History of Chile* (Chicago, 1893), 329ff.

3 Office of Naval Intelligence, *War Series Bulletin IV*, *passim*, in NWC. This document, based on reports submitted by two junior officers attached to the *Baltimore*, evaluates the progress of the Chilean civil war in 1891.

4 Navy Dept., *Annual Report*, 1891; *Navy Register*, 1891.

5 McCann to Tracy (dispatch), March 31, 1891, in Cipher Record No. 40, Navy Arch.

6 McCann to Tracy, March 10, 1891, in Cipher Record No. 40, Navy Arch.

graduate, secured assistance from Blaine's friend, W. R. Grace, a prominent shipowner and former mayor of New York.[7] With Grace's cooperation, Trumbull bought five thousand rifles and a supply of ammunition and had the lot shipped to California. At San Francisco, the shipment was stowed in the hold of the *Robert and Minnie*, an American-flag schooner which Trumbull had chartered to carry the arms to San Diego for transfer to a rebel merchantman.[8]

Such were the components of an explosive incident touched off in San Diego in early May. Attorney-General W. H. H. Miller received word of the illegal arms shipment on May 6 from a federal marshal in San Diego. Having investigated the matter, Marshal George E. Gard felt sure that the shipment was destined for the insurgent steamer *Itata*, recently arrived from Iquique.[9]

Gard's report reached Miller in President Harrison's absence. After consulting Secretary Tracy, the attorney-general telegraphed the President in Seattle for authority to have the *Itata* seized where she lay for violation of federal neutrality laws. Harrison wired back his approval, whereupon Miller ordered his agents to proceed against the steamer immediately.[10]

Accordingly, a marshal boarded the *Itata* and declared the ship under seizure. Meanwhile the *Robert and Minnie* had slipped out of San Diego, bound for parts unknown.[11] The schooner's escape seems to have precipitated the ensuing actions of the *Itata*'s captain. Making the marshal his prisoner, he ordered mooring lines cast off and then headed the steamer for the open sea. After steaming southward for some eight miles, the captain lowered a boat and sent the marshal ashore.[12]

Near the island of San Clemente off the coast of Southern California, the two ships met to complete the transshipment which had been interrupted by federal agents. This accomplished, the *Itata* again stood out to sea and shaped course for Valparaiso.[13] From that moment, the

7 Osgood Hardy, "The Itata Incident," *Hispanic–American Historical Review*, V (May, 1922), 195ff.; hereinafter cited as *HAHR*. Hardy cites an article from the Los Angeles *Times*, May 8, 1891.

8 H. C. Evans, *Chile and Its Relations with the United States* (Durham, N.C., 1927), 214; hereinafter cited as Evans, *Chile and Relations*.

9 W. Cole to Miller (telegram), May 6, 1891, in File No. 2714–2924, Navy Arch.

10 Miller to Harrison (telegram), May 6, 1891, and Harrison's reply of even date in File No. 2714–2924, Navy Arch.

11 Gard to Miller (telegram), May 7, 1891. File No. 2714–2924, Navy Arch.

12 Gard to Miller (telegram) May 7, 1891, File No. 2714–2924, Navy Arch.

13 Navy Dept., *Annual Report*, 1891. The arms were aboard the *Itata* when she returned under escort to San Diego in July, 1891.

insurgent steamer became the concern of the Navy as well as that of the Department of Justice.

In Washington, the cabinet convened to discuss the next move. Tracy and Miller sought the recapture of the *Itata* on the premise that, because of her seizure, the vessel was legally the property of the United States. Although some of the members expressed opposition, Tracy persuaded them before long of the advisability of retaking the ship, by force if necessary.[14]

The secretary moved promptly to carry out the cabinet's decision. In view of the large-scale defection of Chilean naval units to the insurgents, he directed the *Charleston*, the most powerful cruiser available, to pursue the *Itata* and bring the fugitive back to justice in San Diego. The *Charleston* departed in haste from Mare Island, sped through the Golden Gate, and set course for Acapulco Bay on the Mexican coast where her captain, Commander George Remey, hoped to intercept his quarry.[15]

Meanwhile, the insurgent regime at Iquique dispatched the redoubtable cruiser *Esmeralda*, now flying congressionalist colors, to make full speed for Acapulco Bay, meet the *Itata* there, and escort her to the safety of Chilean waters. Unknown to their crews, the *Charleston* and the *Esmeralda* were closing on each other at a relative speed of about 38 knots![16] As soon as Remey sighted the rebel cruiser near Acapulco, he identified her ensign and ordered the *Charleston* cleared for action. The insurgent captain followed suit, and all hands braced themselves for the roar of gunfire. It never came because the *Itata* failed to appear. The steamer, following her course to Valparaiso, passed Acapulco well to seaward of the cruisers.[17]

Realizing after a while what had happened, Commander Remey headed the *Charleston* for Iquique to report to Admiral McCann and request further orders. On his arrival, Remey found McCann absorbed in the problem of arranging a truce between the belligerents with the congressionalist foreign minister, Isidorio Errazuriz, as requested by Patrick Egan, Harrison's minister to the Balmacedist government. An abler seaman than diplomat, the admiral failed to win the congressionalist re-

14 Hardy, "Itata," citing *Daily Alta Californian*, May 8, 1891.
15 C. M. Remey, *The Life and Letters of George C. Remey* (Washington, 1937), 771–73; Mitchell, *Modern Navy*, 44; Peck, "Twenty Years of the Republic," 369ff.
16 Navy Dept., *Annual Report*, 1891.
17 Remey, *George C. Remey*, 771–73. A detailed account of the fiasco appears here.

gime's agreement to a cease-fire, but on another count he scored a diplomatic victory.[18] Ever since the *Itata's* escape from San Diego, McCann had been badgering the insurgents for an official statement of their attitude towards the steamer's flight. In June, his efforts bore fruit. The provisional government disavowed "the act of the *Itata*," and promised to place the ship, with guns and ammunition aboard, at the disposal of the United States. On June 4, the admiral reported to Secretary Tracy: "*Itata* placed at my disposition this morning." [19]

On receipt of McCann's message, as Tracy put it, "no time was lost in changing the *Charleston's* orders." The secretary instructed the admiral to have Remey meet the *Itata* outside the harbor of Iquique and escort her to San Diego.

During the run north, relations between the ships' companies grew quite cordial. The Chileans transferred a supply of fresh meat to the *Charleston* for the crew's mess, a compliment which Remey's officers returned by passing over to the *Itata* a number of casks of California wine. On July 4, the insurgent steamer reentered San Diego harbor in the wake of her American escort.[20]

The *Itata* incident generated a wave of hostility to the United States in Chile. To congressionalists, the seizure of the ship confirmed their suspicion of Harrison's pro-Balmacedist leanings. Although the steamer herself meant nothing to them, the arms she had carried represented the means of victory. Consequently, when the Harrison administration decided to return the *Itata*—stripped of her cargo—to Iquique in September, the gesture failed to warm the rebels' hearts, even though their government had bartered for the steamer's release.

To Tracy and Attorney-General Miller, on the other hand, the decision to free the *Itata* appeared wise and generous. They considered it a demonstration of the American spirit of compromise; an attitude shared by an important segment of the press. "The *Itata* is to be returned to Chile in accordance with . . . a compromise effected . . . between ex-Mayor Grace of New York and the Chilean Constitutional Repre-

18 Egan to Blaine, June 27, 1891, in Dispatches, Chile, Dip. Arch.; J. B. Moore to Harrison (memorandum), May 27, 1891, in Volwiler (ed.), *Correspondence;* McCann to Tracy, June 12, 1891, in Bureau of Navigation Executive Book No. 2, in which McCann confessed that he was "unused to diplomacy."
19 McCann to Tracy (telegram), June 4, 1891, in Tracy Papers; *House Executive Documents,* 52nd Cong., 1st Sess., No. 91, pp. 253–54. A search party at Iquique found five thousand rifles and a substantial supply of ammunition in the *Itata's* hold, all of which had been transferred from the *Robert and Minnie.*
20 Remey to Tracy (telegram), July 4, 1891, in Tracy Papers.

sentative on the one hand, and Secretary Tracy and Attorney-General Miller on the other." [21]

The publicity given this affair held personal significance for General Tracy. Newspaper accounts called attention to the weight of his influence on national policy and established him as a man of action, determined to uphold American prestige. Tracy's behavior in the matter of the *Itata* betrayed, too, his intense nationalism which, coupled with his legalistic approach to problems, was to involve the Navy in a series of provocative situations before the end of the Chilean struggle.

A second wave of anti-American sentiment arose in Chile over the question of asylum for political refugees, once the insurgents' victory seemed assured. In February, 1891, congressionalists protested loudly when United States Minister Patrick Egan granted sanctuary to ex-President Balmaceda in the legation at Santiago. Not that various South American ministers were barring refugees of the old regime from their thresholds—they were not—but Egan became the main target of abuse, not only from the triumphant congressionalists, but also from their sympathizers in the former capital's foreign colony, especially the British element.

Prior to his arrival in the United States, Egan had been prosecuted in English courts for his part in the Irish nationalist campaign for Home Rule. Britons in Santiago, who believed Blaine had appointed this Anglophobe minister to Chile in order to gain commercial advantage for the United States, warned their Chilean neighbors that as long as Egan remained, the Harrison administration would never recognize the provisional regime. As evidence of Washington's prejudice against Chile's new government, prominent Britons cited Egan's hospitable treatment of Balmaceda and Tracy's conduct during the misadventure of the *Itata*. When the insurgent leaders in Iquique learned of the position Tracy had taken concerning political asylum aboard warships, moreover, they had further reason to accept the views of Santiago's British clique. [22]

From the beginning of the war in Chile, Secretary Tracy had foreseen the danger inherent in a vague policy of asylum, especially when applied to men-of-war. In March, 1891, therefore, he outlined a set of principles for American commanders in the area to follow. "The obliga-

21 San Francisco *Evening Bulletin*, September 10, 1891; Washington *Star*, September 10, 1891.
22 Volwiler (ed.), *Correspondence*, Harrison to Blaine, No. 226; Osgood Hardy, "Was Patrick Egan a Blundering Minister?" *HAHR*, VIII (February, 1928), 66–81; Curtis, *From the Andes*, 411ff.; Pike, *Chile and U.S.*, 66–70.

tion to receive political refugees and to afford them asylum is . . . one of pure humanity. It should not be continued beyond the urgent necessities of the situation, and should in no case become the means whereby the plans of contending factions are facilitated." [23] Setting forth this doctrine in a letter to Rear Admiral George Brown, the secretary concluded: "You are not to invite or encourage such refugees to come aboard your ship but, should they apply to you, your action will be governed by considerations of humanity and the exigencies of the service upon which you are engaged." [24]

Brown followed Tracy's orders literally. After the downfall of Balmaceda, he allowed nineteen refugees to board the *Baltimore* and his flagship, the *San Francisco*. These unfortunates enjoyed the shelter of the cruisers for most of the summer of 1891. On September 4, by order of Secretary Tracy, the *Baltimore* took aboard the flagship's refugees and carried them safely to Peru. Ten days thereafter, Brown admitted more Balmacedists to the *San Francisco* and gave them passage to Callao. [25]

Apparently, German naval commanders in Chilean waters were acting under similar instructions. The Balmacedist president-elect, Claudio Vicuña, and the loyalist Admiral Oscar Viel found safety aboard the cruiser *Leipzig*. The British and French displayed no such solicitude for the welfare of refugees, however. British officers barred them from Her Majesty's ships, while French units remained well offshore, as if to avoid the issue altogether. [26]

In a corollary to his policy of asylum, Tracy warned American officers to treat insurgent vessels correctly. Conscious of the resentment provoked by the *Itata* episode, he directed his ship captains to regard congressionalist warships as legitimate men-of-war of a foreign state, unless these vessels engaged in distinctly piratical operations. [27]

The secretary's attitude towards political refugees angered the congressionalists as much as had Egan's pampering of Balmaceda. But this was only the beginning; in August, two fresh developments gave the Chileans additional grounds for distrusting American naval policy. The

23 Tracy to Brown, March 26, 1891, in Tracy Papers.
24 *Ibid.;* Moore, *Digest,* II, 851–52. These principles were incorporated in *Navy Regulations,* 1893.
25 Navy Dept., *Annual Report,* 1891; Moore, *Digest,* II, 852. Cf. Pike, *Chile and U.S.,* 66–70.
26 Navy Dept., *Annual Report,* 1891.
27 *Ibid.;* Moore, *Digest,* II, 852.

first of these centered on the operations of the *Baltimore* while escort-ing an American-flag cable-layer, the *Relay*, off the port of Iquique.

A New York firm, the Central and South American Telegraph Com-pany, had applied to the authorities in Iquique for permission to com-plete its new cable to Valparaiso, prior to the establishment of the pro-visional government. Following the formation of the insurgent regime, Admiral McCann endorsed the company's application and requested the regime's approval of his intention to use the cable as soon as possible, for the purpose of expediting his communications with Tracy.

The insurgents turned down the admiral's request, whereupon Mc-Cann summoned the captain of the *Baltimore*, Commander W. S. Schley, to his quarters. Ordering Schley to escort the *Relay* to a point well outside the harbor over the unconnected ends of the Valparaiso cable, the Admiral directed him to keep the *Baltimore* standing by the cable-layer while the latter spliced them. Accordingly, the *Baltimore* led the *Relay* to the indicated position. There the *Relay* picked up the cable sections and connected them with a loop which extended beyond the limit of Chilean territorial jurisdiction. The *Baltimore* circled slowly around the *Relay* during this lengthy operation.[28]

Outraged at McCann's disregard of their authority, the officials at Iquique declared the actions of the *Baltimore* and *Relay* unlawful and provocative. In his report of the matter, General Tracy pointed up the absurdity of the accusation. The American vessels had, he argued, steamed more than five miles from the Chilean shoreline before the *Relay* stopped to pick up the first segment of cable, which in any event was American property. Furthermore, continued the secretary, Schley's conduct throughout the operation merely reflected a proper concern for the safety of his compatriots aboard the *Relay*. What Tracy failed to explain was why McCann felt he needed the provisional government's permission to use the cable, if it lay outside Chile's territorial juris-diction.[29]

During the furor caused by the *Relay's* actions, a second occurrence

---

28 W. S. Schley, *Forty-Five Years*, 214–15. Schley's account varies in detail with Tracy's version as published in his annual report and with Curtis' description in *From the Andes*, 409. According to Tracy and Curtis, Schley took the *Baltimore* out of port to escort the *Relay* on his own initiative. It seems unlikely, how-ever, in view of McCann's presence, that Schley would have taken this action without his superior's approval at least. In emphasizing the admiral's responsibility for the cruiser's part in the incident, therefore, Schley's report seems more ac-curate.

29 Navy Dept., *Annual Report*, 1891.

added to the Chileans' suspicion of the American naval mission. In August, a rumor spread through Valparaiso to the effect that congressionalist generals were contemplating a massive landing at nearby Quintero Bay as the first phase of an all-out offensive against the port city.[30] The rumor reached the ears of Admiral Brown and sparked his curiosity. Deciding to see for himself, he ordered the flagship's captain to weigh anchor on August 20. The *San Francisco* steamed to Quintero Bay, circled it once or twice, and returned to her anchorage at Valparaiso in the afternoon of the same day. On the run back to port, Brown noticed two insurgent picket boats approaching his flagship and directed the captain to steer clear of them. A loud protest arose over the news of Brown's inspection of the landing area. Influenced by their distrust of Egan and the Navy, the insurgents accused Brown of espionage on behalf of the loyalists. Probably as a result of inaccurate reporting by picket boat lookouts, moreover, the congressionalist leaders complained that Brown had permitted loyalist aides of Admiral Viel to observe from the bridge of the flagship.[31]

Brown denied these charges completely. In his opinion, they derived from false statements made at the English Club of Valparaiso for the sake of strengthening congressionalist ties with Britain and frustrating America's commercial aspirations in Chile. As to the rest, Admiral Brown insisted that he had taken no foreigner on his ship except a German officer from the *Leipzig*, that he had passed no information to the Balmacedists, and that he had ordered his crew not to discuss the *San Francisco's* voyage to Quintero Bay with anyone.[32]

The cruiser's movements on August 20 received wide publicity, not only in Chile, but also in the United States. Tracy supported Brown's version of the story without reservation, as did a number of American editors. Others shared the suspicion of Brown's intentions as expressed by the Chilean press. Before long, conflicting views of the matter had a full airing in the newspapers.[33]

30 *Ibid.* Admiral Brown's official report of his voyage to Quintero Bay appears here.
31 *Ibid.* Cf. Pike, *Chile and U.S.*, 68ff.
32 Navy Dept., *Annual Report*, 1891.
33 *Ibid.* For pro-Chilean accounts, see Hancock, *History of Chile*, 368ff.; Evans, *Chile and Relations*, 225–30; numerous articles on the subject in *The Nation* and New York *Times*, August through October, 1891, especially *The Nation* (New York), October 8, 1891. See also, New York *Evening Post* May 16, 1891. A number of editorials in full or qualified accord with the official report of Brown's conduct appeared during the summer and autumn of 1891 in New York *Herald*, New

During the last week of August, the State Department announced the administration's decision to grant official recognition to the new Chilean government. If Harrison and Blaine had hoped thereby to improve relations, they were disappointed. The congressionalist regime continued to protest the alleged misconduct of the Navy and to condemn Egan's persistent harboring of Balmacedists in the legation. Believing the complaints unfounded, Harrison publicly endorsed Tracy's statement of the Navy's exemplary behavior in Chilean waters.

As the notes of protest from Iquique piled up on his desk, the President's ire mounted. Blaine had taken to his sickbed in Bar Harbor; one of his assistants had also become ill, and the other was preparing his resignation. The situation in the State Department added to Harrison's burden, and the oppressive heat of the Washington summer sharpened his temper. The President revealed his state of mind in a letter to Blaine in September. Referring to the Chilean leaders, he declared in Rooseveltian language, "The trouble with these people and their kindred seems to be that they do not know how to use victory with dignity and moderation; and someday it may be necessary to instruct them." [34]

Meanwhile, at Harrison's request, Tracy was helping him oversee the work of the State Department in connection with Chile. Newsmen quickly sensed the general's growing influence on matters of state and tried to sound him out, but he refused at the time to satisfy their curiosity.

By mid-October, the congressionalists had gained control of both Santiago and Valparaiso. Writing Tracy from the latter city, Commander Schley remarked how peaceful the waterfront seemed from the quarterdeck of the *Baltimore*. The populace, reported Schley, had celebrated the return of peace in orderly fashion. British, French, and German men-of-war had already withdrawn from the area; and the *San Francisco* was making ready for sea. Only the *Baltimore* would remain. In conclusion, Schley added: "Everything quiet. The presence of a

---

York *Tribune*, Washington *Star*, Brooklyn *Daily Eagle*. For scholarly interpretations, see Tyler, *Policy of Blaine*, 141ff.; J. B. Moore, "The Late Chilean Controversy," *Political Science Quarterly*, VIII (September, 1893), 467–94. In *Chile and U.S.*, Pike agrees with Moore that Brown was innocent of espionage but was foolish to visit Quintero Bay. The brief treatment of the incident that appears in La Feber's *New Empire*, on the other hand, finds Brown guilty of spying and relaying information to the Balmacedists!

34 Volwiler (ed.), *Correspondence*, Harrison to Blaine, September 6, 1891; Navy Dept., *Annual Report*, 1891; La Feber, *New Empire*, 133.

vessel is no longer demanded. Balmaceda committed suicide September 19." [35]

Despite this reassurance, General Tracy thought it wise to keep one warship at Valparaiso for the time being. As soon as the crew realized that the *Baltimore* would not be sailing soon, the question of liberty arose. On October 16, Commander Schley yielded to the pleas of his men. Convinced of the serenity of conditions in the city, he ordered two boats lowered for the purpose of taking the liberty party ashore.

The cruiser's boats reached the quayside at about one-thirty that afternoon. Predictably, a number of the men gravitated to bars in the less respectable section of Valparaiso. They soon discovered that the citizenry was not so peaceably inclined as their captain had believed.[36]

Secretary Tracy's report of the events that followed the landing of the liberty party stated that the seamen were attacked by Chileans at approximately 6:30 in the evening. He found the *Baltimore's* men wholly innocent of starting the riot that began as a barroom brawl.

According to Tracy, two of the Americans were drinking in the True Blue Saloon shortly after coming ashore. For unexplained reasons, a fight broke out between them and "several" Chilean sailors. In the face of superior numbers, the *Baltimore's* men ran out of the saloon and into the street where they were surrounded by furious townspeople. Forcing their way through the crowd, they hastily boarded a passing street car.[37]

Thereupon, the report continued, a Chilean sailor stopped the car; and the shouting mob dragged the beleaguered pair to the ground. The clamor brought their shipmates to the scene on the run, followed by the Valparaiso police. Instead of attempting to quell the riot and rescue the victims, declared Tracy, the police forced all Americans still standing

---

35 Schley to Tracy, September 25, 1891, in Bureau of Navigation Executive Book No. 2, Navy Arch.; Schley, *Forty-Five Years,* 220ff.

36 Peck, "Twenty Years of the Republic," 371–72. Cf. Hancock, *History of Chile,* 369.

37 Navy Dept., *Annual Report,* 1891. For the attitude of the pro-adminstration press, see editorial comment during the fall and winter of 1891 in New York *Herald,* New York *Sun,* Philadelphia *Press,* and Brooklyn *Daily Times.* Other accounts supporting Tracy's stand appear in E. B. Potter (ed.), *The United States and World Sea Power* (Englewood Cliffs, N.J., 1955), 398ff.; Mitchell, *Modern Navy,* 44; Knox, *History of the U.S. Navy,* 326; Theodore Roosevelt, "The Foreign Policy of Benjamin Harrison," *The Independent* (New York), August 11, 1892, 2–3. In general agreement with Tracy's version is Tyler, *Policy of Blaine,* 145–46.

Benjamin Franklin Tracy, secretary of the navy from 1889 to 1893, recognized the latent naval responsibilities of a growing United States and began the work that would give America a capable, modern navy.

Theodore Roosevelt, assistant secretary
of the navy (1897–98), readily espoused
Mahan's theories and used them as a
basis for his actions prior to the Spanish–American War.

Admiral Stephen B. Luce, another of
Mahan's followers, helped establish the
Naval War College in 1884 in order to
provide officers with post-graduate training in the science of naval warfare.

Captain Alfred Thayer Mahan, whose
revolutionary work *The Influence of Sea
Power upon History* (1890) inspired
three secretaries of the navy and numerous other advocates of a modern
navy, argued that naval warfare could
be an exact science.

U.S.S. *Atlanta*, one of the ABCD's *(Atlanta, Boston, Chicago, Dolphin)*, America's first steel protected cruisers.

U.S.S. *Texas*, a sister ship to the *Maine*. In these two warships, technology outran policy in that both were too large and too powerful for what the United States thought its international policy was at that time. The *Texas* took an active part in the battle at Santiago.

William E. Chandler,
secretary of the navy, 1882–85.

William C. Whitney,
secretary of the navy, 1885–89.

Hilary Herbert,
secretary of the navy, 1893–97.

John Davis Long,
secretary of the navy, 1897–1902.

Captain Stephen B. Luce (second from left) and three other officers in the captain's cabin on board the flagship U.S.S. *Hartford* in Hampton Roads, Virginia, March 1, 1877.

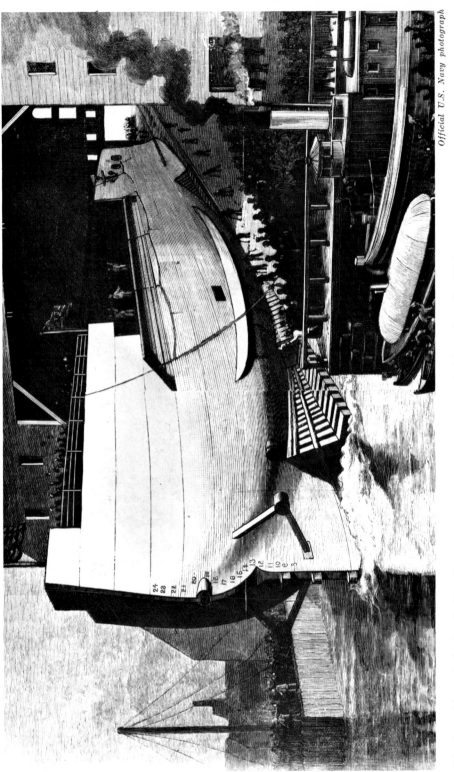

The launching of the battleship *Maine* at the Brooklyn Navy Yard, November 18, 1890.

The *Maine* passing Morro Castle as she entered the harbor of Havana.

U.S.S. *Kentucky* (top)
and the
U.S.S. *Indiana*.

to march to jail at bayonet-point, leaving their wounded mates at the mercy of the enraged mob. In all, eighteen seamen from the *Baltimore* sustained more or less serious injuries before the turmoil subsided, and two lost their lives.[38] The police arrested thirty-six American sailors, examined them in secret, and then released them pending further investigation.

Schley opened his own inquiry the following morning. Local officials gave him little satisfaction, saying only that his men had been guilty of drunken provocation. No diplomatist, the commander allowed the port authorities to maneuver him into a pointless debate over the degree of the sailors' intoxication.

Within the week, Commander Schley dispatched a report of his findings to Tracy. In it he made the improbable statement that his men had been sober on the day of the riot. Accusing the mob of causing the disorder and the resulting casualties, Schley maintained that the police too were at fault. He argued, moreover, that the disturbance was premeditated, offering in evidence the testimony of his men to the effect that they had been attacked simultaneously in various locations.[39]

Errazuriz and Manuel Matta, the recently appointed foreign minister of Chile, undoubtedly wished to employ the *Baltimore* incident as a means of affirming their country's sovereignty and its complete independence of the United States. In general, the Chilean press took the same line, asserting the guilt of the Americans and protesting the efforts of the northern "Colossus" to pin the blame on Chileans. The editor of a Valparaiso paper implied that the *Baltimore's* removal of Balmacedists from the jurisdiction of Chile justified the attack on the ship's liberty party, even if the mob had instigated it which, he insisted, was not the case.

This version of the incident held that two of the *Baltimore's* bluejackets had assaulted a Chilean seaman, knocked him down, and thrown rocks at him. When the Americans saw a hostile crowd gathering, they tried to flee but were seized by patriotic citizens. At this point, the account continued, forty policemen arrived, arrested thirty American and ten Chilean sailors, and marched them off to jail. One American

38 For the martyrdom of Boatswain's Mate C. W. Riggin, one of the *Baltimore's* fatalities, see R. D. Evans, *Sailor's Log*, 277; Curtis, *From the Andes*, 411; New York *Recorder*, February 9, 1893. From Valparaiso, Riggin's body was taken to Philadelphia, where it lay in state in Independence Hall.
39 Schley to Tracy, October 22, 1891, in Cipher Record No. 40, Navy Arch.; Mitchell, *Modern Navy*, 45.

had been killed in the melee and five seriously injured; one Chilean had suffered slight wounds. There was no reasonable doubt that the Yankees had provoked the riot.[40]

Referring to Schley's evaluation, Foreign Minister Matta declared bluntly, "The statement that the North American seamen were attacked in various localities at the same time is deliberately incorrect." [41] Anti-administration editors in the United States also took issue with Schley and Tracy, reasoning that the liberty party could not have remained sober for five hours and was probably guilty as charged by the Valparaiso police. At least one American naval officer concurred tacitly in this opinion. When informed that the Navy Department had established the sobriety of the bluejackets, Captain John Coleman shook his head and observed, "Well, mebbe so, mebbe." [42]

Scholars of this period of Chilean history have interpreted the "*Baltimore* outrage" as a symptom of the resentment felt in Valparaiso of Harrison's tardy recognition of the new regime, combined with the popular indignation over the recent activities of the United States minister and the Navy. Considering the provocative attitude of Tracy's officers, argues one historian, the attack on the liberty party was not surprising. He agrees with Schley, on the other hand, that leaders of the Valparaiso mob had indeed planned the riot in advance, probably in a series of strategy meetings in the city's saloons.[43]

Although Secretary Tracy had accepted Schley's version of the incident, he realized that the commander was not the man to handle the American case at Valparaiso. Accordingly, once he had digested differing accounts in the newspapers, he ordered Commander Robley Evans—then commanding the gunboat *Yorktown*—to proceed to Valparaiso and relieve the *Baltimore*. At the end of November, shortly after the arrival of the gunboat, Schley weighed anchor and headed his cruiser seaward.[44]

In preliminary discussions with local officials, Evans presented his case with firmness and tact. The question of the degree of intoxication

40 Pike, *Chile and U.S.*, citing *El Mercurio* (Valparaiso), October 17, 1891. Cf. La Feber, *New Empire*, 133–34.

41 *House Executive Documents*, 52nd Cong., 1st Sess., No. 91. pp. 105ff.

42 Quotation from *The Nation* (New York), October 19, 1892. This periodical and the New York *Evening Post* consistently opposed the policies of the Harrison administration.

43 Hancock, *History of Chile*, 368–69; Luis Galdames, *Estudio de la Historica de Chile* (Santiago de Chile, 1911), 466–67. Cf. Pike, *Chile and U.S.*, 73–76.

44 Navy Dept., *Annual Report*, 1891.

prevailing among the *Baltimore's* men, he pointed out, had no bearing on the central issue. Drunk or sober, American seamen on liberty were entitled to receive the protection of the municipal police.[45]

As the case dragged on in the Valparaiso court, the citizens grew increasingly hostile. On one occasion a group of them stoned Evans' gig but failed to goad him into retaliation. On another, Chilean torpedo-boats held maneuvers after dark near the *Yorktown's* anchorage, making "practice runs" on the American ship and firing torpedoes that narrowly missed her hull. Evans reacted in characteristic fashion; he set general quarters on the *Yorktown*, lodged a strong protest with Chilean naval authorities ashore, and informed them of his intention to open fire on the torpedo-boats if such manifestations continued. They did not. On the contrary, the commander's determination appears to have softened the attitude of port officials. In any event, they allowed a number of Balmacedist refugees to board the *Yorktown*, following Evans's display of fortitude.[46]

Meanwhile, war fever was rising in Washington. Word of the *Baltimore* incident struck the capital like a thunderclap. Harrison and Tracy regarded the attack on the sailors as a cowardly insult to the uniform of the United States and insisted on vigorous prosecution of the case. Blaine took a larger view of the matter, seeing it as a threat to Pan-American harmony, and attempted to persuade the indignant President to approach the Chilean government with moderation and caution.[47]

When Schley's report reached Tracy's desk on October 22, Blaine was away from his office on sick leave. On Harrison's instructions, General Tracy drafted a note to Egan over the signature of Assistant Secretary of State William F. Wharton, who dispatched it to Santiago on the next day. The message directed Egan to consider carefully the Chilean side of the dispute but, if the evidence substantiated Schley's statement, to demand full reparation immediately.[48]

Under the circumstances, Tracy thought the text extremely mild, as did those of his colleagues who were inclined to sensitivity in matters

45 Volwiler, "Harrison, Blaine," 639–41; Mitchell, *Modern Navy*, 45.

46 Edward A. Falk, *Fighting Bob Evans* (New York, 1931), 154–64; Knox, *History of the U.S. Navy*, 326ff.

47 Volwiler, "Harrison, Blaine," 640–43; Curtis, *From the Andes*, 411–13; Roosevelt, "Foreign Policy of Harrison," 1–3. According to Roosevelt the attack on the Baltimore's men was "due merely to the fact that the unfortunate victims wore the uniform of our Republic."

48 *House Executive Documents*, 52nd Cong., 1st Sess., No. 91, containing Wharton's instructions to Egan. See also, Volwiler, "Harrison, Blaine," 640–44.

involving the nation's prestige abroad.[49] Others, less aggressively minded, feared that the note might lead to a rapid deterioration of relations with Chile. Blaine agreed; on his return to the State Department, he complained that Tracy's message had committed him to a policy of which he could not approve.[50]

Replying through the Chilean envoy in Washington, Pedro Montt, Foreign Minister Matta declared that the American note was unacceptable to his government. He reminded President Harrison that Valparaiso authorities were in process of investigating the *Baltimore* affair and that the municipal court had exclusive jurisdiction over the case. In conclusion, Matta observed, nothing had occurred to impair friendly relations between Chile and the United States![51]

Matta's response infuriated the President and Tracy. The latter deemed it "so insulting . . . that it might almost have been a cause for war in itself. It sought to justify the assault on the sailors and dodged the issue in every way possible." [52] On December 9, Harrison reacted by announcing to Congress that he would call on it "for such action as may be necessary," if the Chileans failed to satisfy promptly all American expectations.[53]

Blaine continued to urge his chief to be patient. Throughout November and December, he worked persistently to restrain Harrison from making warlike statements and, at the same time, to maintain cordial relations with Pedro Montt. The secretary of state favored a waiting game at this point especially, because he expected the new ministry of President-elect Jorge Montt to replace the provisional regime at Iquique in January, 1892. [54]

The conflict of opinion in Harrison's cabinet over the Chilean situation, not to mention Tracy's growing influence on matters of state, caused considerable speculation. Concerning the apparent rift in the cabinet, Commander Evans noted in his diary the gist of a telegram from W. R. Grace to the Grace and Company agent in Valparaiso: "He wires that Harrison is for war, that the Navy Department is making every preparation for war and that Blaine, while in favor of war under certain conditions only, cannot stem the tide, and that

49 Tyler, *Policy of Blaine*, 147n.
50 *Ibid.* Cf. Curtis, *From the Andes*, 411.
51 Egan to Blaine, October 28, 1891, in *House Executive Documents*, 52nd Cong., 1st Sess., No. 91.
52 Tracy quoted in Curtis, *From the Andes*, 411.
53 *Messages and Papers*, IX, 186.
54 Tyler, *Policy of Blaine*, 148–51; Peck, "Twenty Years of the Republic," 243.

unless Chile makes ample apology at once nothing can prevent war." Ending the notation with a statement of his own intent, Evans declared: "Taking all things under consideration, the crew of the *Yorktown* will sleep at the loaded guns tonight and every night until I get better news." [55]

The anti-administration press, on the contrary, attempted to smear Blaine as a warmonger. In defense of the secretary of state, H. T. Peck termed such criticism "intemperate and inappropriate. . . . It is impossible to hold this view. Mr. Blaine's attitude was a firm one, yet it is certain . . . he was exerting his influence to hold back the President. Mr. Harrison was, perhaps unconsciously influenced by the thought that a foreign war would . . . re-elect him." [56]

An interesting evaluation of the situation in Washington appears in a letter of Theodore Roosevelt's friend, Sir Cecil Spring-Rice, secretary of the British Legation, to a correspondent in London.

We are on the verge of war here, owing to inconceivable stupidity on our side and trickery on the other. . . . Blaine has prevented war with Chile so far and may do so still, but the President and the Navy are bent on it.[57]

The President and the Secretary of the Navy wish for war; one to get re-elected, the other to see his new ships fight and get votes for more.[58]

A New York editor gave the thoughts expressed by Spring-Rice a different twist.

A war with Chile would certainly develop one name as a compromise candidate between Blaine and Harrison. And that dark horse might be the horse marine, the alert, active and accomplished . . . Benjamin F. Tracy, who would have more to do with the immediate making of war with Chile than all the rest of the cabinet combined.[59]

55 Evans, *Sailor's Log*, 277. This must have been a tense period for Evans and his crew; the *Yorktown* was the sole non-Chilean warship in Valparaiso at the time.

56 Peck, "Twenty Years of the Republic," 372.

57 Quoted in Volwiler, "Harrison, Blaine," 645. For another testimonial to Blaine's anti-war attitude, see Hilary A. Herbert, "Grandfather's Talks about His Life under Two Flags," unpublished, undated typescript in Southern Historical Collection, University of North Carolina Library, Chapel Hill, 310–13; hereinafter cited as Herbert, "Grandfather's Talks."

58 Stephen Gwynne, *The Letters and Friendships of Sir Cecil Spring-Rice* (Boston, 1929), II, 118.

59 New York *Morning Advertiser*, January 19, 1892. The editorial policy of this paper reflected the views of "independent" Democrats.

Other editors speculated as to the extent of Tracy's influence on administration decisions. A number of them predicted that he would soon replace
Blaine in the State Department; a few felt that he was already managing
foreign, as well as naval, policy; and one editorial labeled him Harrison's
"premier." [60]

Newsmen quickly seized upon hard evidence of the President's reliance on General Tracy, especially during Blaine's frequent absences
from the State Department. As one reporter wrote: "Will Tracy take
Blaine's place? It is regarded as significant that the orders to Egan
should go through him to Acting Secretary of State Wharton." [61]

As a spate of wild rumors heightened the tension in Washington,
relations with Chile worsened. On December 11, Matta dispatched an
irate telegram to Pedro Montt, making plain his hostile reaction to
Harrison's message to Congress and the accompanying report from
Secretary Tracy. Two days later, the foreign minister circulated copies
of his telegram among Chilean legations everywhere before releasing
the text to the press in Santiago.

Matta had couched his wire in tactless language: "The statements
on which both report and message are based are erroneous and deliberately incorrect. . . . There is, moreover, no exactness or sincerity
in what is said at Washington." [62] Although instructed by his superior
to convey the contents of the telegram to the State Department and to
release it to the American press, Montt took alarm at the wording and
tried to conceal it.[63]

Inasmuch as the text of Matta's wire appeared in the Chilean press,
Montt's efforts were in vain. The message received wide publicity in
the United States, inflaming public opinion to the boiling point. Even
Blaine reacted sharply to Matta's breach of diplomatic propriety; he
broke off all communication with the Chilean regime, "beyond the
barest formalities." [64]

On New Year's Day, 1892, the odds on a peaceful settlement rose

60 For example, see New York *Mail and Express,* June 4, 1891; Brooklyn *Daily
Eagle,* August 9, 1891; New York *Herald,* September 5, 1891. In 1895, two years
after Tracy had returned to private life, a groundswell of modest proportions arose
in New York to promote his nomination for the presidency in 1898. The general's
law partner, A. J. Boardman, informed him of this development while Tracy
was attending ceremonies in commemoration of the opening of the Kiel Canal in
Germany. Boardman to Tracy, undated, 1895, in Tracy papers.
61 New York *Herald,* September 5, 1891, for quotation, and January 19, 1892.
62 A. B. Hart, *Practical Essays on American Government* (New York, 1893),
121–22. Cf. Tyler, *Policy of Blaine,* 149ff.; Hardy, "Itata," 195.
63 Peck, "Twenty Years of the Republic," 372ff.; Tyler, *Policy of Blaine,* 150–52.
64 Tyler, *Policy of Blaine,* 154.

briefly as word reached the State Department from Egan that Jorge Montt had formed a ministry at Santiago. Luis Pereira, Matta's successor in the foreign office, advised Blaine that he was forwarding to Washington a summary report of the court proceedings in the *Baltimore* case. At the same time, Pedro Montt conveyed to Blaine the new government's expression of regret over the matter and its assurance of swift justice for the guilty parties.[65]

When he heard this, Blaine moved. Hoping to find the Montt regime more receptive than its predecessor to Harrison's original terms, he asked Egan to ascertain President Montt's attitude toward disavowal of the Matta telegram. Egan replied that he had put the question to Montt and received an evasive answer, whereupon Blaine drafted a new note for Harrison's signature, repeating as tactfully as possible the former demands. Chile must apologize, make reparation for the *Baltimore* outrage, and withdraw Matta's incendiary message.[66]

President Harrison considered Blaine's draft altogether too bland. Revising the note, he sharpened the secretary of state's wording to give it the character of an ultimatum. Harrison restated his terms and warned the Chilean government that unless it made an acceptable response at once, the United States would sever diplomatic relations.[67]

These were fighting words; they evoked a strong jingoist reaction from the American public. Secretary Tracy's desk was soon cluttered with letters from citizens in various parts of the country, asserting their loyalty and readiness for war with Chile. One enthusiast wrote: "The Press Club has just inspected the cruiser *San Francisco* with satisfaction. The loyalty on the West Coast is very impressive. They only await the call." [68] From New York, Theodore Roosevelt expressed himself in customary fashion: "The United States is absolutely in the right and Chile absolutely in the wrong!" He described Harrison's position as one of "dignified firmness and wise liberality." [69]

Not all Americans shared this chauvinist sentiment. One contemporary interpreted Harrison's ultimatum as the act of a bully: "This message was looked upon by the American people as the precursor of an actual declaration of war . . . , and it looked as if little Chile was doomed." [70]

---

65 *Ibid.*, 154–55.
66 *Ibid.*; Hardy, "Itata," 195ff.
67 Tyler, *Policy of Blaine*, 154; Hardy, "Itata," 195ff.
68 J. S. Page to Tracy, January 25, 1892, in Tracy Papers.
69 Roosevelt, "Foreign Policy of Harrison," 2.
70 Thomas Campbell-Copeland, *Harrison and Reid: Their Lives and Records* (New York, 1892), 197.

Another writer, known as an authority on Chilean-American relations, condemned administration policy more bluntly:

The difficulty of deciding which side was right in a domestic war would have been ample excuse for not meddling at all. But having Egan and new cruisers, in an atmosphere filled with buncombe, we chased, and fumed, and cursed, and vowed vengeance dire; and accumulated little by little, a huge moral and political and commercial blunder.[71]

By January 21, when Blaine reluctantly dispatched the President's ultimatum to Santiago, the Navy was ready for war. For months, General Tracy had presided over the Navy Department's preparations for fleet action against Chile. In September, 1891, Tracy had summoned Mahan to Washington for special sessions of the secret board of strategy. Thereafter, the captain, Folger, and Soley met frequently with the secretary to discuss plans for operations in Chilean waters. Subsequently, Mahan wrote Luce of these meetings in a letter which suggested his annoyance at Tracy's determination to play his own game. "I was . . . directed to study the military side of the question, to be ready to prepare plans, or to express opinions as a result of my reflections; but Mr. Tracy kept matters in his own hands . . . and acted without consultation as he chose." [72] This was a far cry from the Tracy Admiral Porter had described in 1889 as a slow mover and a willing listener, eager for advice! Tracy had assumed full responsibility for readying the Navy for combat, put the yards on a seven-day week, and himself worked around the clock drafting plans and directives and parrying the questions of curious newsmen.[73]

Few people guessed the magnitude of the general's plans for war with Chile. "These were carried out so quietly that it never has been known just how far we went. The reason that we were . . . able to keep what we were doing from the public was that all the preparations . . . were controlled by one person, who carried on all his transactions with principals, not agents." [74] The "one person" was General Tracy. Once he had ordered every effective vessel on the Navy List made

71 Hardy, "Was Egan a Blundering Minister?" 66–67. Cf. *The Nation* (New York), September 10, 1891.
72 Mahan to Luce, September 3, 1901, in NHF, Luce Collection.
73 Volwiler, "Harrison, Blaine," 643–47.
74 Curtis, *From the Andes*, 412. Tracy's nonofficial summary of his preparations for war appears here and, as far as the author knows, nowhere else. Curtis quotes him directly.

ready for immediate service, Tracy arranged personally for the purchase of large quantities of coal in London, New York, and California.

Selecting Montevideo to serve as the Navy's coaling station for Chilean operations, he obtained permission to use the necessary facilities there and chartered colliers to transport the coal to them. In this connection, one of the "principals" Tracy referred to was Collis P. Huntington, president of the Southern Pacific Company. In January, 1892, the general concluded an agreement with Huntington which would permit the Navy Department to charter the collier *San Benito* for $500 per day for the duration of the emergency. This vessel was to carry five thousand tons of coal purchased on the west coast to Montevideo.[75]

As to the strategy devised for operations against the Chilean fleet, let Tracy speak for himself:

According to this plan, the first order was to concentrate the fleet. A point of concentration was agreed on, and this was to be telegraphed to the three fleet commanders with the orders . . . to begin operations. Admiral Gherardi was to be in command of the combined fleets.

After the fleets had concentrated, they were to proceed to Chile, drive the Chilean men-of-war under the guns of the fort in Valparaiso, then attack the whole coast of Chile. The coal mines in the southern part were to be seized, thus cutting off the coal supply for the warships of the enemy, and all other details were to be looked after.[76]

Although the specifics of Secretary Tracy's preparations were carefully concealed from the press, the intensified activity of the naval establishment could not be kept secret. Tracy's forehandedness drew the applause of expansionists in government circles, especially Henry Cabot Lodge and Theodore Roosevelt, who declared: "From the moment when hostilities became possible, the Navy Department had been quietly preparing a thoroughly adequate naval force with an energy and success that argues well for the conduct of this department in any future crisis." [77]

In the days following the dispatch of Harrison's ultimatum, "the air on all sides was filled with talk of war." [78] As time passed with no reply from Santiago, the President threw down his final challenge; on Monday, January 25, he urged Congress to consider a declaration of war. To

75 *Ibid.;* Huntington to Tracy, January 24, 1892, in Tracy Papers.
76 Tracy is quoted in Curtis, *From the Andes,* 412–13.
77 Roosevelt, "Foreign Policy of Harrison," 2.
78 Hardy, "Itata," 197.

the astonishment of informed observers, this brought results. Within five days, the Chilean government signified its complete acceptance of Harrison's terms.[79] The crisis was over.

Unknown to Washington, President Montt had decided to yield when he received the American ultimatum on January 23; but he and Foreign Minister Pereira had not had sufficient time in which to draft their reply prior to Harrison's message to Congress. Harrison's complaint of Chile's delaying tactics, contained in the fourteen-page message he delivered to Congress only two days after the arrival of the ultimatum in Santiago, is difficult to justify at best.

To Chilean observers, President Harrison's rapid-fire actions in January merely confirmed their conviction that the rupture in relations with the United States resulted primarily from Harrison's desire for a second term, and secondarily from the determination of Tracy's clique of admirals to obtain funds for naval expansion. Neither Montt nor Pereira wanted war; they appreciated the danger of challenging an America recently converted to the gospel of Mahan and bent on fulfilling its new Manifest Destiny. At first, however, both men underestimated the belligerence of the Harrison administration, a miscalculation which reports from Chilean legations in Europe in early January indicated might lead to war.[80]

On January 4, Montt's envoy in London relayed to Santiago the information that the British Foreign Office no longer regarded Harrison's aggressiveness as a typical example of Yankee bravado, but now believed that the United States would declare war unless Chile apologized at once. Similar warnings to assume a contrite posture reached Santiago from the legations in Paris and Berlin. When the American demands were handed Montt, therefore, he had no illusions about the seriousness of the situation and, in all probability, no need to be reminded of it by Harrison's bellicose message to Congress.

For the purpose of this study, an evaluation of the positions taken in the dispute with Chile by the American principals seems in order. What motivated their outlook and actions during the hectic months of crisis? Blaine left the impression of a statesman desiring peace at almost any cost; even the regime at Santiago appeared to be counting on him to keep the peace. After all, Pedro Montt had advised his superiors that "we have nothing to worry about from Blaine." [81]

---

79 Bemis, *Secretaries of State*, VIII, 156ff.
80 Pike, *Chile and U.S.*, 82-83.
81 *Ibid.*, 76-77, quoting Montt.

To many contemporaries, on the other hand, Harrison and Tracy sounded overly aggressive; to some they were downright warmongers. Did they want war and, if so, for what reason? Were Blaine's supporters correct in ascribing to Harrison a hankering for war to win reelection? And were they justified in accusing Tracy of trying to provoke Chile into action merely to secure additional naval appropriations from Congress?

The evidence suggests their innocence of these charges. To both men, war represented the last resort. The difference between their approach and Blaine's was essentially that of the military mentality versus the diplomatic. The reactions of all three to the *Baltimore* incident make this clear.

Behind Blaine's determination to restrain his colleagues' militancy lay years of preparation for the first Inter-American Conference which, he hoped, would lead not only to hemispheric solidarity but to commercial advantages for the United States. When he learned of the attack in Valparaiso, consequently, his interest in maintaining harmony with all Latin American states overshadowed his indignation at the outrage and influenced the policy of the State Department towards Chile.

Harrison, on the contrary, had less concern for Pan-American accord than for national prestige. His awareness of the nation's developing status as a ranking world power undoubtedly amplified his resentment of an act he looked upon as an insult to the flag. Obsessed with the idea of validating America's claim to such stature, Harrison sought European recognition of his country's greatness by way of humbling Chile. To that end, although he did not intend to foment war, he resolved not to yield in order to avoid it.

General Tracy shared the President's diagnosis and, owing to his personal involvement with the Navy, was even more eager than his chief to apply pressure. It should be pointed out, however, that Tracy considered a naval war with Chile a somewhat risky proposition. A contest of this nature would require dangerously extended lines of supply and communication; it might lead to hostilities with other Latin American states; and it would surely involve extremely difficult exercises in logistics. He remembered, moreover, that only a few years ago Chile had ranked above the United States in sea power.

On the day following Chile's capitulation to Harrison's ultimatum, a reporter asked Secretary Tracy for his interpretation of a remark made by W. R. Grace that every member of the cabinet except Blaine had favored declaring war on Chile. The reporter's paper had recently printed this observation and he wanted to verify it. Speaking for himself only, the general replied heatedly: "I did not know I was a war man; I rather thought I was peaceably inclined, but I am also inclined to maintaining the dignity of the United States government and its power to protect its civilians, soldiers, and sailors when abroad. If that leads to war, then I am for war; if it leads, as I believe it will, to peace, then I am for peace." [82]

For the most part, the American press gave Blaine credit for avoiding war with Chile. Whether or not this opinion reflected objective editorial analysis is impossible to ascertain. In the light of evidence probably unavailable to contemporary journalists, it seems far more logical to conclude that the Montt government yielded in consequence of the challenge posed by Harrison, backed up by Tracy's preparation of the fleet for offensive operations, and not as a result of Blaine's deft statesmanship. [83]

---

82 Tracy quoted in New York *Times*, January 30, 1892.
83 Brooklyn *Daily Eagle*, January 30, 1892.

VII
MIDPASSAGE TO RETIREMENT

THE SECOND HALF OF TRACY'S STEWARDSHIP BEGAN IN THE tense days of the Chilean emergency. Throughout the stormy midpassage of his tour, he saw the department smoothly and efficiently through one crisis after another, bringing the Navy to an unprecedented state of peacetime preparedness before Chile came to terms in January, 1892. From then to the day he stepped out of office in March of the following year, the general continued to work for naval progress, especially in the areas of administrative reform and fleet expansion, while displaying his versatility as Harrison's man Friday.

The political situation in 1891 was not conducive to large appropriations for new ship construction. The elections of the preceding November, which reduced to six the Republican majority in the Senate, had returned 235 Democrats to the House, as against 88 Republicans.[1] And, although the Democratic platform included a strong naval plank, party leaders frowned on the idea of carrying out an expansion program which would redound to the benefit of a Republican administration.[2]

For this reason, the general had to be content with relatively minor advances. On March 2, Congress passed a bill in response to his plea for federal support of state naval militias. Providing for payment of an annual subsidy to each state willing to form and train a pool of reserve seamen, the measure anticipated the organization of groups made up of "sea-faring men, yacht-club members, and ex-officers and men of

1 For additional comment, see Peck, "Twenty Years of the Republic," 296ff.
2 Sprout, *Naval Power*, 190.

the Navy," who would receive formal training annually for a period of thirty days and be subject to federal service in wartime.[3] The bill encouraged the secretary to provide warships, whenever practicable, for indoctrinating the militia units at sea.

Although the naval militia experiment—under state auspices—failed to evolve into a national reserve, it aroused enthusiasm in residents of participating states.[4] Senator Nelson Aldrich for one announced his determination "to see to it that the Naval Militia of Rhode Island should be fully provided for" and requested Tracy's assistance in scheduling exercises for its enrollees.[5]

Conversely, Congress ignored the secretary's plea for improved methods of recruiting seamen and promoting officers. The Navy must be enabled to offer prospective recruits greater inducements, he had pointed out, in order to attract men of high caliber; and the first step should be to raise pensions to the level prescribed for the Army. Otherwise, the service could neither procure seamen for long-term enlistments nor reduce the currently high rate of desertion. Nevertheless, Congress took no action on Tracy's request for the means of raising the standard for acceptance of enlisted personnel.[6]

The general's scheme for a more efficient system of officer promotion fared no better. He had appointed a board to study the situation and had applied its findings to his proposal. The present system, he explained, clogged the lower grades and placed undue emphasis on longevity; officers usually stayed at the rank of lieutenant up to the age of fifty, after which they were apt to be promoted rapidly in the twelve years remaining prior to mandatory retirement. To correct this condition, Tracy proposed to substitute merit for seniority as the criterion of advancement of officers through the lower grades to the rank of captain and to empower the President to nominate the best of them for promotion to the flag ranks of commodore and admiral.[7] But again Congress disregarded his recommendation.[8]

3 Navy Dept., *Annual Report*, 1889, 1891; Mitchell, *Modern Navy*, 32.
4 Secretary Josephus Daniels established a reserve corps of naval veterans in 1914. See Sprout, *Naval Power*, 319, citing *Annual Report*, 1914.
5 Aldrich to Tracy, June 21, 1891, in Tracy Papers.
6 Navy Dept., *Annual Report*, 1891.
7 *Ibid.*
8 The Personnel Act of 1899 provided a partial solution to the problems of officer promotion; see Mitchell, *Modern Navy*, 31.

Equally adamant in refusing to appropriate funds for new construction, Congress authorized not one significant warship between April and December, 1891. As if to offset the resulting breakdown in Tracy's battleship program, the press acted to keep popular interest alive by publicizing the warships abuilding during this period. As it happened, much of the material for this publicity came from across the Atlantic.

Convening at London in March, the Institute of British Naval Architects discussed current developments in American naval construction. The noted English designer J. H. Biles, who admired the products of Tracy's program, bestowed "unlimited praise" on the battleships of the *Oregon* class. He considered them "distinctly superior to any European vessels of the same displacement, and . . . quite a match for any ships afloat." [9] As for the cruiser *Columbia*, Biles observed, "The building of such a ship as Number 12, which we have nothing to cope with, certainly is an indication of what America is capable of, both in conception and construction. . . ." [10] A second speaker, Admiralty Chief Constructor John White, compared the boldly independent trend of modern American design, as embodied in the *Oregon*, with that of a decade earlier, when the Navy Department was still purchasing plans for men-of-war from European designers.[11]

New York editors embellished British accounts of the convention's proceedings with interpretive comment, as exemplified by an editorial appearing in the *Sun*: "It is evident that Secretary Tracy has given British naval authorities something of a fright. Hitherto, Great Britain has worried over the possibilities of the French Navy, and only in the last few months has it found a fresh source of concern. There is at last an American Navy." [12] Such remarks, of course, pleased the general; and he was especially gratified when ex-Secretary Whitney congratulated him on the enthusiastic reception given the three *Oregons* and the *Columbia*.[13]

But the secretary had no illusions about the relative strength of the

9 London *Times*, March 21, 1891; Harrison Loring to Tracy, March 31, 1891, in Tracy Papers. Loring was a prominent, contemporary naval architect.
10 Biles's remarks about Number 12, the *Columbia's* prechristening hull designation, are quoted in Tracy's article, "Our New Warships," *North American Review*, CLII (June, 1891), 647. See also, "Addresses," Boston speech, April 8, 1891, in Tracy Papers.
11 Tracy, "New Warships," 648.
12 New York *Sun*, April 20, 1891.
13 Whitney to Tracy, April 7, 1891, in Tracy Papers.

fleet. Despairing of additional authorizations in the immediate future, he recommended to Congress the formation of a reserve force of merchant vessels adaptable to naval service in wartime.

Shipowners and their business associates became interested in Tracy's proposal as soon as they realized that it promised to award mail subsidies to steamship lines whose vessels measured up to naval specifications. The wisdom of this plan was demonstrated in 1898: when it appeared that the Navy lacked sufficient ships to mobilize for war against Spain, the department pressed a number of fast passenger steamers into service as auxiliary cruisers.[14]

Meanwhile, the secretary's abiding faith in "Harvey-ized" nickel-steel armor had led to continued testing of the alloy at the proving grounds. The satisfactory reports submitted by ordnance men conducting the tests prompted Tracy to invite both domestic and foreign steel producers to enter samples of their armor plate in a series of competitive experiments to be held at Annapolis. The Navy's contractors complied willingly and voiced their pleasure at the outcome. Andrew Carnegie spoke of the tests gleefully: "Our nickel steel excelled the Cruesot plate . . . our French competitor is behind us!"[15]

On April 8, the general announced a program of navy yard reform that made headlines. Speaking at the opening of a new Republican club in Boston, he lashed out with unexpected candor at the custom of hiring civilian workmen on the grounds of political preference. Describing it as "an ulcer on the naval administrative system," he resolved to abolish the practice, regardless of repercussions in his party's leadership.[16] Amazed at Tracy's open defiance of political tradition, editors of newspapers represented at the Boston meeting reacted in various ways. The New York *Sun* voiced the sentiment of the majority, hailing the speech as "a notable public utterance," which at last "dealt the anticipated blow to the spoils system in our navy yards," while others expressed reservations as to the secretary's motives.[17] But all doubts of his sincerity were

---

14 W. R. Jones to Tracy, April 22, 1891, in Tracy Papers. This was one of many inquiries concerning the requirements steamship lines would have to meet in order to win subsidies. Jones wrote on behalf of the American Shipmasters' Association.

15 William Abbott to Tracy (Bethlehem Steel Company letterhead), March 2, 1891, and Andrew Carnegie to Tracy, May 8, 1891, both in Tracy Papers.

16 "Addresses," Boston speech April 8, 1891, in Tracy Papers. For editorial reactions, see especially, New York *Herald*, Philadelphia *Press*, and New York *Sun*, April 9, 1891.

17 New York *Sun*, April 9, 1891.

quickly dispelled; the first phase of the reform plan became effective immediately after Tracy's return to Washington.[18]

The spring of 1891 saw the beginning of the most comprehensive administrative reform in naval history as the general's program evolved step by step in a series of directives addressed to yard commandants. First, he instructed all currently employed foremen to vacate their positions. He then established an examining board of technicians to determine the fitness of the suspended foremen—as against that of new applicants—by testing their practical aptitudes without regard to general education. In the future, Tracy informed the commandants, competitive examinations alone would govern the selection of yard foremen.[19]

For filling vacancies below the grade of foreman, the secretary instructed commandants to appoint registration boards which were to classify existing workmen and applicants according to trades, to subject them to preliminary examinations, and, finally, to register acceptable men, in order of their registration dates, for certification to appropriate departments. Former yard employees, as well as veterans of the Army and Navy, would be given priority by these boards, which were warned specifically to make no reference to the political inclinations of candidates. Tracy made clear the responsibility of commandants for enforcing to the letter the rules of registration; they were obliged to see to it that their boards would in no case "give preference to a man on account of his political or other affiliations."

Once an applicant won certification under the new procedure, he reported to the designated department for work. The head of the department concerned was required to give the prospect a "fair and impartial trial" for at least two weeks before deciding to hire him or not. The registration board's function was to classify and certify candidates; only the department head was empowered to employ workmen.[20]

The general's merit system drew the general support of naval officers, editors, and reformers. But just as soon as the details appeared in the press, the navy yard reform became a highly sensitive political issue. Aghast at the loss of a primary source of patronage, politicians of both parties privately denounced the action; predictably, the angriest response to Tracy's measure came from the Republican leaders of districts in which yards were situated.

---

18 New York *Herald*, April 9, 1891.
19 Navy Dept., *Annual Report*, 1891.
20 *Ibid.*

Rumors and speculation distorted the nature of the registration procedure and called into question Tracy's reason for creating it. One editor attributed his shift from toleration to prohibition of a hitherto accepted practice to strong pressure from Soley and the bureau chiefs.[21] Another ascribed the general's reform to political expediency. According to the latter source, Republican leaders had persuaded Tracy to terminate the operation of the spoils system in the navy yards because they felt it was costing the party more votes than it produced. Also, stated this editor, the Democratic victory of 1890 had forced the Republicans to propitiate the reform element, and the hierarchy had seized on the idea of cleaning up the yards as a likely gesture.[22]

H. F. Gosnell, an authority on the Platt organization in New York, considered the general's motives superficial.

> The work of acting as an employment agent for a political party was not always pleasant, and it was probably the irksomeness of this task that led . . . Tracy . . . to adopt a registration system. It is surprising that such a step was taken by someone so close to Platt, but responsibility sobers some party men and General Tracy had other things to consider besides "the good of the organization." [23]

Most contemporary observers passed favorable judgment on Tracy's program; none condemned it. Even the usually hostile New York *Evening Post* gave him faint praise: "It is regarded as a great moral victory when Secretary Tracy makes the admission that a merit system of some kind is necessary." [24] A week later, when the new procedure went into effect at the Brooklyn Navy Yard, the *Post* changed its tune and endorsed the plan wholeheartedly.[25]

Reformers naturally applauded the general's program, welcoming it as a boon to the nation.[26] Speaking for the Civil Service Commission, Theodore Roosevelt remarked: "Mr. Tracy's policy is of an importance impossible to overestimate. He deserves the heartiest praise from all friends of reform." [27] The New York Civil Service Reform Association

21 *Army and Navy Register* (Washington), April 11, 1891.
22 New York *Herald*, April 5, 1891.
23 Gosnell, *Boss Platt*, 253–54.
24 New York *Evening Post*, April 9, 1891.
25 *Ibid.*, April 16, 1891.
26 See especially, *Harper's Weekly*, April 15, 1891; *Army and Navy Journal* (New York), April 18, 1891; New York *Tribune*, April 9, 1891; New York *Times*, April 10, 1891; Boston *Transcript*, May 18, 1891.
27 Roosevelt is quoted in New York *World*, April 12, 1891.

echoed Roosevelt's opinion, as did leaders of the reform wings of the Republican and Democratic parties, including Seth Low, president of Columbia College, who declared: "Your important action . . . deserves the thanks of every lover of his country." [28]

Tracy's influential Republican friends did not agree. Tom Reed urged him to reconsider and to increase the number of political hirelings at the yard in Kittery, Maine. When the general refused, Reed lamented, "It is very unfortunate for the District, I am afraid." [29] Taking a still dimmer view of the new hiring procedure, Tom Platt implored Tracy: "For Heaven's sake, don't issue any more Civil Service orders, at least until after election. If you want to do everything to beat the ticket, all right, but our friends are getting pretty discouraged." [30]

Local Republican leaders protested loudly as the system overtook one installation after another. In the fall, when the commandant of the Brooklyn Navy Yard dismissed a group of party henchmen, district ward captains adopted a formal resolution to the effect that "the future success of President Harrison and the Republican party demands the immediate removal of Benjamin F. Tracy as Secretary of the Navy." [31] Discharged workmen were less formal in venting their disgust with Tracy, as one of his admirers informed him while describing the dismissal of a Republican employee from the Brooklyn yard: "Quarterman Shannon called you some fearful names . . . he is bitter toward you and is only one of many like him, only he talks louder." [32]

Unruffled by such complaints, General Tracy maintained close contact with the yard commandants as the new regulations took effect. He scanned the opposition press daily for reports of violations and, whenever one appeared, he sent Assistant Secretary Soley to the yard in question to investigate the alleged infraction. Before long, owing to Tracy's vigilance, the merit system was running smoothly.[33]

The general's detractors to the contrary, his record contains no evidence of external influence on the decision to remove the navy yards from the political orbit. Indeed, his correspondence with Reed, Platt,

---

28 Low to Tracy, April 17, 1891, in Tracy Papers. Reference to the New York Civil Reform Association is made in *Annual Report*, 1891.
29 Reed to Tracy, August 1, 1891, in Tracy Papers.
30 Platt to Tracy, Sept. 18, 1891, Tracy Papers.
31 C. W. Fish to Tracy (telegram with unidentifiable clipping attached), November 20, 1891, in Tracy Papers.
32 G. Sims to Tracy, May 27, 1891, in Tracy Papers.
33 Tracy to navy yard commandants (circular letters), June-July, 1891, in Tracy Papers; Navy Dept., *Annual Report*, 1892.

Lodge, and other Republican chieftains invalidates the notion that they had induced him to police the yards as a bid for the reform vote; their letters manifest chagrin at the very idea of yard reform. It is plain that the secretary instituted the merit policy with one object in mind—the welfare of the service.

Tracy's correspondence in 1891, particularly the letters he received throughout the year from Tom Platt, reveal his waning patience with factional leaders.[34] To the dismay of the New York boss, requests for favors on behalf of friends were turned down without exception by his former lieutenant.[35] Especially galling to Platt was the general's determination to deprive the party of the advantage it had enjoyed through a partisan approach to the business of appointing midshipmen to the Naval Academy. "I have frittered away what influence I may have had," complained Platt, "writing in behalf of every worthy young man who has come to my attention, on the theory that all the letters would go into the wastebasket anyway." [36] Other party leaders received similar treatment.[37] As Tracy informed the President's son, Russell Harrison, the most effective means of weeding out political influence at the Academy was to reject candidates whose prestige in the party exceeded their academic ability.[38]

Although the general stayed close to his desk following his convalescence at the White House, he found it necessary on occasion to leave Washington on official business. In the fall of 1890, for instance, he had accompanied President Harrison on a railroad junket through the Middle West.[39] During August, 1891, Tracy set off again, this time without his chief and by sea, to attend a naval review he had arranged at Bar Harbor, Maine, in honor of the White Squadron's homecoming.[40]

When the secretary arrived aboard the U.S.S. *Dispatch* at the designated anchorage off Bar Harbor, the ships of the squadron were already dressed and the review underway. Crowding the rails of the *Atlanta*,

34 Brooklyn *Daily Eagle*, April 17, 1891.
35 Platt to Tracy, January 15, 1891, in Tracy Papers. Platt's particular friend in the service was Commander A. S. Crowninshield, whom Secretary Hilary Herbert would appoint chief of the Bureau of Navigation in 1897.
36 Platt to Tracy, July 11, 1891, in Tracy Papers.
37 See, for example, Tracy to Quay, October 15, 1891, in Tracy Papers, rejecting the senator's request to have registration waived in the case of one of his henchmen who had applied for a yard job.
38 Tracy to Russell Harrison, undated, in Letterbook No. 2, Tracy Papers.
39 Various clippings—especially, Indianapolis *Journal*, October 7, 1890, in Scrapbook No. 4, Tracy Papers; Muzzey, *Blaine*, 465ff.
40 Numerous clippings, August, 1891, Scrapbook No. 6, in Tracy Papers.

Boston, and *Chicago* were numerous civilian notables of public and private life, including Senator Hale, the members of the House Naval Affairs Committee, and New York banker Spencer Trask.[41] The President, who had been forced to remain in Washington, sent his regrets: "The unusual number of American warships . . . will make the review very brilliant . . . and I am sorry to miss it." [42]

From the general's viewpoint, one discordant note prevented the review from being the brilliant event that Harrison had predicted. At Bar Harbor, as at Port-au-Prince three months earlier, Admiral Walker failed to convey his respects to Admiral Gherardi, who was still commander of the North Atlantic Squadron. Gherardi felt slighted at the repeated snub and ignored Walker during the review. Annoyed at the continued feuding between two competent senior officers, Secretary Tracy resolved to investigate the background of their quarrel as soon as he returned to his office.[43]

With Soley's help, Tracy found reports of Walker's alleged insubordination in a number of articles in back issues of the New York *Times*, which did not, however, explain the reason for the admiral's attitude. Determined to get at the root of the matter, the General wrote Walker a terse letter requesting his version of the case. The latter replied at once, claiming that the exaggerated accounts of his feud with Gherardi had been manufactured by the *Times* out of bitterness toward the department, and assuring the secretary that his lawyer, W. H. Stayton, would clarify the matter shortly.[44]

According to Stayton, the editors of the *Times* felt they deserved special treatment in connection with the department's press releases, inasmuch as the paper, though Democratic in editorial opinion, had consistently supported Tracy's conduct of naval affairs. Since the department had not lived up to their expectation, the editors had decided to criticize the Navy whenever an opportunity arose. And, since they had no pretext for smearing Tracy or Soley, the editors chose the prominent Admiral Walker as their scapegoat.[45]

Stayton's explanation far from satisfied the secretary, but he had nothing further to go on at the time. Well aware of Walker's reputation

41 *Ibid.*
42 Volwiler (ed.), *Correspondence*, Harrison to Blaine, August 22, 1891. For accounts of the review, see Boston *Transcript*, August 13, 1891; New York *Recorder*, August 17, 1891; Baltimore *American*, August 29, 1891.
43 W. H. Stayton to Tracy, September 7, 1891, in Tracy Papers.
44 Walker to Tracy, September 7, 1891, in Tracy Papers.
45 Stayton to Tracy, September 7, 1891, in Tracy Papers.

as a "political officer," Tracy knew he could stop the rumors of insubordination quickly by transferring the admiral to an overseas command, but he hesitated to do so for two reasons. First, such action would deprive the Navy of the invaluable experience of its only squadron of evolution commander; and second, the general had no wish to encourage outside pressure on naval business by bowing to the exhortations of the *Times's* editorial staff. He made up his mind, therefore, to keep Walker on duty at home for the time being and to delegate to Soley the task of improving the department's relations with the *Times*.[46]

Vexing as it was, Gherardi's quarrel with Walker was nothing compared to Mahan's long-standing battle with his superiors—particularly Rear Admiral Ramsay, who remained in charge of the Bureau of Navigation. When Ramsay threatened to assign Captain Mahan to sea duty while the Chilean crisis was developing, the general insisted again that he had greater need of Mahan's services in Washington. Plans were underway for reopening the War College in 1892, but in the meantime the captain was dividing his time between consultations in the secretary's office and research for his articles and a new book on war at sea.[47] Tracy wanted Mahan near at hand, not only for the sake of his writing, which the general considered essential to the effective promotion of naval expansion and the isthmian canal, but also because of Mahan's importance to the secret strategy board.[48]

Among other anti-intellectual seniors in favor of sending Captain Mahan to sea, Admiral Ramsay knew virtually nothing of the activities of the strategy board. Secretary Tracy would not reveal the nature of Mahan's work at the department in 1891, but he did notify Ramsay that the captain's presence would be required for the duration of the Chilean emergency. The extent of the planning undertaken by Mahan, Folger, and Soley is unknown even today, though there is reason to believe that they had instructions from Tracy to prepare for eventualities more hazardous than a naval war with Chile, as the captain's correspondence implies: "The progress of that duty is as follows: I drew up a paper containing my views in case of England and sent it over six weeks ago to Folger. I wrote yesterday for *data* needed to take up the cases of Spain and Germany, and the West Indies generally." [49]

46 Walker to Tracy, August 26, 1891, in Tracy Papers.
47 Tracy to Mahan, undated, 1891, in Tracy Papers; Puleston, *Mahan*, 112. At this time, Mahan was working on a manuscript dealing with the naval wars of Revolutionary France and the Second French Empire.
48 Mahan, "U.S. Looking Outward," 819.
49 Mahan to Tracy, January 2, 1891, in Tracy Papers.

Admiral Ramsay had no choice but to comply with the secretary's wishes; however, before January ended, another threat to Mahan's shore assignment materialized when Admiral Walker offered him command of the *Boston*. Considering Walker's constant support of the War College, the captain felt obliged to accept the offer if Tracy approved, even though it meant interrupting his literary work.[50] Since Mahan's willingness to take command of the cruiser was prompted by a sense of obligation rather than a yen for sea duty, Tracy easily dissuaded him from accepting.

In early February, 1892, shortly after Chile had capitulated to Harrison's demands, Admiral Ramsay felt free to detail Captain Mahan to a warship and advised him accordingly.[51] When the captain argued that he could do more for the Navy by continuing to write ashore, Ramsay cut him short, declaring: "It is not the business of naval officers to write books." [52] At this, General Tracy came to Mahan's rescue a third time; quietly overruling his bureau chief, he ordered the captain's shore duty extended.[53]

Contrary to the opinion held by many of his seniors, Mahan does not appear to have evaded transfer to sea for personal reasons. More scholar than seaman, he had the scholar's urge to disseminate knowledge of an all but untapped field of study. As he had pointed out to Tracy a year earlier, most of the history of naval warfare had yet to be written; and, if American officers were to become familiar with their primary function, the void must soon be filled. "The professional success my own book had, in England and here," explained Mahan, "is due less to its merit than to the utter barrenness of naval literature bearing on the art of war." [54]

By the same token, the general would never have reversed Ramsay's orders simply to cater to Mahan's personal preference. No one was more conscious than the captain of Tracy's disregard of personal considerations where the good of the service might be affected.[55] The trouble with Chile had furnished ample evidence of the secretary's singleness of purpose, as Mahan observed when the crisis evaporated. "The energy with which he pushed . . . preparations had much to do with the final pacific outcome. . . . Chile simply temporized to see how much

50 Mahan to Tracy, January 2, 1891, in Tracy Papers.
51 Mahan to Tracy, September 9, 1891, in Tracy Papers.
52 Ramsay is quoted in Mahan, *Sail to Steam*, I, 311.
53 Puleston, *Mahan*, 114–15.
54 Mahan to Tracy, March 14, 1891, in Tracy Papers.
55 Mahan to Luce, September 3, 1901, in NWC.

we would stand, and had our naval efforts been less vigorous . . . , there would have been a collision." [56]

In November, 1891, the secretary submitted his annual report to the President. Summarizing the diversified activities of the Navy's squadrons over the past year, he called attention to the heavy demands made on them by conditions in many parts of the world. To give the fleet the strategic mobility it needed to meet these demands, Tracy re-emphasized the advisability of building a transisthmian canal in the near future—probably in Nicaragua. He recommended also the construction of two more battleships of the *Oregon* class, a second *New York*-class armored cruiser, one torpedo-cruiser, and a flotilla of light torpedo-boats.

If the press reflected popular opinion accurately, stated the general, the public desired "efficient naval protection" and for good reason. One had only to note the advance of foreign imperialism, he reasoned, to understand why such protection had become a national necessity. "The establishment of complete commercial supremacy by a European power in any state in the western hemisphere means the exclusion of all American influence and the virtual destruction . . . of independent existence. With the great maritime powers it is only a step from commercial . . . to territorial control." [57] Tracy concluded his report with a brief review of recent progress in the development of naval weapons. Among other advances, he mentioned the optimistic outcome of continuing tests of smokeless powder samples and the building of a factory for the manufacture of torpedoes. The E. W. Bliss Company had, he announced, completed a plant in Brooklyn which would soon be turning out torpedoes in volume for the Navy.[58]

In the President's third annual message, Harrison reasserted his support of General Tracy, requesting Congress to appropriate funds for the construction of a fleet of the "best modern type" large enough to insure the safety of American lives and property wherever they might be. "The world needs no assurance of the peaceful purposes of the United States, but we shall probably be in the future more largely a competitor in the commerce of the world, and it is essential to the dignity of this nation . . . that its Navy should be adequate . . . upon the Atlantic and . . . the Pacific." [59]

Congress opened debates on Tracy's proposals in April, 1892, and as

56 Puleston, *Mahan*, 114. Cf. Livezey, *Mahan on Sea Power*, 146–47.
57 Navy Dept., *Annual Report*, 1891.
58 *Ibid.*
59 *Messages and Papers*, IX, 200–201.

the discussions progressed, seemed disposed to cooperate, to a degree at least. Boutelle, still chairman of the House Naval Affairs Committee, wired the general on April 12: "Navy bill seems likely to come up today—send as soon as possible to House draft of amendment two battleships, one armored cruiser, two light-draft gunboats, ten torpedoboats." [60] The secretary complied with pleasure; excepting the substitution of two gunboats for one torpedo-cruiser, which Boutelle undoubtedly made as a gesture to isolationists in the House, the amendment was in line with Tracy's original recommendation. But he knew from experience the distance the new measure must travel before coming to a vote, and he realized that he might well have to settle for less than Boutelle's modification promised.

Sure enough, the Navy Act of 1892 authorized only one battleship and an armored cruiser. The reduction did not concern Tracy as much as it might have, however, because the specifications of the vessels described in the measure denoted a departure in American design which gratified him.

Perhaps unwittingly, Congress had appropriated funds for building the two mightiest men-of-war of their types ever laid down in the United States. Significantly, the battleship clause in this act set no limit on fuel capacity or cruising range. By approving a capital ship without restricting her range to the mileage prescribed for the *Oregons* in the act of 1890, Congress signified at last its tacit acceptance of the offensive doctrine developed by Luce and Mahan and embodied in Secretary Tracy's policy. As for the cruiser authorized in the new measure, the general boasted: "Her offensive and defensive qualities greatly surpass those of any vessel afloat or in course of construction." [61] Doubtless Tracy's enthusiasm accounts for any exaggeration of the cruiser's prowess in this statement!

The new battleship, soon to be christened *Iowa*, had a designed displacement of 11,340 tons and a main battery of four 12-inch rifles. Heavier than the *Oregons* by one thousand tons, the *Iowa* would mount guns smaller by one inch in caliber for greater efficiency in handling. Her secondary armament specifications called for the emplacement of eight 8-inch rifles and six 4-inchers. The ship's power plant would deliver a speed of 17 knots, about a knot higher than the rate designed for the *Oregon* class. But the most advanced feature of the *Iowa's* plans

60 Boutelle to Tracy (telegram), April 12, 1892, in Tracy Papers.
61 Navy Dept., *Annual Report*, 1892.

was the provision for expanded bunker capacity: it would allow the battleship to carry two hundred more tons of coal than her predecessors could and thus render her capable of operating far beyond the one thousand-mile limit set by Congress in 1890.[62]

The cruiser, appropriately named *Brooklyn*, resembled the *New York* in design but was to be heavier and faster. The blueprint for the *Brooklyn* specified a displacement of 9,215 tons, an armament of eight 8-inch and twelve 5-inch rifles, and a flank speed of 21 knots. Her fuel capacity would enable the ship to "go easily from New York to San Francisco without recoaling." [63]

General Tracy had the new vessels equipped with the best materials and weapons that an aggressive development program could provide. Fortunately, the ever-present armor problem proved less of a deterrent than it had in 1891. Although the general's early efforts to import nickel ore from Canada duty-free had involved him in bewildering exchanges with protectionists in Washington, the government in Ottawa, and operators of Canadian mines, he had acquired sufficient nickel to assure the armoring of all ships presently authorized or under construction.[64] By this time, both Bethlehem Steel and Carnegie, Phipps were forging nickel-steel armor in growing volume. Moreover, the secretary's persistent testing of the alloy and of related refining processes encouraged the contractors to improve the quality of the armor plate they were producing for the Navy Department.[65]

In his report for 1892, Tracy announced a substantial increase in the number and variety of weapons over the last three years. When he came to office, not a single operational torpedo had been available; now the Navy's arsenal contained one hundred of these lethal projectiles. Progress had occurred in the diversification of conventional armament as well; Tracy predicted that rapid-fire guns of up to six inches in caliber would soon be added to the batteries of new men-of-war. Also, domestic munitions firms were delivering armor-piercing shells "in abundant quantities" which, according to the general, were superior to those of European manufacture. These advances, together with the successful testing of smokeless powder and high explosives, satisfied

---

62 *Ibid*. See also, Mitchell, *Modern Navy*, 26.
63 Navy Dept., *Annual Report*, 1892.
64 See, for instance, Tracy to William McKinley, March 15, 1890, in Tracy Papers; Toronto *Globe*, March 22, 1892.
65 Navy Dept., *Annual Report*, 1892.

Tracy that the firepower of United States warships was reaching parity with the standard set by the strongest of the foreign navies.[66]

Outlining the operations of the fleet in 1892, the secretary reported unusually extensive and diverse activities for a period of peace, owing to existing circumstances and coming events. Every serviceable unit was on an active assignment of one kind or another, involving lengthy cruising in remote areas.

Commander Evans' *Yorktown* experienced as busy a year as any warship in commission. On completion of his mission at Valparaiso, Evans headed his gunboat for a refit at Mare Island where he received orders from Tracy to proceed to Alaska as soon as the *Yorktown* was ready for sea again and to assume command of the recently formed Bering Squadron.[67] The hasty formation of this task force originated in Anglo-American attempts to reconcile a quarrel over sealing rights in the Bering Sea—an issue centering on the supposedly illegal seizure of Canadian sealing vessels by American revenue cutters. Speaking for his prime minister, Lord Salisbury, British Ambassador Sir Julian Pauncefote accused the United States of violating the freedom of the seas and demanded that Washington make amends. Secretary Blaine, much of whose argument was supplied by Tracy, replied that the seizures were justified inasmuch as the Canadians had been slaughtering seals—bulls and cows alike—in the water, which inhumane practice, if allowed to continue, would surely mean the extermination of seal herds rightfully belonging to America.

When, in May, 1891, negotiations between Blaine and Pauncefote reached a stalemate, they agreed to prohibit all sealing in Alaskan waters for one year in order to allow time for working out a permanent settlement. Having failed to overcome the impasse by the following April, the statesmen decided to renew the *modus vivendi* and to enforce it as stringently as possible.[68]

66 *Ibid.;* various letters indicating progress of tests of smokeless powder and high explosives, 1891-92, in Tracy Papers.

67 Navy Dept., *Annual Report*, 1892.

68 Differing versions of the Bering Sea negotiations appear in Moore, *Digest*, I, 894–96; Foster, *Diplomatic Memoirs*, II, 20–42; R. D. Mowat, *Life of Lord Pauncefote* (Boston, 1929), 133ff. Tracy has recorded the results of the research he undertook at the President's request in his article, "The Behring Sea Question," *North American Review*, CLVI (January, 1893), 513-15. For the material he furnished Blaine for use in clarifying the position of the United States in the dispute, see Professor H. W. Elliott to Tracy, October 15, 1891, *et al.*, concerning the habits

This decision led Tracy to propose the assignment of a special service squadron to patrol the Bering Sea. Blaine disapproved of the idea and advised the President to veto it.

If we get up a war cry and send naval vessels to the Bering Sea, it will re-elect Salisbury. England always sustains an administration with the prospect of war pending.

On the other hand . . . I am sure that war would prove of no advantage to you. New York and Massachusetts are steadily against war with England unless the last point of honor requires it.[69]

But, less than a month after Blaine made these interesting observations, illness compelled him to resign from the cabinet; and John W. Foster succeeded him in the State Department. Consultations with Secretary Tracy and Mahan's nemesis, Rear Admiral Ramsay, convinced Foster of the wisdom of establishing the patrol, subject to Harrison's approval.[70]

Hence, with the President's blessing, General Tracy appointed Evans commander of the Bering Squadron and detailed to it enough warships to prevent sealing in the Bering Sea for a full year. He informed the commander at the same time of the British Admiralty's participation in the patrol—a cooperative gesture instigated by Tracy—to the extent of assigning H.M.S. *Garnet* and *Nymphe* to Evans' new command. Furthermore, the general assured Evans, the squadron would have the services of the revenue cutters *Bear, Corwin,* and *Rush,* on loan from the Treasury Department. When fully mobilized, the Bering force consisted of the five aforementioned vessels as well as the flagship *Yorktown* and the naval ships *Adams, Mohican,* and *Ranger.*

Prior to the onset of winter, the Bering Squadron steamed 63,000 miles, smoking out vessels sealing or carrying gear for that purpose

---

of Bering seal herds, and J. B. Moore to Tracy, July 11, 1891, both in Tracy Papers. Elliott, a member of the staff of the Smithsonian Institution, was an expert on seals, while Moore, an assistant secretary in the State Department, was a scholar of international law. For a notable interpretation of the American case, see C. S. Campbell, Jr., "The Anglo-American Crisis in the Bering Sea," *MVHR,* XLVII (December, 1961), 56ff. See also, Harrison to Tracy, April 5, 1892, in Harrison Papers; New York *Evening Post,* March 25, 1892; Washington *Post,* May 8, 1892; New York *Times,* May 14, 1892; New York *Mail and Express,* March 25, 1892.

69   Volwiler (ed.), *Correspondence,* Blaine to Harrison, March 6, 1892.

70   Prior to Blaine's resignation from the State Department, he was forced by his illness to absent himself for lengthy periods, during which Tracy, Ramsay, and Foster held a series of conferences on the naval aspect of the Bering controversy. See Philadelphia *Public Ledger and Daily Transcript,* March 10, 1892; Tyler, *Policy of Blaine,* 340-41.

within the restricted area. Naval parties boarded ninety-eight Canadian and American ships suspected of poaching and recovered over 460 skins from them. The *Corwin* seized the supply ship *Coquitlan*, while Evans himself caught the sealers *Winifred* and *Henrietta* red-handed and sent all three under the *Corwin's* escort to Sitka for condemnation.[71]

A letter Tracy received in December from an irate whaling captain attested to the vigilance—or overzealousness, as the writer saw it—of the Bering Squadron. During the summer before, complained the master of the American whaler *Jane Gray*, his ship had been stopped three times and searched from stem to stern by boarding parties whose ardor surpassed their courtesy. Having been searched and released first by the *Corwin* and then by the *Yorktown*, the *Jane Gray* was subjected to harsher treatment in mid-August when Commander H. C. Johnson of the *Mohican* refused to believe that whaling gear was unsuited to sealing, and escorted the hapless ship to Sitka, where the court promptly set her free.[72]

Naval operations in 1892 were not confined to the Bering Sea. Early that summer, Tracy directed Admiral Gherardi to transfer his flag from the North Atlantic Station to a special service squadron then being formed for the purpose of displaying the flag along the east coast of Latin America. To lend the detail the degree of prestige he felt it warranted, the secretary assigned the *San Francisco, Charleston, Boston,* and *Baltimore* to Gherardi's new command and ordered the *Yorktown* to join the cruisers on her return from Alaska in the fall.

A second source of friction—the boundary dispute between Venezuela and British Guiana—induced the general to keep the *Chicago, Concord,* and *Kearsarge* on patrol in Venezuelan waters in the event of a possible move in that direction on the part of the Royal Navy. Later, when he saw no imminent threat materializing in the area, he detached the *Chicago* for service with Admiral Walker, who was then in command of a task force made up of the *Atlanta* and *Bennington*. In August, Tracy dissolved this squadron and dispatched the *Bennington*, in company with the *Newark*, to Italy with instructions to participate in cere-

71 Navy Dept., *Annual Report*, 1892; Volwiler (ed.), *Correspondence*, Harrison to Blaine, April 20, 1892. In many cases, the court at Sitka ruled that ships charged with sealing were innocent and, therefore, released them.
72 Edmund Kelley to Tracy, December 20, 1892, in Tracy Papers. Kelley, master of the *Jane Gray*, resided in upstate New York, not far from Tracy's farm at Apalachia. Five weeks before he wrote his letter of protest to Tracy, Kelley's version of the Bering Squadron's conduct appeared in a Binghampton, New York, newspaper. See Binghampton *Republican*, November 14, 1892.

monies commemorating the birth of Columbus. Three months thereafter, he sent the *Constellation* to Naples where she was to take aboard works of art selected by the Italian government for display at the forthcoming Columbian Exposition in Chicago.

Just before Christmas, the *Boston* left Gherardi's squadron to steam around the Horn and report to Admiral Brown's Samoa-bound Pacific Squadron, from which Tracy would later detach her to take station with the *Adams* at Pearl Harbor. The latter, together with the *Ranger* and *Mohican*, had been recalled from Alaska for duty under Brown, whose flagship was the *Alliance*. To maintain surveillance of the Bering during what he hoped would be a quiet winter, the general directed the *Pinta* to operate with the revenue cutters regularly assigned to the region. Meanwhile, the *Thetis* and *Albatross* steamed slowly across the Pacific, surveying the route for a cable which would one day connect San Francisco with Honolulu. Beyond Hawaii, the five warships of the Asiatic Squadron—*Monocacy, Lancaster, Palos, Marion,* and *Petrel*—watched the trouble spots of the Far East.[73]

In addition to their normal shipboard duties, the commanders of the far-ranging men-of-war were expected to dispatch to the secretary periodic intelligence reports. Their evaluations supplied the department with a wealth of information concerning political, economic, and military developments in Latin America, western Africa, India, China, Japan, Korea, Australia, and Mongolia. The areas covered in these reports reveal not only the extent of the Navy's intelligence system, but also the profound interest manifested by a newly imperialist government in the underdeveloped territories of the world.[74]

Soon to share in the varied activities of the growing fleet, the new cruiser *Columbia* slid down the ways at Philadelphia on July 26 amid resounding applause from a crowd of onlookers including the secretary, who could barely conceal his delight at the launching of one of his favorite projects. The spirit of the occasion stirred reporters as well, one of whom proclaimed, "Uncle Sam will make peace a sight cheaper than any sort of trouble." [75]

Tracy hoped to have the *Columbia* in commission by April, 1893,

73 Navy Dept., *Annual Report,* 1892; Ramsay to Tracy (telegram), September 8, 1892, in Tracy Papers.
74 An abundance of intelligence data submitted to Tracy by officers of ships visiting these areas may be found in Cipher Dispatch Records, 1892–93, in Navy Arch.
75 Quoted from editorial, New York *Recorder,* July 27, 1892. For further comment, see New York *Times* and New York *Press,* same date.

when the international naval review was scheduled to be held in Hampton Roads as an adjunct to Chicago's Columbian Exposition. As early as January, 1892, excitement at the thought of this event was building up rapidly throughout the fleet; a number of admirals were already vying with one another for command of the combined United States Squadrons to be assembled at Norfolk for the review.[76] Admiral Walker, whom Tracy had detailed to duty under Gherardi in the South Atlantic in hopes of scotching further rumors of their feud, submitted his request for the honor a year in advance. The general turned him down, explaining that he lacked the desired seniority; unknown to Walker, Tracy had slated Gherardi for overall command of the American force.[77]

In July, the War College again claimed the secretary's attention. Captain Mahan had expressed anew his concern for the future of the institution in letters to Tracy and Soley, despite its brightening outlook. Although the secretary had promised Mahan that the College would remain on Goat Island for only one more session, pending the completion of new quarters at Coaster's Harbor, and had acted to prevent Ramsay from assuming control by placing the College under Soley's jurisdiction, Mahan remained dissatisfied with its status.[78] More promotion of the curriculum was necessary, in the captain's opinion, and the position of the institution's president must be clarified. Ever mindful of his unpopularity, Mahan denied having any personal stake in the College: "Personally, I am willing to step aside," he wrote, "but in the interest of the College, it will be necessary so to define the position of its head as will insure his self-respect as such." [79]

Tracy's positive response to this plea increased Mahan's obligation to him. His efforts to heighten the prestige of the College in the service, on Capitol Hill, and among the nation's editors won him the captain's enduring gratitude. In October, with the academic session safely underway, Mahan presented the general with a copy of his recently published biography of Admiral Farragut, enclosing a note of appreciation: "I have to thank you, and it is at once fitting and a pleasure to make this acknowledgement of my indebtedness to you." [80]

76 Philadelphia *Inquirer*, January 16, 1892.
77 Navy Dept., *Annual Report*, 1892.
78 Puleston, *Mahan*, 114–15. For Mahan's report of the College's operation after the reopening, see Mahan to Soley, October 2, 1892, in NWC.
79 Mahan to Tracy, July 8, 1892, in Tracy Papers; Mahan to Soley, October 29, 1892, in NWC.
80 Mahan to Tracy, October 10, 1892, in Tracy Papers.

The sense of security engendered in Mahan by Tracy's steadfast support was shattered in November when the Democrats won the election. Within a month, the captain learned that Grover Cleveland would probably appoint Congressman Hilary Herbert of Alabama secretary of the navy. Thoroughly alarmed by this news, Mahan pleaded with Tracy to prevail on Herbert to retain him at Newport in any capacity that would permit him to continue writing.[81]

Mahan's fear of Herbert originated in an exchange that took place between them in 1888 while the latter was serving as chairman of the House Naval Affairs Committee. At the time, Herbert had flatly rejected the captain's request for political assistance on behalf of the War College, a rebuff that caused Mahan to write an angry letter to a friend in which he alluded to Herbert as "pig-headed" and "impossible." [82]

Tracy was unable to persuade Herbert to do as the captain wished. Expressing reservations as to the value of the College and the character of its head, the Democrat refused to commit himself in advance of the inauguration to any line of procedure. Admiral Ramsay won in the end; two months after Tracy left office, Mahan returned to sea duty.[83]

Despite Mahan's well-founded uneasiness during the lame-duck period of the Harrison administration, he added substantially to the body of naval and expansionist literature. In a second series of articles, he reinforced his earlier stand for the annexation of Hawaii and the construction of an isthmian canal by forecasting the imminent emergence of Japan as a sea power of consequence. Even before the Sino–Japanese War of 1894–95 broke out, the captain conjured up the "yellow peril" image and exploited it to foster naval expansion. Garnishing his presentation with provocative references to the exposure of the Pacific coast to oriental aggression, he called for the acquisition of Hawaii and for a "great extension of our naval power" to "protect this outpost of Western Civilization." [84]

For some time after Tracy retired, Mahan kept on writing in this vein. As translations of his principal works appeared abroad, his repu-

81 Mahan to Tracy, January 23, 1893, in Tracy Papers; Captain H. C. Taylor to Luce, December 28, 1892, in NWC. Taylor succeeded Mahan as president of the College.
82 Mahan to J. C. Roper, in Mahan Papers, Puleston Collection.
83 Mahan, "Reminiscences," 4; Puleston, *Mahan*, 136.
84 See, for example, Mahan, "Hawaii and Our Future Sea Power," 5; New York *Times*, January 31, 1893. Quotation is from Mahan's article.

tation as a naval theoretician became international in scope. Soon he would receive the acclamation of academicians as well as navalists in the form of honorary degrees awarded him, first by Oxford, Cambridge, and McGill Universities, and later by Harvard, Yale, and Columbia.[85]

As Harrison's administration neared its end, Tracy disposed of his unfinished business in order to leave his desk clear for the man who would succeed him. Indeed, the press of such business had prevented him from participating actively in his chief's unsuccessful campaign for reelection.[86] Among the matters awaiting his attention was a request from the Academy of Natural Sciences in Philadelphia for the services of Lieutenant Robert E. Peary as leader of an exploratory expedition to the Arctic Circle. The general complied gladly, granting Peary a three-year leave of absence in which to make his contribution to knowledge of the Far North.[87]

Having attended to the tag ends of his routine by December, Tracy turned to the task of reviewing his stewardship in the last of his annual reports to the President. Since the latter's inauguration, he reported, nineteen steel warships had entered active service and nineteen more had been laid down in various shipyards. True, Tracy had obtained fewer ships than had Whitney, but those authorized during the general's term added up to greater tonnage and firepower.

For the coming year, the general requested one additional battleship, two torpedo-cruisers, and thirty small torpedo craft. His comments in this connection reflected the impact of the policy revolution of 1890 on the national attitude toward sea power:

> Our true naval policy for the future is to construct principally . . . first-class cruisers and battleships and their accessories. The progress . . . by which the United States has emerged from . . . helplessness at sea, and by the employment of its own resources, has distanced its more experienced competitors, marks an epoch in the naval development, not only of this country, but of the world.[88]

Warning against complacency in the future, the general concluded:

85   Mahan, *Sail to Steam*, I, 312ff.
86   W. S. Gowdy to Tracy, September 9, 1892, and Tracy's endorsement thereon, September 13, 1892, in Tracy Papers. Gowdy, as chairman of the Indiana State Republican Committee, had invited Tracy to take part in Harrison's campaign in the Middle West.
87   Boston *Herald*, November 21, 1892.
88   Navy Dept., *Annual Report*, 1892.

"While our progress has been startlingly rapid . . . , other nations have not been idle, and the United States is not yet in a condition of adequate defense. The aggressive policy of foreign nations has continued, and this country . . . will soon be forced into a position where it cannot disregard measures which form a menace to its prosperity and security." [89] As these words suggest, Tracy planned in terms of the world of the future and the leading role America would play in it. The sum of his accomplishments as secretary, from his initiation of the battleship program to the preservation of the War College and the reform of the navy yards, represents a contribution to the Navy yet to be surpassed in time of peace. The events following his retirement left no doubt of the durability and significance of the lessons he taught.[90]

89 *Ibid.*
90 Editorial opinions of Tracy's administration appeared in 1893 in the following newspapers: New York *Recorder*, January 4; New York *World*, January 3; Brooklyn *Daily Eagle*, January 6; New York *Press*, January 13; San Francisco *Evening Bulletin*, January 4; St. Louis *Post-Dispatch*, January 8. For a recent appraisal, see John Mahon, "Secretary of the Navy Benjamin F. Tracy," *New York Historical Quarterly* (April, 1961), 179–201.

VIII

HIATUS: 1893-1894

G<small>ROVER</small> C<small>LEVELAND'S</small> <small>SECOND TERM OF OFFICE, BEGINNING IN</small> March, 1893, interrupted the expansionist policy which one Republican administration had formulated and another would carry to a successful conclusion within the decade. The new President's anti-imperialist attitude during the first half of this term, coupled with the emergence of grave domestic problems, dismayed navalists who feared that Tracy's battleship program might be discarded as a false start.

This was the era of populism, economic depression, and the fight for free silver—an era in which Americans had less concern for security at sea than for the depletion of the country's gold supply and the prevalence of agrarian unrest. To conservatives particularly, the prospect of the root-and-branch reforms espoused by the Populists appeared far more menacing than the possibility of foreign aggression.

In the election of the previous November, Cleveland had won some 5,540,000 popular votes, as against Harrison's 5,190,000 and Populist James Weaver's 1,027,329. By capitalizing on their man's campaign for moderate tariffs and sound money, the Democrats had captured majorities in both houses of Congress.

The most immediate question facing the administration was how to cope with the financial crisis inherited from its predecessor. For three years, gold had been flowing out of the United States, owing to the heavy selling of American securities by British investors who had taken fright at the failure of Baring Brothers' Bank in London. In the same period, federal revenues fell off sharply, a decline usually attributed to the McKinley Tariff Act of 1890. To make things worse, the formerly large treasury surplus had all but vanished in consequence of Harrison's open-handed pension grants to Grand Army veterans. On May 5, as the federal gold reserve dropped below the $100,000,000 mark, panic swept the New York Stock Exchange; by October, the reserve was down to $80,000,000, with no relief in sight.

One effect of the President's curative measures bears directly on naval expansion and thus deserves mention here. His efforts to stabilize the economy, which drew considerable criticism that summer, split the ranks of the Democrats in Congress and thereby paved the way to an off-year Republican victory in November, 1894. With the Republicans in control of Congress, the Navy moved ahead once more.

It was the abnormal economic state of the country, rather than his isolationist impulse, that induced Cleveland to call a halt to battleship construction. The record indicates that he would have allowed the program to continue, despite his distaste for Harrisonian imperialism, if financial conditions had been more favorable.

The President's choice of Hilary Abner Herbert to head the Navy Department suggests his willingness to enlarge the service—at least for defensive purposes. Herbert had for years maintained a bipartisan approach to naval legislation in the House of Representatives and usually voted for expansionist bills.

Born in Laurensville, South Carolina, in 1834, the "Congressional Secretary" graduated from the University of Alabama and, three years later, from the University of Virginia Law School. He practiced law in Greenville, Alabama, until the Civil War began, whereupon he entered the Confederate Army as a lieutenant. After serving in this grade for three years, Herbert was promoted to colonel and given command of the 8th Alabama Regiment, just in time to see action in the Wilderness campaign. Wounded in a skirmish, he was taken prisoner by a Union patrol and held until 1864 when he was exchanged and, shortly thereafter, honorably discharged from military service.

Resuming his law practice, Colonel Herbert remained in Greenville for eight years before moving to Montgomery. His legal talent soon brought him to the attention of the political circle at the state capital, leaders of which opened the avenue to his election to the federal House of Representatives in 1877. Here he served his district well for the next sixteen years, interesting himself primarily in naval affairs. Three times a member and once chairman of the House Naval Committee, Herbert was probably as well qualified as any secretary in history to head the Navy Department.[1]

Like Tracy, Herbert received his appointment as a result of political compromise. Cleveland had originally picked Richard Olney of Massachusetts for the Navy post; but, when Olney stated his preference for the Department of Justice, the President-elect named him attorney-general instead. Consequently, Cleveland placed Herbert in the department declined by Olney even though two other Southerners—John G. Carlisle and Hoke Smith—had already accepted positions in the cabinet.[2]

For the most part, the press welcomed the appointment. Two New York editors questioned it, however, one of them terming the choice of Herbert a "great surprise," and the other expressing concern for the Alabaman's "inclination . . . to magnify the importance of naval prowess." [3] Doubters aside, Secretary Herbert quickly proved himself capable, honest, and energetic, if somewhat less dynamic than Whitney or Tracy.

The brief ceremony of relieving Tracy of his duties on March 7 was marked with cordiality on both sides.[4] Then followed six hectic weeks, filled with demands on Herbert's time from callers asking favors of one kind or another. "Lovely and eloquent Southern ladies," appealing to him as a Confederate veteran on behalf of relatives seeking work in naval establishments, virtually reduced him to tears. Nevertheless he adhered to the letter of the Civil Service Law in filling vacancies in the department, and requested the Commission to provide replacements.

But Herbert was not above favoring his party within limits, as his modification of Tracy's registration system of labor procurement demon-

1 See sketch of Herbert in *DAB*, VII, 572–73. Brief biographical sketches are also in Philadelphia *Evening Telegram*, February 23, 1893; Troy (N.Y.) *Daily Press*, February 24, 1893.

2 Herbert, "Grandfather's Talks," 310–13, in Herbert Papers; Troy *Daily Times*, February 24, 25, 1893; New York *Times*, February 3, 1893. Carlisle was secretary of the Treasury; Smith headed the Department of the Interior.

3 New York *Daily Mercury*, February 24, 1893. For editorial comment of the Democratic press, see Birmingham *Age-Herald*, February 24, 1893; Pensacola (Fla.) *Daily News*, February 25, 1893; New York *Evening Post*, February 23, 1893; Washington *Sentinel*, February 25, 1893. More objective support for Herbert appeared in the Republican and independent newspapers, especially, Baltimore *Sun*. November 28, 1894; New York *Times*, February 23, 1893; Rochester (N.Y.) *Post Express*, February 17, 1893.

4 Herbert, "Grandfather's Talks," 316.

strated. In order to give Democratic applicants for jobs in the navy yards "a fairer chance," he cut down the time allowed candidates for keeping their names on the registration rolls.[5]

As the new secretary settled down to his routine tasks, he learned with pleasure of the President's decision to appoint William G. McAdoo assistant secretary. Formerly a Democratic representative from New Jersey in the House, McAdoo had joined Herbert in supporting the 1883 measure that authorized the ABCD's. Six years thereafter, the two Democrats finally endorsed the bill containing Tracy's battleship program, though for a time both had urged retention of the traditional monitor-raider formula. When they took office in 1893, neither Herbert nor McAdoo subscribed wholeheartedly to the capital ship theory; their conversion to Mahan's doctrine had yet to come.[6]

The naval review previously arranged by Tracy highlighted Herbert's third month in office. He had rescheduled the event for May, instead of April, and shifted the stage from Hampton Roads to New York Bay. By May 1, units of the British, French, Russian, Spanish, and Italian fleets had already met Admiral Gherardi's handpicked men-of-war in Chesapeake Bay near the mouth of the Potomac, where all the ships were to form up for the voyage to New York.

Herbert set out on the *Dolphin*, which Tracy had designated the secretarial yacht and refitted to his successor's taste, to lead the colorful array of warships north. On the evening after his arrival at the river mouth, the secretary held a reception aboard the *Dolphin* in honor of the visiting admirals from abroad. The Marine band, under the direction of John Philip Sousa, played for the entertainment of the guests during dinner and, at one point, struck up the Gilbert and Sullivan ditty which advises its hearers to "Stick close to your desk and never go to sea, and you may be the ruler of the Queen's Navee!" According to the host, not even Britain's representative blinked an eye at the selection.

Forty-eight hours later, the *Dolphin* passed through the Narrows in New York Bay, with Gherardi's squadron steaming in column on one quarter and the European warships paralleling the Americans on the

---

5 *Ibid.*, 320.
6 Navy Dept., *Annual Report*, 1893, 1896. For Herbert's and McAdoo's contributions to Chandler's expansionist program in 1882 and 1883, see *Congressional Record*, 50th Cong., 2nd Sess., 1437. For their initial opposition to the battleship clause in the Act of 1890, see *Congressional Record*, 51st Cong., 1st Sess., 3161, 3221–23, 3256–71. Both men later endorsed the clause when the House defeated an attempt to replace it with a monitor provision. For a brief analysis of their stand, see La Feber, *New Empire*, 229–30, 230n.

other. The sight attracted large, enthusiastic crowds of spectators on the shores of Brooklyn and Staten Island as President Cleveland boarded the *Dolphin* for the official reception preceding the second day of the review.[7]

The success of the event justified Tracy's belief that it would heighten public interest in the Navy. Both foreign and domestic newspapers gave the review full play, comparing the participating foreign vessels with those flying the Stars and Stripes in regard to everything from heavy guns to seamen's uniforms. Perhaps the most significant effect of the occasion, however, was the awakening of Herbert to the might of the European fleets represented at New York. What he had seen there caused him to question his former opposition to the battleship program.

As the year progressed, Herbert made a number of friends among his naval and civilian associates. He found the President "exceedingly pleasant," though reluctant to delegate authority to department heads whom, in Herbert's opinion, he was inclined to treat as clerks. Secretary of State Walter Q. Gresham became the Alabaman's closest friend in the cabinet. Gresham consulted him frequently, primarily for information received from naval intelligence officers whose reports the secretary of state deemed more reliable than his own consular dispatches.

The caliber of personnel in the department pleased Herbert. McAdoo cooperated with him closely, and even the bureau chiefs worked in harmony with the secretary, undoubtedly in deference to his former status as chairman of the House Naval Affairs Committee. Herbert regarded all the chiefs as men of ability, especially Rear Admiral Ramsay of the Bureau of Navigation, of whom he wrote: "I have never known a man more upright and just-minded than Admiral Ramsay." [8] Small wonder that Mahan feared the loss of his shore berth on Tracy's retirement!

Among other officers, the secretary's intimates included Captain George Dewey, who at the time headed the Bureau of Equipment and Repair, and Captain William T. Sampson, chief of the Bureau of Ordnance. But curious as it appears in the light of Herbert's esteem for Ramsay, whose dim view of the capital ship theory and the War College he had shared in the past, Captain Mahan came to exert greater influence on the secretary than did the admiral or any other officer.

The decisive factor in Herbert's conversion to the strategic principles

---

7 Herbert, "Grandfather's Talks," 328-31, in Herbert Papers.
8 *Ibid.*, 321-25.

set forth by Mahan was the latter's latest book, *The Influence of Sea Power upon the French Revolution and Second Empire*, which the secretary read in the spring of 1893. The captain's reasoning impressed Herbert as favorably as it had Tracy, and he too resolved to incorporate it in his first annual report to the President.[9]

The secretary's changed attitude was as yet unknown to Mahan, who was preoccupied with the transfer of the War College from Goat Island back to Coaster's Harbor. Because of the length of time involved in the move, the captain had decided not to schedule a session for 1893, though he realized that by closing the College however briefly he was according its enemies a golden opportunity to keep it closed permanently.

Mahan had reason to fear the outcome of his decision. Certain bureau chiefs led by Ramsay attempted to convince Herbert of the uselessness of the College. Unconscious of the secretary's new frame of mind, Ramsay and his cohorts thought they had their battle won when Herbert listened to them with a polite show of interest and then reminded them of his former hostility to the institution. But the chiefs did not know that this outlook had formed as a matter of principle; Herbert's rejection of Mahan's plea for support of the College reflected his distrust, as a congressman, of any institution created by executive rather than legislative action.[10]

In the period before the secretary began corresponding with Mahan, Admiral Luce also appreciated the threat posed to the College by the weighty influence of the bureau chiefs. By the end of April, he and other supporters of the school had concluded that the chiefs would prevail on Herbert to abolish it. Luce discussed the situation with Henry Cabot Lodge and Theodore Roosevelt, who described the conference in a letter to Mahan: "Last evening, Lodge . . . , Admiral Luce and I held a solemn council of war. I fear all hope for the War College has gone; our prize idiots—Herbert and the others—have thrown away the chance to give us an absolutely unique position in naval affairs." [11]

Roosevelt underestimated Secretary Herbert; he had a mind of his own despite his willingness to hear out the bureau chiefs. Once he had

9 Herbert to Mahan, October 4, 1894, in Mahan Papers, Puleston Collection; Sprout, *Naval Power,* 218; C. C. Taylor, *Mahan, Alfred Thayer* (New York, 1920), 34–35; La Feber, *New Empire,* 230. The Boston firm of Little, Brown and Company published this two-volume work of Mahan's in 1893.

10 Taylor, *Mahan, A. T.,* 34–35; C. J. Bernardo and E. H. Bacon, *American Military Policy: Its Development since 1775* (Harrisburg, Pa., 1957), 272.

11 Roosevelt to Mahan, May 1, 1893, in Mahan Papers, Puleston Collection.

done so, the secretary surprised them by refusing to decide the fate of the War College until he had an opportunity to see it in operation after the reopening in 1894.

Mahan had in the meantime become so agitated about his future that he submitted a formal request to the department for three more years of shore duty, promising to retire at the end of the third, which would coincide with his completion of forty years of service. The request reached Ramsay's desk and went no farther; the admiral had already prepared orders detailing Mahan to command of the *Chicago*, then fitting out in Brooklyn for duty as flagship of the European Squadron.[12]

Luce, Roosevelt, and Lodge interceded on the captain's behalf, utilizing all their considerable resources to prevent interruption of his writing —but to no avail. Ramsay refused to budge; he insisted on sending Mahan to sea. And Herbert, in spite of his respect for the captain's work, felt constrained to back up the Chief of the Bureau of Navigation. On May 11, Captain Mahan assumed command of the *Chicago*.

The War College, though temporarily without a head, was far from lost as its friends feared it would be following Mahan's departure. On the contrary, as Herbert informed Ramsay in August, he had changed his opinion of the College since his last days in Congress, and would henceforth lend it his support.[13]

The secretary's report for 1893, moreover, revealed his full acceptance of the capital ship theory. Published in November, the document astonished many of his associates who recalled his earlier aversion to battleship construction. The arguments Herbert now presented in favor of heavy ships not only reflected the extent of the transformation he had undergone in less than a year, but might have come from Mahan himself!

Referring to the failure of light Confederate commerce raiders to offset the advantage held by heavier Union blockaders, the secretary denounced the policy of building unarmored cruisers and called for the authorization in the coming year of "at least one battleship" and a half-dozen torpedo-boats. Notwithstanding the downward spiral of the national economy, Herbert's estimates were higher by $3,000,000 than the appropriations made in 1893. Vigorous enforcement of the country's foreign policy in peacetime, declared the secretary, necessitated the increase at once. "We must . . . keep our Navy in such a condition

12 Taylor, *Mahan, A. T.*, 35; Puleston, *Mahan*, 134-35.
13 Puleston, *Mahan*, 142.

. . . as to give weight to whatever policy it may be thought wise on the part of the government to assume." As if to emphasize America's emergent imperialism, Herbert pointed to the nation's "close interests with China and Japan" and predicted its inevitable involvement in Latin America and the islands of the Pacific. "Indeed, the continent to the south of us, and both oceans . . . now demand the presence of American ships to a greater extent than ever before, and this demand . . . will steadily increase." [14]

The secretary's battleship proposal, made at a time of acute economic distress, had little chance of adoption. Resumption of the program would have required the government to spend more money than the current condition of the treasury warranted and, as the reaction of the congressional majority illustrated, would contradict Democratic tradition. Cleveland withheld his endorsement of Herbert's recommendation, warning Congress that heavy naval construction must await the return of prosperity. Disregarding Herbert's protests, Congress authorized only four small vessels during the year ending in December, 1894 —three light gunboats and the experimental submarine *Plunger*.[15]

Few advances in any aspect of naval development occurred in the first half of Herbert's term. Old problems persisted, while new ones arose to tax the ingenuity of the administrators. Inherited headaches, such as the absence of a national reserve force, the inefficiency of the officer promotion system, and the inadequacies of the recruiting procedure, tormented Herbert as they had his predecessors.[16] Even more serious was the defective organization of the department, which had experienced no material change since 1890.

Naval business was distributed among eight bureaus of supposedly equal rank; each was headed by a senior captain, a commodore, or a rear admiral. Perhaps the most sensitive of these commands was the Bureau of Navigation, which supervised the detailing of all line personnel and the movements of warships. The Naval Academy and the Hydrographic Office came under its jurisdiction, though the War College continued to function under the secretary's office, as Tracy had directed.

The corps of engineers and their charges—main propulsion and aux-

14 Navy Dept., *Annual Report*, 1893, 1894. Cf. Sprout, *Naval Power*, 218ff.; La Feber, *New Empire*, 230–31.
15 *Messages and Papers*, IX, 451; *House Reports*, 53rd Cong., 2nd Sess., No. 728; Navy Dept., *Annual Report*, 1894.
16 Navy Dept., *Annual Report*, 1893, 1894.

iliary power plants—were the province of the Bureau of Steam Engineering; the Bureau of Equipment—formerly Equipment and Repair—took care of electrical units, rigging and cordage, anchors and chains, navigational and signaling devices, and libraries aboard ships or ashore. Also classified under "equipment" were the *Nautical Almanac* and the Naval Observatory.

The Bureau of Ordnance supervised the procurement, installation, and maintenance of naval guns, ammunition, and related *matériel*, while the recently reconstituted Bureau of Construction and Repair was responsible for the design, building, and refitting of ships. Secretary Herbert acted in October, 1893, to consolidate under one roof certain components of design and construction by transferring the authority over gun turrets and ammunition hoists from Ordnance to Construction and Repair. The change, which proved lasting, seemed logical inasmuch as these items of equipment affected the structural character of a ship and thus properly belonged to the latter bureau.[17]

Navy yards, drydocks, and associated facilities were the concern of the Bureau of Yards and Docks, which also controlled the system of civilian labor procurement. The Bureau of Supplies and Accounts had the onerous task of purchasing, distributing, and keeping custody of the bulk of naval stores, including food and uniforms. In addition, this command handled the payrolls and accounts of the Navy.

The eighth bureau, Medicine and Surgery, attended to the medical needs of the service. The Chief Surgeon, who was in charge of naval physicians, surgeons, nurses, and enlisted medical corpsmen, bore full responsibility for the condition of food and sanitation afloat and ashore.

Two subordinate agencies rounded out the organization of the department. The Office of Naval Intelligence presided over the gathering and evaluation of strategic information from all quarters of the globe by naval attachés and ships' officers. Equally important was the work of the Department of Law which, under the direction of the judge advocate general, interpreted Navy Regulations and reviewed records of court-martial proceedings in its capacity as the legal branch of the service.[18]

17 F. E. Chadwick, "Navy Department Organization," *NIP*, XX (1894), 493ff. Commander Chadwick, chief of the Bureau of Equipment and Repair (later Construction and Repair) in 1894, had criticized the system severely in a number of letters to Tracy, April, 1889, to November, 1892, in Tracy Papers. For the transfer of responsibility for turrets and hoists, see Navy Dept., Bureau of Construction and Repair Memorandum, October 18, 1915, in Herbert Papers.
18 Chadwick, "Navy Dept. Organization," 493–96.

Commander French E. Chadwick, a faithful correspondent of Tracy's who became a bureau chief in 1894, condemned the entire system of departmental organization as one of "unsurpassed crudity" which placed the "heavy duty of reconcilement of divergent views . . . upon the Secretary . . . much of whose time is taken up with questions which under any proper system need never come before him." In the commander's opinion, it was not the business of the secretary—seldom appointed for his knowledge of naval matters—to make decisions of a highly technical nature. Nor did Chadwick condone the division of authority in the bureaucracy, which disrupted "unity of control" and caused duplication of bureau activities—not to mention endless red tape.

To rectify the situation, wrote Chadwick in an article for the Naval Institute's *Proceedings* in 1894, the number of bureaus should be reduced and the whole department reshuffled. He presented a radical plan which, among other changes, called for the creation of a general staff. This, stated the commander, would have the dual effect of centralizing the more sensitive functions of the department and of relieving the secretary of the burden of deciding military and technical questions. According to Chadwick's scheme, the staff would oversee naval operations and the formulation of war plans while maintaining communications with all men-of-war on active assignments.[19]

Captain Mahan subsequently expressed agreement in principle with Commander Chadwick's ideas. Deploring the lack of coordination among naval agencies, which Mahan regarded as the natural product of the existing system, he emphasized the necessity of forming an instrument for evaluating the mass of information supplied by the War College, the Office of Naval Intelligence, and other sources. At this time, the secretary alone had the authority to analyze strategic requisites and to apply the results at the policy level. And, since civilian administrators usually came to office via the route of political expediency, declared the captain, they could not be expected to reach valid judgments at that level—let alone solve technical problems.

Mahan singled out for special criticism the absence of teamwork among the bureau chiefs. True, the secretary was empowered to hold each chief accountable for the proper operation of his command; but he lacked the means of tying together the individual—and often dovetailed—efforts of all eight. Consequently, as nothing more was demanded of a chief than satisfactory conduct of his bureau's affairs, the system

19 *Ibid.*, 495.

tended to insulate one bureau against another. This meant that the efficiency of the department, to which every man in it was theoretically dedicated, might suddenly deteriorate, simply because no individual or group had been designated to report the condition of the organization to the secretary. In short, Mahan concluded, unless things soon took a turn for the better, the future welfare of the department would depend solely on the talents of its civilian heads, rather than on a firmly established method of procedure able to survive the shocks of political fortune.[20]

By 1894, the long-standing issue of officer promotion had received so much publicity that Congress appointed a committee to investigate the matter. At the committee's hearings, officers had the opportunity to air their own ideas as to the best way of improving the system. While some suggested increasing the number of advancements to upper grades and others favored placing less competent men on a reserved list, which would remove them from the ladder to higher rank by relegating them to limited duty ashore, all agreed that the blockage in lower grades must be eliminated and the requirements for promotion be clarified. Among the proposals made to the committee, a plea for the establishment of a merit system, in which a duly appointed selection board would upgrade only the worthiest of those qualified for promotion by longevity, received considerable support from senior officers. Extending this line of thought, their juniors suggested creating a fixed number of vacancies each year in every grade by removing a corresponding number of the less valuable men.[21]

During the investigation, spokesmen for the line officers challenged the right of their colleagues in the staff corps to advancement to the upper grades. Staff officers, it seemed, aspired to rank as high as that open to men of the line, but had no desire to yield their separate and distinct classifications. After much debate, a compromise solution was offered by a commander of the line: he recommended merging in one branch the principal seagoing elements of the service—line officers, engineers, and marines; other members of the staff corps—doctors, paymasters, and constructors—would as in the past fend for themselves.

When the hearings ended, the committee retired to chambers in

20 See Mahan's memorandum in "Circular for the Information of Officers," 1903, in NWC.
21 W. L. Rodgers, "Examination of the Testimony Taken by the Joint Committees of the House and Senate in regard to the Reorganization of the Navy," *NIP*, XX (1894), 747ff.

order to prepare a report. There the question rested for the time being; not a single change was instituted to render the promotion system more efficient, nor was an inquiry made to determine the best means of attracting superior enlisted recruits to the Navy. If nothing else, however, the committee hearings had provided a safety valve for the airing of real or imagined grievances on the part of officers.[22]

In the meantime, several new problems were bedeviling Secretary Herbert. When the warships laid down in Tracy's term began joining active squadrons toward the end of 1893, Herbert found to his dismay that the naval establishment lacked the facilities for servicing a rapidly growing fleet. To correct this deficiency, he drafted an urgent appeal to Congress for additional yards and fueling stations, particularly on the Pacific coast.

The congressional reaction to the secretary's call for help demonstrated above all the prevalence of parochial jealousy in national politics. Senators and representatives from eastern states made clear their opposition to any measure which would require heavy expenditures for building naval facilities outside their individual constituencies, no matter how badly such bases were needed by the Pacific and Asiatic Squadrons. Even the most imperialist-minded of these congressmen refused to entertain the thought of authorizing construction of west-coast navy yards. Large as it loomed, the imperialist spirit came second to local interests.[23]

Related to this problem—and just as embarrassing—was the absence of drydocks capable of accommodating the new battleships and heavy cruisers soon to be placed in commission. Of the three drydocks in the United States in 1893, not one was large enough to handle vessels of the *Oregon* class. And, although eighteen more would be in operation within five years, as late as 1897 the *Indiana* had to steam to Halifax for drydocking! [24]

In the fall of 1893, another source of concern materialized with the arrival of a letter from an attorney representing certain employees of Carnegie, Phipps and Company. The lawyer alleged that the company was foisting defective armor plate on the Navy. Herbert acted at once to investigate the charge personally, with the assistance of his ordnance chief, Captain William T. Sampson.

22 *Ibid.* See also, Navy Dept., *Annual Report,* 1894.
23 Mitchell, *Modern Navy,* 33.
24 Navy Dept., *Annual Report,* 1894, 1895; Long, *New Navy,* II, 111–17.

Exhaustive tests of samples of the plate recently delivered by Carnegie, Phipps convinced Herbert and Sampson that the armor was not
defective as charged. On the contrary, the samples proved at least 5
per cent higher in grade than the quality specified by contract. The
outcome of the tests did indicate, however, that the plate in question
fell short of the quality to be expected from the new processes employed at the Carnegie forging plant. Close questioning of company
personnel brought to light evidence of a fraud perpetrated by a group
of Carnegie employees who hoped to win government premiums for
delivering armor superior in grade to the minimum contract limit. To
this end, they had removed specimen plates set aside for the naval inspectors' acceptance tests, improved their quality by special treatment,
and returned them. Believing that the plates thus treated were typical
of the whole shipment, the inspector passed the lot with a higher rating
than the untreated bulk of it deserved.[25]

Satisfied with the validity of their findings, Herbert and Sampson
presented the evidence of fraud to Congress, whereupon the House
appointed a committee to hear the testimony of all concerned. The committee's report, which was published in 1894, substantiated Herbert's
conclusions and prompted him to ask Cleveland to levy a fine on the
contractor equal to 15 per cent of the cost of all plate Carnegie had
produced for the department. But the President, feeling that the company had suffered almost as much damage as the government had at
the hands of unscrupulous steel workers, reduced the penalty to 10
per cent—or $140,000. [26]

Returning to his regular duties after the inquiry, Captain Sampson
discovered that his colleagues in the Bureau of Ordnance had become
alarmed at reports of excessive inaccuracy in recent gunnery exercises.
Ordnance men had heard complaints of this nature as early as 1890
but had usually ignored them in view of the supposed excellence of
shipboard gunnery training. Nevertheless, a growing number of critics
of naval marksmanship continued to point out serious deficiencies. Contemporary target practice procedure accounted in large measure for
the inflated reputation of the Navy's gunners. Gun crews customarily
fired at small targets, on which "near misses" were often counted as

25 B. J. Hendrick, *Andrew Carnegie* (New York, 1932), II, Appendix I, *passim;*
Nevins, *Cleveland,* 637; Allard, "Influence upon Steel Industry," 105. Allard treats
the armor frauds case as a minor aberration. For criticism of Herbert's omission of
the frauds in his second annual report, see New York *World,* November 28, 1894.
26 Nevins, *Cleveland,* 637-38; *House Reports,* 53rd Cong., 2nd Sess., No. 1468.

hits by officers in charge out of mistaken kindness to their shipmates. Consequently their "gun-decked" score-sheets exaggerated the actual level of accuracy attained.[27]

The profession was not completely blind to this condition, as numerous articles by naval critics show. These authors demanded that closer ordnance calculations be required of gunnery officers and that all enlisted men—regardless of rating—be put through a systematic series of target practices. In addition, they called on the department to equip all warships with range finders and stadimeters and to furnish naval guns with electrical primers and firing attachments.[28]

In the articles on this subject appearing at the time, the tone of many suggests that the long-standing debate between the advocates of the heavy gun and those of the ram bow had yet to be resolved. New support for the ramming tactic was stimulated by the circumstances of a collision in June, 1893, between two crack British battleships on daylight maneuvers off the coast of Tripoli. The speculation among American officers occasioned by the disaster centered on the lethal effect of H.M.S. *Camperdown's* ram, which had sliced open the *Victoria* —Vice Admiral Sir George Tryon's flagship—and sent her to the bottom in minutes, a feat that heavy armament might never have accomplished. Furthermore, according to rumors emanating from the Admiralty, the *Victoria's* exceptionally heavy forward guns had caused her to turn turtle before sinking.

Of more fundamental significance was the nature of the maneuver responsible for the collision. Tryon had ordered a dangerously complex evolution which had no practical application in combat; it appeared to be a grandstand play calculated to impress his commanders with his ingenuity and daring. The tragic outcome of the maneuver dramatized the necessity of making tactical evolutions as clear and simple as possible.[29]

The British catastrophe distracted Americans temporarily from a crisis taking shape in Hawaiian politics bearing strong naval overtones. In March, Cleveland's withdrawal of Harrison's annexation treaty from the Senate provoked the wrath of expansionist editors who promptly

27 See, for instance, John Spears, "The American Navy," *Chatauquan* (May, 1890), 11ff.; "Prize Essay Discussion," *NIP*, XX (1894), 670–71.
28 Navy Dept., *Annual Report*, 1894. See also, W. R. Herrick, "The Naval Policy of Theodore Roosevelt" (M.A. thesis, Columbia University, 1959), 39.
29 Potter and Nimitz (eds.), *Sea Power*, 337; Richard Hough, *Admirals in Collision* (New York, 1960), *passim*.

accused the President of undermining the Dole regime and abandoning the islands to the mercy of a foreign naval power.[30] The administration, they reported, planned to restore Queen Liliuokalani in the near future; and word of the plan had already reached London. If the plot to reestablish the monarch succeeded, predicted the editors, Her Majesty's government would regard it as a signal for British warships to land marines at Honolulu and proclaim a protectorate over the islands.[31]

Newspaper accounts of Cleveland's Hawaiian policy, though often distorted, had some substance. Recent dispatches from Honolulu had convinced him of the islanders' distaste for a government dominated by Hawaiian-American sugar interests. Apparently motivated by humanitarian as well as isolationist considerations, the President then took steps to substitute the monarchy for Dole's republic. He instructed his minister to Hawaii, Albert S. Willis, who had replaced Minister Stevens, to terminate the American protectorate and, subject to certain conditions, to offer the Queen her former throne.

Willis persuaded Liliuokalani to accept Cleveland's terms; she agreed to assume the debts of the Dole government and to abide by the Hawaiian Constitution of 1887 if the administration would support her return to power. But, just as these negotiations seemed complete, Sanford Dole refused to abdicate on the grounds that the United States had no right to influence the trend of Hawaiian political affairs. This ended Cleveland's attempt to restore the monarchy; unwilling to force the issue, he condemned Dole's seizure of power and reasserted the administration's opposition to annexation. In August, 1894, he extended formal recognition to the Hawaiian Republic.[32]

Captain Mahan entered the annexation controversy in March with an article which presented the annexationist point of view in a new light. Hawaii, he declared, was the key to military and commercial control of the North Pacific "in which the United States has the strongest right to assert herself"; possession of the chain would "deny any maritime enemy . . . a coaling station well within 2,500 miles . . . of our coastline from Puget Sound to Mexico." In Mahan's opinion, if a foe were barred from refueling in Hawaii, he would have to depend on coaling stations distant from the Pacific coast by at least

---

30 Pratt, *Expansionists of 1898*, 146ff.
31 For examples, San Francisco *Call*, March 10, 1893; New York *Commercial Advertiser*, March 13, 1893; *Portland Oregonian*, March 18, 1893; *Literary Digest*, VI (March 4, 1893), 388–90, 500; *Review of Reviews* (March, 1893), 131ff.
32 Pratt, *Expansionists of 1898*, 146–50.

3,500 miles—"an impediment to sustained operations well-nigh prohibitive." [33]

The prominent isolationist reformer Carl Schurz counterattacked at once with an article of his own. Schurz reasoned that acquisition of such an overseas outpost would certainly invite foreign aggression. Besides, he continued, democracy could not flourish in the tropics. Indeed, if Americans yielded to the lure of tropical expansion in their march to Manifest Destiny, they would suffer "total abandonment of their conservative traditions and . . . rapid deterioration in character," and would face a "future of turbulence, demoralization, and final decay." [34]

The Senate acted in May, 1894, to interrupt the debate over Hawaii by voting heavily in favor of adopting a resolution opposed to both annexation and intervention. The vote deprived Cleveland of the full victory he could have claimed if he had succeeded in restoring the Queen to the throne, but it did at least check the ambitions of the imperialists for the time being. [35]

Naval operations in the Pacific reflected the political developments. In compliance with one of Secretary Herbert's first orders in the spring of 1893, Admiral Walker had proceeded in the *Philadelphia* to Pearl Harbor, where he relieved Admiral Skerrett and remained for more than a year. On August 12, 1894, Walker headed his flagship for San Francisco, as directed by Herbert, without awaiting relief.

During the homeward passage, Walker wrote the secretary of his fear that British men-of-war operating near Hawaii would take advantage of the *Philadelphia's* recall to stage a restoration of the Queen. The admiral's concern was justified; a royalist revolt broke out later in the year, and before the republican government had time to suppress it, back to Pearl Harbor steamed the *Philadelphia*! [36]

Meanwhile, an insurrection in Brazil was keeping ships of the Atlantic squadrons equally busy. At the time, Brazilians were living out their period of transition from monarchy to republicanism under the autocratic rule of a series of dictators, whose policies had by the fall of 1893 culminated in open rebellion.

33 Mahan, "Hawaii," 153–54.
34 Carl Schurz, "Manifest Destiny," *Harper's Monthly,* LXXXVIII (March, 1893), 753–54.
35 *Congressional Record,* 53rd Cong., 2nd Sess., 5499–5500.
36 Navy Dept., *Annual Report,* 1894; Pratt, *Expansionists of 1898,* 190, citing *Foreign Relations* (1895), 818–20, 852.

Led by malcontent Admiral José de Mello, the rebels won to their side the bulk of Brazil's fleet. Hoping to compel the resignation of the legal chief of state, President Floriano Peixoto, Mello sent warships to the Bay of Rio de Janeiro and was preparing to blockade Rio and bombard the coast. Believing he had the president trapped, Admiral Mello invited the Cleveland administration to recognize the rebel faction as a legitimate belligerent and appealed at the same time for the support of Brazilian royalists by promising to reestablish the Empire. The promise was a mistake; it ruled out whatever chance Mello had of obtaining recognition from the United States because, despite his efforts on behalf of Queen Liliuokalani, Cleveland despised monarchy as thoroughly as he did imperialism. Once Mello realized that Washington would not legalize the status of his forces, he gave up his plan to bombard the coast.

When the fighting began, Herbert had responded to United States Minister T. S. Thompson's request for naval protection by dispatching to Rio Commodore O. F. Stanton's South Atlantic Squadron. On his arrival, the commodore made official calls on both Peixoto and Mello, for which curious behavior he was promptly recalled to Washington by Secretary Herbert, who then ordered Admiral A. E. K. Benham to assume command of the squadron at Rio.

Benham had instructions to protect American shipping and cargoes by whatever means he deemed necessary. Accordingly, when an insurgent man-of-war fired on a barge laden with American goods, he ordered the *Detroit* to fire a warning shot across the rebel's bow. This brought things to a head; there followed a sharp exchange between Benham and an insurgent commander from which the former emerged triumphant. Benham's action not only assured the safety of cargoes being lightered from carriers to wharves, but it also convinced Mello of the hopelessness of his attempt to maintain a blockade. The insurrection died shortly afterwards.[37]

America's display of sea power in the Bay of Rio de Janeiro impressed Assistant Secretary McAdoo profoundly, as he announced in mid-April, 1894, to a Democratic gathering in Boston. Presumably speaking for the administration, McAdoo sounded strangely aggressive for an official representative of a self-styled isolationist administration. Referring to the "universal" acceptance of Mahan's theories, the

37 Navy Dept., *Annual Report*, 1894; L. F. Hill, *Diplomatic Relations between the United States and Brazil* (New York, 1937), 274–78.

assistant secretary unashamedly took up the cudgel for imperialism. "Our vast resources, our advancing civilization . . . make us a factor in the affairs of our neighbors. During the recent trouble in Brazil, the United States . . . put into Brazilian waters the most powerful fleet which ever represented our flag abroad." The effect of this armada, declared McAdoo, was to boost the nation's prestige throughout Latin America. "It was a notice to the world that . . . we were keenly alive to our expressed declarations. With the phenomenal growth of our population, the increase of our commerce," he went on, in tones worthy of Roosevelt, "there comes a stimulus from the sight of that splendid squadron . . . carrying our flag with pride over decks cleared for action, as it steamed up the Bay of Rio." In the future, the speaker prophesied, owing to the country's industrial capacity, "we should . . . prevail, and this is thoroughly understood abroad."

On the other hand, warned the assistant secretary, the Navy had yet to measure up to the demands of national security. Echoing Tracy, he stressed the advisability of building a two-ocean fleet. Since the trend of international events foreshadowed an increase in the number of "constant upheavals" besetting such areas of interest to the United States as the Bering Sea, the Far East, and Central and South America, a one-ocean navy would not suffice.[38]

The successful rebirth of the War College in 1894 substantiated McAdoo's assertion of the general acceptance of the arguments employed by Luce and Mahan to foster professionalism in the service. A few weeks prior to the reopening, Secretary Herbert visited Coaster's Harbor to welcome Mahan's successor, Captain H. C. Taylor. In his address for the occasion, Herbert bestowed his official blessing on the College and expressed gratification at its evolution from a school of theory to an essential planning agency where, in addition to theoretical study, "practical information is being amassed without which the Navy Department cannot possibly, in the event of war, utilize the naval resources of our country." [39]

At the close of the 1894 session, Captain Taylor summarized the work of the College, which had come a long way since Luce first opened the door of Newport Alms House to a few student officers in 1888. The curriculum described by Taylor included a number of new offerings

38 W. G. McAdoo, "The Navy and the Nation," Boston address, April 15, 1894, reprinted in *NIP*, XX (1894), 399–402, 418–19.
39 A reprint of Herbert's speech appears in *NIP*, XXXVI (1901), 575ff. See also, Navy Dept., *Annual Report*, 1894; Philadelphia *Press*, November 28, 1894.

besides those instituted in the early days of the College. Students could now avail themselves of courses in steam engineering, weapons of offense and defense, construction, and electricity, as well as seminars in strategy, tactics, international law, intelligence evaluation, and military science.[40]

In the session just ended, announced the captain, the College had also required students to analyze and work out solutions to specific war problems in order to "promote professionally a mental activity" which would "provide valuable material results." These projects, Taylor explained, would benefit the Navy "in the realm of both strategy and tactics, and . . . furnish a backlog of operational programs of great value in the event of sudden aggression in the future." Further, "the search for . . . solutions will inevitably lead" officers "into close intimacy with the art of war," an intimacy Taylor felt was enjoyed by too few of his colleagues.

Another new feature of the curriculum was the integration of war games in the regular College program. Although introduced during Mahan's presidency, the games had not in the past gained a permanent place on the schedule. For want of more appropriate training ships, Taylor had borrowed steam launches from the North Atlantic Squadron and manned them with student officers for the purpose of simulating heavy warships on tactical maneuvers. These exercises, he pointed out, demonstrated in practice the necessity for careful planning of tactical evolutions, with special attention to the limitations set by speed, turning circle, and other characteristics of all units involved. As the captain put it, the launches were used primarily to eliminate "visionary formations from the list of possibilities." [41] Perhaps he had Admiral Tryon and the *Victoria* in mind.

Concluding his summary with a vigorous defense of the War College, Captain Taylor called for recognition of its increasing importance to the service. The institution had already begun to fill the gap occasioned by the absence of a central strategic planning agency in the department, while continuing to function as the most advanced source of professional education. The faculty had on file numerous corrected plans for defending the coast against specified naval powers. As they accumulated, these plans would constitute a body of reliable defensive doctrine, after

40 "Extracts from Captain H. C. Taylor's Closing Address at the Naval War College," *NIP*, XX (1894), 796ff.
41 *Ibid.*, 797–98.

the fashion of the Prussian system in the Bismarckian era. And, promised Taylor, the College would supplement existing offensive programs with updated information supplied by the Office of Naval Intelligence.

The quality of the planning envisaged by Captain Taylor depended on the ability of the College faculty which, he declared, must be composed of the best instructors available. Nowhere else could naval officers learn "the immutable laws that govern the conduct of war." If for no other reason, the War College must be sustained and developed further to enable it to carry out this mission as effectively as possible.[42] Secretary Herbert appreciated the wisdom of Taylor's views—indeed, he shared them with a growing number of Navy men. Gradually, by dint of its multiple contributions to the service, the War College moved toward a permanent place in the naval establishment.

Aside from the rebirth of the College and the promotional success of the naval review, few signs of progress brightened the first half of Herbert's administration. December, 1894, marked the end of two years of frustration for him and for other naval expansionists. Yet the imperialist spirit persisted and before it reached its apex would carry the standard-bearer of Democracy along with it. Although few observers realized it at the time, the hiatus in Tracy's battleship program had come to an end.

42 *Ibid.*, 798.

IX

THE REVOLUTION RESUMES

FOREIGN AND DOMESTIC CIRCUMSTANCES ALIKE INFLUENCED the resumption of battleship construction in 1895. In the Far East, Japan emerged from the war with China as a maritime power of consequence, one whose imperialist aspirations might in the future provoke a clash with the United States. To the South, Venezuela's quarrel with Britain over the boundary of British Guiana threatened to involve America in a defense of the Monroe Doctrine against the strongest naval power on earth. Nearer at hand, persistent nationalist agitation in Cuba for freedom from Spanish rule had by February become an armed revolt.

Naval operations over the past two years had underlined the immensity of the task facing the service. Clearly, the Navy lacked the strength to police areas of national interest in two oceans and still keep itself in trim for meeting a major emergency. To informed Americans, the situation—compounded by the crises arising in 1895—indicated the need for an immediate increase in sea power. Admiral Luce, for one, expressed the opinion that the government should within three years construct a fleet of eighteen battleships and appropriate supporting units.[1]

At home, several factors reawakened the public to the desirability of naval expansion. One was the work of Captain Mahan, whose name was rapidly becoming a household word. Another derived from the

1 S. B. Luce, "As to Navy Yards and Their Defense," *NIP*, XXI (1895), 638. The admiral's proposal contemplated, in other words, the construction of fourteen battleships in addition to those already authorized—the three *Oregons* and the *Iowa*.

173

popularity of the naval display at the Chicago Exposition and the international review in New York Bay, both of which had attracted huge crowds in the preceding year. But the decisive consideration in the renewal of the battleship program was the very condition that had stalled it in the first place; it was the depression—at its worst as 1895 opened—that impelled President Cleveland to reconsider his suspension of heavy naval construction.

So far, his attempts to bring about recovery had met with little success. Not only had the repeal of the Sherman Act failed to check the flow of gold from the treasury, but the negotiation of a series of loans from J. P. Morgan had created new enemies of the administration. In addition, Attorney-General Olney's use of force to settle the Pullman strike had intensified social unrest and extended it to industrial centers.

Against this somber backdrop, Secretary Herbert offered the President a partial solution to the economic problem. He pointed out that large-scale naval building would stimulate industrial activity and provide jobs for the idle in shipyards, steel mills, armor forging plants, and numerous related manufacturing and commercial agencies. Failure to resume the battleship program soon, warned Herbert, would jeopardize the existence of recently established facilities on which the Navy had come to depend with the advance of technology and would cause their forces of skilled labor to disband. Spokesmen for management and labor agreed for once; both were demanding naval contracts for the sake of investments and jobs.[2]

The armor contractors, declared Herbert, whose product had as yet no application other than naval, would suffer especially if the Navy Department placed no further orders. Conversely, the department would require more armor shortly if the warships already authorized were to be completed, though the existing contracts would be fulfilled and due for renewal before the need could be satisfied.[3]

The secretary's reasoning impressed Cleveland. Heavy naval construction might not cure the country's economic ills, but it should at least work against further decline. Acting on this assumption, the President endorsed Herbert's request for three additional 10,000-ton battleships and twelve torpedo-boats ranging from one hundred to three hundred

2 Herbert, "Grandfather's Talks," 342; *Congressional Record*, 53rd Cong., 3rd Sess., 3113; New York *World*, November 28, 1894.
3 Herbert, "Grandfather's Talks," 342.

tons in displacement, though he had discouraged authorization of the more modest program submitted by the secretary a year earlier.[4]

Herbert found the Republican-dominated House of Representatives equally receptive to the thought of identifying naval expansion with economic recovery, once he had warned the members that failure to vote for his program would mean bankruptcy for many large shipyards, to the detriment of national security. To the secretary's surprise, the congressmen seemed willing to appropriate $12,000,000 for three capital ships at a time when the depression was most acute and no emergency appeared imminent. Perhaps they felt the measure would bring a degree of prosperity to their constituents and thus redound to their own political advantage.

Following a vigorous debate, in which the representatives displayed unprecedented awareness of strategic principles, the House voted to authorize the ships proposed by the secretary. The naval bill encountered stiffer resistance in the Senate; here the number of battleships was reduced to two and the torpedo-boat program cut in half. At length, in order to save the measure before the session ended, the House agreed to the reduction. In all, the Navy Act of 1895 provided for the construction of two battleships, six torpedo-boats, and eight smaller craft of various types.[5]

Although the Senate had deprived Herbert's program of one battleship, the two authorized proved heavier and more expensive than he had anticipated. The final plans for the *Kearsarge* and *Kentucky* specified a displacement of 11,520 tons each and a top speed of 17 knots; the estimated cost of both vessels amounted to $10,000,000. Ordnance specifications for the *Kentuckys* were the most impressive ever drafted in America. They called for a main battery of four 13-inch rifles, as against the 12-inchers mounted on the *Iowa*, and for a secondary armament of four 8-inch guns, supplemented by numerous rapid-fire cannon.

The decision to equip the battleships with exceptionally heavy guns gave rise to the problem of weight distribution. To help solve it, Herbert created the board of design and named Admiral Walker president. After consulting the chiefs of the two bureaus concerned, Ordnance, and Construction and Repair, the board advised the secretary to adopt a plan—approved by all hands—which would locate the 13-inchers in pairs in two double turrets, one forward and one aft.

4 *Messages and Papers*, IX, 540–41. See also, Millis, *Arms and Men*, 165.
5 Navy Dept., *Annual Report*, 1894, 1895. See also, New York *World*, November 28, 1894; New York *Times*, May 16, 1895.

Ordnance and construction men disagreed, however, about the emplacement of the 8-inch guns of the secondary battery, though they had already decided to install the rapid-fire cannon in broadside casemates, port and starboard. Herbert's advisers pointed out that in order to achieve a satisfactory arc of fire with only two double turrets of two 8-inchers each, the guns should be mounted on the center line. The chief of the Bureau of Construction and Repair sought to accomplish this by placing them above and behind the 13-inch turrets, which would thus enable the 8-inch gunners to fire over the heavier rifles. Sampson's ordnance experts advanced a more radical scheme, one which would superimpose each of the smaller turrets on one of the 13-inch structures. On the advice of the board of design, Herbert accepted the latter plan for further consideration, though it was the first proposal ever made to place all turrets on the center line, with secondary guns superimposed on the main turrets. Within twenty years, the superimposed double turret would become a standard feature of battleships. The *Kentuckys* introduced two other innovations which were universally accepted by 1915—the recast, oval turret, and the application of electrical power to turret machinery.[6]

As the secretary observed, the Act of 1895 connoted a departure from traditional policy inasmuch as it made no mention of cruisers. The omission reflected an international trend; Herbert learned from naval intelligence that the popularity of cruisers had declined in seventeen foreign countries while that of torpedo-boats had increased correspondingly.

According to the chief intelligence officer, European strategists had come to regard the speedy torpedo-boat as an effective and inexpensive weapon to use against the costly and relatively slow battleship. He informed Herbert that none of the seventeen fleets investigated had fewer than twenty-two such craft built or building, as opposed to the dozen in service or authorized in the United States, and that the number of torpedo-boats under construction abroad equalled or surpassed that of all other types combined.[7] Naval engagements of the Sino–Japanese War had conveyed, too, many lessons to strategists and designers and had influenced to a degree the temporary subordination of the cruiser.

6 Navy Dept., Bureau of Construction and Repair Memorandum, October 18, 1915, in Herbert Papers; hereinafter cited as C & R Memo, 1915.
7 Navy Dept., *Annual Report*, 1895; New York *Times*, December 2, 1895.

The performance of this type at the Yalu River and Wei-hei-Wei did not measure up to that of the torpedo-boats engaged.

Theodore Roosevelt wrote Herbert in December of a letter he had received from an unidentified friend serving in China as a "European military attaché." The friend had seen the beaten Chinese fleet limping into Port Arthur, reported Roosevelt, "immediately after the big naval fight" at Yalu and had subsequently inspected the damage inflicted on its units by Japanese guns. "If it had not been for the excellent iron-clads, which did most of the fighting under control of foreigners," quoted Roosevelt, "not a ship would have returned." The attaché described the "havoc" aboard the Chinese men-of-war as "terrific." Everything above the water line had been "riddled with shells and splinters; decks . . . were spattered with blood . . . and you can imagine the stench in the filthy iron hulls heated by the sun."

This observer had reached several conclusions which Roosevelt relayed to Secretary Herbert. From what he had seen from Port Arthur, the attaché considered the most powerful unarmored cruisers incapable of outfighting ironclads, even though he found that armor-piercing shells had little effect on the former. As to ordnance, he concluded that rapid-fire guns up to six inches in caliber were "very effective," but that topside torpedo tubes had proved too vulnerable in action to be of value. His tour of the vanquished fleet convinced him of the absurdity of carrying small boats in combat; when hit, the boats were apt to disintegrate into splinters injurious to deck personnel. By the same token, he condemned the installation of woodwork on fighting ships; the extent of the damage caused by fire aboard Chinese warships ran in direct proportion to the amount of wood in their superstructures.[8]

The secretary's construction program for 1896 was affected by the findings of this and other observers of the war in Asia. Omitting cruisers for the second time, he recommended building two additional battleships and twelve more torpedo-boats. The House, which remained under Republican control, responded by voting with a rare degree of unanimity not two, but four, capital ships! Once again, the Senate reduced the number of battleships to two, owing to the determined opposition of Populist leaders. Nevertheless, following heated debate, a compromise measure was worked out by Senator Quay, with the assistance of Lodge

8 Roosevelt to Herbert, December 12, 1894, in Herbert Papers.

and Boutelle, authorizing three battleships and ten torpedo-boats. Congress enacted the modified bill on June 9, 1896.[9]

The battleships authorized by the act, the *Alabama*, *Illinois*, and *Wisconsin*, were designed to approximate the *Kentuckys* in displacement, firepower, and speed. The board of design, which began work on the new ships' plans during the Senate debates in May, submitted the completed, preliminary blueprints to Herbert on June 10. Expressing second thoughts about the superimposed turrets, which were under consideration for all five battleships, the board had found the scheme sound enough in theory but dangerous to apply at the time. The department had insufficient knowledge of the techniques required of gunners for avoiding the interference of gunfire from turrets situated atop one another. Urging further investigation of such safeguards in the near future, the board recommended a modified secondary battery for each of the five vessels, to consist of fourteen 6-inch guns in broadside. The main battery of four 13-inchers would be located as originally agreed in two double turrets, fore and aft. The secretary approved the modification on June 11, adding a memorandum to Admiral Walker concerning the elimination of woodwork from the hull plans.[10]

In general, the press favored the enactment of Herbert's program for 1896; some editors hailed it as a sure indication that Congress had at last aligned itself with Mahan's brand of naval expansion. The New York *Times* termed the program "moderate," and commented, "No more gunboats or cruisers are required, and Mr. Herbert's statistics from foreign navies sustain his present demand, which is only a regular installment of the scheme of construction adopted years ago." The *Times* editorial proceeded to praise Herbert for his capacity to absorb the lessons of the war in Asia and to profit from naval experimentation in Europe.[11]

The secretary's annual report presented a tabulation of the strength of the world's maritime powers in battleships of all classes. According to his figures, which reappeared in the St. Louis *Republic*, the United States stood sixth in 1896, with eleven capital ships building or authorized. Britain retained first place with fifty-seven in commission or under construction, followed by France with thirty-two, Russia with

9 Navy Dept., *Annual Report*, 1896; *Congressional Record*, 54th Cong., 1st Sess., 6195, 6326; Davis, *Second to None*, 89.
10 C & R Memo, 1915; Navy Dept., *Annual Report*, 1895; New York *World*, November 28, 1894.
11 New York *Times*, December 2, 1895.

eighteen, Italy with seventeen, and Germany with sixteen. Spain now ranked after the United States—on paper, at least—with three battleships, though the Spanish Navy boasted seven armored cruisers to America's two and five more torpedo-boats.[12]

British battleships of recent design, displacing from 12,450 to 15,000 tons, were heavier than their American counterparts. The newest of them, H.M.S. *Prince George*, had just passed her acceptance trials. The shipyards of England and Scotland were busily engaged in completing other types as well; they had within the year launched seven light cruisers and delivered four torpedo-boat destroyers—a type as yet unfamiliar in America.

Of the French battleships under construction at the time, the most formidable was the first of the *Gaulois* class, faster by one knot than the *Oregons*, about equal in tonnage, but less heavily armed. France launched two heavy cruisers in 1896, and the Ministry of Marine had on order one additional battleship and three light cruisers.

Third-ranking Russia commissioned two battleships during the year, the *Rotislav* and *Ssissoi Weliki*, for assignment to the Black Sea Fleet. Lighter than the *Alabamas*, these vessels were also slower and weaker in armament. Like other units of the contemporary Imperial Navy, they were outmatched by the men-of-war of modernized western fleets.

The intelligence data on which Herbert's analysis was based revealed the high potential of Japan's naval forces. Their experience in the war with China had induced the Japanese to abandon their former reliance on high-speed cruisers in favor of long-range capital ships. Following the conclusion in 1895 of the Treaty of Shimoneseki, which ratified the Japanese victory, Russian-inspired diplomacy compelled Japan to retrocede to China the Liaotung Peninsula, in violation of the treaty. Motivated by a desire for revenge on the Tsarist regime, therefore, the government in Tokyo placed orders abroad for six modern battleships.[13]

At home, in the meantime, the Navy Department had taken steps to supplement the fleet in case of war. Acting on the plan initiated by Tracy in 1893, Secretary Herbert had registered a number of merchantmen for emergency service as "casual cruisers." Over a dozen of

12 Navy Dept., *Annual Report*, 1896. See also, St. Louis *Republic*, December 6, 1896. The *Maine* and *Texas*, though soon to be reclassified as armored cruisers, were shown on the table as second-rate battleships.

13 Navy Dept., *Annual Report*, 1895. See also, D. E. Cummings, *Admiral Richard Wainwright and the U.S. Fleet* (Washington, 1962), 67ff. Wainwright served as chief intelligence officer at this time.

these auxiliaries were slated for wartime duty in the Atlantic, and nine more were subject to call for operations in the Pacific. To compensate their owners, the secretary had promised to award them mail subsidies.

But, Herbert pointed out, Congress had yet to appropriate sufficient funds to arm the registered merchant ships adequately. The sum of $400,000, which the department had received by virtue of the Act of 1895, fell short of the amount needed to pay for all the 4- and 6-inch guns destined for installation on these vessels. As a result, complained the secretary, owners of fast passenger liners such as the *Paris* and *New York* were drawing on their subsidies, even though the ships were still unfit for service in an emergency. Herbert appealed to Congress for additional money with which to rectify the situation as soon as possible.[14]

Hoping to obtain the manpower required for the auxiliary vessels, the secretary asked Congress to raise the legal allowance of regular seaman, to establish a federal reserve, and to support the state militia organizations which, by now, represented thirteen states on two coasts and on the Great Lakes. Congress ignored all but one of his requests; it continued to subsidize the militia units.[15]

Herbert's recommendations for 1897 differed somewhat from his previous construction programs. On the grounds that the battleships previously authorized drew too much water to permit them to enter Gulf coast ports, he requested Congress to vote three battleships having a maximum draft of twenty-two fleet. These vessels would have access to the harbors of Tampa, Pensacola, Mobile, and Key West, and to the eastern pass into the Mississippi, all of which were closed to the deeper-draft capital ships of foreign powers.

In addition, the secretary proposed construction of twelve torpedo-boats for the purpose of strengthening the United States in a type which was becoming increasingly popular in Europe. Less than a week before Herbert retired from office, Congress rejected his call for light-draft battleships and appropriated funds for building only three torpedo-boats.

14 Navy Dept., *Annual Report*, 1895; Philadelphia *Press*, November 28, 1894. According to the *Press*, Herbert was mistaken about the subsidies which, stated the editor, would not become operative prior to November, 1895. Cf. Baltimore *Sun* and New York *Times*, November 24, 1894. Since 1893, the following steamship lines had registered vessels with the Navy Department: the International Navigation Company, the Pacific Mail Line, the Red D Steamship Company, the Cuba Mail Line, and the Panama Railroad Company.

15 Navy Dept., *Annual Report*, 1896; Washington *Post*, December 1, 1895.

Apparently, congressmen were satisfied with the current state of the Navy.[16]

Predictably, Herbert's attempt to secure funds for what expansionist editors looked upon as a reasonable annual demand drew the applause of many newspapers, but not all representatives of the nation's press shared such enthusiasm. A Midwestern editor, taking issue with Herbert's "Social Darwinism," scoffed at the notion that the country would not "be safe until it has . . . a navy equal to that of any power in the world." On the contrary, he declared, "The very last thing we have to fear is a war, unless . . . we . . . provoke it. We have now a navy more than adequate for all possible needs." To expand the fleet further would be to encourage the growth of militarism—"a spirit destructive of American institutions, . . . a plain imitation of the worst evil which this government was created to escape." [17]

From the beginning of his term, Secretary Herbert had endeavored to economize wherever possible. He had saved money for the government by abolishing the speed-premium system which, in the interest of rapid construction, had in the past often enriched contractors with bonuses. But he refused to pinch pennies at the expense of national security, as his estimates attest. At the close of 1895, Herbert estimated the Navy's bill for new construction at $12,455,025, or $2,343,300 in excess of the appropriation for the same period. As his last fourteen months in office began, he projected expenditures totaling about $13,500,000, over $3,000,000 more than the last appropriation. He realized that, although the estimate for fiscal 1897 would be substantially less, his successor would receive the credit for cutting costs.[18]

The secretary's quest for economies which would reflect favorably on his own stewardship led him to question the prevailing price of armor plate. Discovering that the contract price and size of the orders placed with Bethlehem and Carnegie were identical, he concluded that the two had conspired to stifle competition. As he prepared to advertise

16 Navy Dept., *Annual Report*, 1896; New York *Evening Telegraph*, December 6, 1896; Philadelphia *Ledger and Daily Transcript*, December 7, 1896; St. Louis *Republic*, December 6, 1896. For the debates on the 1896 program, see *Congressional Record*, 54th Cong., 2nd Sess., 2115.
17 The article quoted in part appeared in St. Louis *Daily Globe*, December 7, 1896. For favorable comment on the program, see Washington *Post*, December 5, 1896; St. Louis *Republic*, December 6, 1896; Newark (N.J.) *News*, December 4, 1896.
18 Navy Dept., *Annual Report*, 1895, 1896; Washington *Post*, December 5, 1896; Herbert, "Grandfather's Talks," 344-45.

for new contracts in the summer of 1895, therefore, he informed both companies that they must reduce the current rate of $600 per ton. The demand was justified, said Herbert, because the contractors' profits had undoubtedly exceeded capital outlays on plant and equipment over the past four years. The steel producers responded with an offer to lower the unit price by $50, which Herbert considered unacceptable and so informed the chairmen of the congressional naval committees.

Having investigated the matter briefly, Congress directed Herbert on June 10, 1895, to ascertain the actual cost of forging armor plate and to determine a reasonable percentage of profit to the producers. When he questioned the steel executives about valuations of production costs, however, they refused to cooperate on the premise that the administration had no right to pry into legitimate business secrets.

By this time, Populist spokesmen in Congress had revealed certain information which they hoped would make an important public issue of the price of armor. First, they charged the steel companies with conspiracy to cheat the government and alleged that public officials were toadying to the firms' executives. In 1894, declared the Populists, the contractors had fraudulently supplied defective armor—an outrage which Cleveland tolerated to the extent of reducing to a token sum the fine demanded by the Navy. Then, the critics disclosed that Bethlehem had contracted to forge armor for the Russian Navy at $250 a ton, or less than half the unit price being paid by the department!

The pressure brought to bear on the secretary as a result of this revelation compelled him to resort to unorthodox methods. Unable to obtain cost and profit figures from domestic producers, and suspecting that steelmen had formed an "international combine," he resolved to undertake secret, personal inspections of European armor plants in hopes of finding the information he sought. What occurred during his trip abroad in the summer of 1896 confirmed his suspicion. Not only did he discover a Carnegie agent among his fellow passengers on the eastward passage, but his tours of British, French, and German plants brought him absurdly high estimates of production costs—valuations planted in advance for his benefit by the ubiquitous envoy from Carnegie, Phipps.

In France, the Minister of Marine informed Herbert that the armorers were in cahoots to suppress their cost figures and advised him to employ more devious means to accomplish his mission. Taking this suggestion to heart, Secretary Herbert hired a "secret broker" to pose as an agent for an armor-seeking government other than that of the United States.

Before sailing for home, Herbert instructed his "broker" to report to him through the American naval attaché at Paris, Lieutenant R. T. Rodgers.[19]

Following his return to Washington that autumn, the secretary received from his agent what seemed to be realistic estimates of foreign armor production costs, as well as related data forwarded by Rodgers from Paris. Comparing these figures with the inflated valuations he had seen in Europe, Herbert concluded that a unit price of about $400 would cover the contractors' costs and assure them a fair profit in the bargain. He informed the chairmen of the naval committees of his findings and recommended that the contract figure be adjusted accordingly, but Congress took no action on the price of armor prior to Herbert's retirement.[20]

The breakdown in the department's negotiations for new armor contracts, which congressional inaction prolonged, had grave implications for a maritime state beset with inflammatory situations in several areas of interest. To Mahan and other strategists, the vulnerability of Hawaii to foreign aggression posed the foremost threat to the United States. German policy by 1896 foreshadowed rapid naval expansion and territorial designs on Pacific islands. At the same time, Japan ranked second only to Great Britain in naval strength in the Pacific. To the strategists' fear of a British seizure of the islands, therefore, the more alarming prospect of German or Japanese annexation had been added, reinforcing Mahan's demand for reestablishment of the American protectorate.

Meanwhile, explosive developments in Nicaragua, Venezuela, and Cuba had presented the administration with additional complications. Any one of the crises arising in these countries might momentarily oblige Cleveland to invoke the Monroe Doctrine and to defend its principles by means of naval force.

In American eyes, Great Britain was responsible for two of the threats to hemispheric tranquility, the first of which had taken shape in January, 1895. Using the arrest of the British consul at Corinto, Nicaragua, as an excuse for forcing the Nicaraguan regime to satisfy outstanding debts to British nationals, Her Majesty's government had sent a nav-

19 Herbert, "Grandfather's Talks," 344–48. Cf. Newark *News*, December 5, 1896; Allard, "Influence upon Steel Industry," 113ff.

20 R. T. Rodgers to Herbert (marked "personal"), November 24, December 20, 1896, in Herbert Papers; Allard, "Influence upon Steel Industry," 114–17; Herbert, "Grandfather's Talks," 346–47.

al squadron with orders to land marines and seize the customs house. This power play provoked a hostile reaction in Washington especially among administration critics, who urged the President to uphold the Monroe Doctrine at any cost. Silverites and Anglophobes of all stripes joined expansionists in the clamor for action in defense of Nicaragua, but to no avail. Cleveland would not be stampeded; he refused to intervene.[21] At this, Henry Cabot Lodge berated the President for following a policy of retreat on all fronts, instead of setting a course which would bring the entire hemisphere—"from the Rio Grande to the Arctic Circle"—under the Stars and Stripes.[22] Then, as if to silence Lodge and his fellow interventionists, the British suddenly withdrew from Corinto.[23]

Despite the British withdrawal, Cleveland's opponents maintained their attack on his foreign policy. Alarmed at their strength and mindful of the oncoming elections, administration leaders cast about for a face-saving issue elsewhere. They quickly discovered a cause in the Anglo-Venezuelan dispute over the boundary of British Guiana—a long-standing controversy involving Venezuela's claim to gold-rich territory which had been transferred to Guiana owing to an arbitrary boundary adjustment made by a British surveyor.

A number of considerations induced President Cleveland to take Venezuela's part in the quarrel. In his opinion, the British were bullying a helpless South American state in defiance of the Monroe Doctrine. By entering the fray, therefore, Cleveland would not only be able to elevate national prestige in the hemisphere, but might also regain the popularity he had lost because of the continuing depression and the Corinto incident. Other factors influenced him too; he had read of imperialist agitation in France for settling the boundary issue by force, and he had heard rumors of German interest in acquiring a dependency in Latin America as soon as an opening materialized.[24]

21 N. M. Blake, "Background of Cleveland's Foreign Policy," *AHR*, XLVII (1942), *passim*; May, *Imperial Democracy*, 33-34, 69; Pratt, *Expansionists of 1898*, 209.

22 H. C. Lodge, "Our Blundering Foreign Policy," *Forum*, XXIII (March, 1895), 52-67.

23 Apparently Cleveland had advance information of Britain's intention to withdraw the squadron from Corinto; this knowledge partly conditioned his attitude in the matter. See Blake, "Cleveland's Foreign Policy," 115; May, *Imperial Democracy*, 33.

24 Pratt, *Expansionists of 1898*, 142ff.; May, *Imperial Democracy*, 34-38. For the official Venezuelan version of the history of the Guiana boundary dispute, see *The Printed Argument on behalf of the United States of Venezuela before the Tribunal of Arbitration* (London, 1899), *passim*; hereinafter cited as *Argument of*

Convinced of the rectitude of his attitude and, perhaps, over-confident of American sea power, the President expressed his support of Venezuela in the first of a lengthly exchange of notes with Britain's Prime Minister, Lord Salisbury. During the game of diplomatic maneuver that followed, Secretary of State Richard Olney—recently moved from the Department of Justice—conducted himself as aggressively as he had in the Pullman strike. He took the position that America had every right to intervene in a situation involving the Monroe Doctrine. Lord Salisbury rejected Olney's reasoning on the ground that the dispute concerned the boundary of a colony which had belonged to the British Empire "long before the Republic of Venezuela came into existence." [25]

Informing Congress on December 17, 1895, of Salisbury's refusal to submit the matter to arbitration, Cleveland announced that Olney had served notice on Britain of America's determination to resist with force any attempt by a European power to impose its will on Venezuela. Olney had made this clear at the conclusion of his note: "Today the United States is practically sovereign on this continent, and its fiat is law upon the subjects to which it confines its interposition." [26]

During the weeks before Salisbury's reply to this message reached Washington, excitement gripped the nation. The President's firm stand won him the backing of imperialists who, like Mahan, hailed the "awakening of our countrymen to the fact that we must soon come out of our isolation. . . ." [27] The passage of the Navy Act of 1896 reflected the congressional reaction to the surge of enthusiasm for naval expansion that accompanied the epidemic of Anglophobia spreading across the country. The merits of Venezuela's case mattered little; Americans were feeling their oats to the extent of welcoming the warlike utterances of such patriots as Theodore Roosevelt, who challenged the British to send their warships: "Let them come, let them bombard our cities. We will take Canada if they do!" [28]

Venezuela. An objective, condensed interpretation appears in Moore, Principles of American Diplomacy, 246–51. See Blake, "Cleveland's Foreign Policy," passim.
25 Quoted in Pratt, Foreign Policy, 349.
26 A. B. Hart, "The Monroe Doctrine in Its Territorial Extent and Application," NIP, XXXII (1906), 788; Moore, Principles of American Diplomacy, 248, quoting Olney.
27 Herrick, "Tracy's Navy," 315; Livezey, Mahan on Sea Power, 109, quoting Mahan.
28 Quoted in Millis, Arms and Men, 167. For interpretations of the clamor raised against Great Gritain, see Pratt, Expansionists of 1898, 209ff.; May, Imperial Democracy, 34–37.

The uproar subsided quickly with the arrival of the prime minister's reply in January, 1896, consenting to Cleveland's demand for arbitration of the boundary quarrel. Salisbury's decision to yield, which had its roots in Europe's opposition to Britain's South African policy, indicated his willingness to sacrifice a relatively trivial advantage to Guiana in order to improve Anglo-American relations. Predictably, Salisbury's countermarch was interpreted in the United States as a surrender which would surely boost American prestige in Latin America and Europe.[29]

Subsequently, the Anglo-Venezuelan controversy came before an international tribunal in Paris, where former President Harrison and General Tracy served as counsel to the government of Venezuela. The tribunal, after hearing both sides of the case, decided to make minor readjustments to the boundary, favoring the Venezuelans in principle and the British in fact.[30]

Prior to Lord Salisbury's concession to Cleveland, an insurrection in Cuba had begun to make headlines in American newspapers. The revolt, which imperialists seized upon as a substitute for Venezuela's cause, had evolved as the ultimate protest to Spanish misrule. The ministry in Madrid had since 1878 been promising to reform the harsh colonial regime on the island but, aside from abolishing slavery, had done little to alleviate the suffering of most Cubans. Spain had forced them to assume the cost of the Ten Years' War, had subjected them to extortion on the part of colonial officials, and had taxed their exports to the point of extinction. Then, in 1894, the United States Congress scheduled a tax on imported raw sugar which, on top of Spanish exactions, produced unbearable economic hardships in Cuba.[31]

When the Cuban nationalists resorted to armed force, Cleveland adopted a serenely conservative outlook, amid popular demonstrations of support for the rebels. Probably to build up circulation, the papers of William Randolph Hearst and Joseph Pulitzer exploited the rebellion, stirring American emotions with one-sided stories of Spanish atrocities. The accounts appearing in the yellow press found a ready response among readers traditionally dedicated to the underdog's fight for liberty.

Inasmuch as Americans of all political beliefs found common ground

---

29 *Argument of Venezuela,* "Frontispiece," iii-xxi; Dulles, *America's Rise to World Power,* 20–32; Pratt, *Foreign Policy,* 347–52.

30 *Argument of Venezuela,* 1–9.

31 Pratt, *Expansionists of 1898,* 209–11. The Ten Year's War ended in a Spanish victory over the Cuban insurgents.

in their sympathy for the oppressed Cubans, indignation at alleged Spanish cruelty ran even higher than had resentment of British arrogance toward Venezuela. Distaste for Spain's colonial policy led humanitarians and liberals of varying degrees to rally around the banner of the new Manifest Destiny in unwonted harmony with imperialists, navalists, and commercial expansionists. After all, was not the acquisition of superior sea power and overseas bases essential to national survival and, therefore, a moral and patriotic duty? And did not the natural law entitle America to round out its boundaries and thus enlarge the sphere of freedom and democracy wherever possible?

The massive affirmative response to these questions ruled out objective analysis of Cuba's plight. Besides, the nation's faith in the Navy's ability to enforce the Monroe Doctrine had already generated a spirit of reckless belligerence.[32] Congress articulated this sentiment in 1896 when both chambers adopted a resolution for Cuban self-rule, and again when the House voted four battleships. Congressional navalists were making the most of the "revival of nationalism."[33]

By autumn, the presidential campaigns were in full swing. The Republican platform reasserted the principles of the Monroe Doctrine, demanded peace and independence for Cuba, and called for an increase in naval power. In addition, declared the party's leaders, construction of a transisthmian canal should begin soon and, to provide bastions for its defense, Hawaii and the Danish West Indies must be brought under American control. The Democrats confined their foreign policy plank to an expression of sympathy for the Cuban nationalists. Emphasizing domestic policy, the Democratic spokesmen referred to naval expansion not at all.

The Republicans won the November elections handily. Their nominee, William McKinley, received 600,000 more votes than William Jennings Bryan, the candidate of both the Democratic and Populist parties. At the same time, the Republicans gained substantial majorities in the Senate and House.

Although the Republican sweep appeared to represent a mandate for extending the battleship program, shrewd political observers thought otherwise. In the first place, despite the strong naval plank in the party's platform, campaign orators had barely mentioned the Navy in their desire to defeat the silverites. Secondly, the President-elect displayed no

32 *Ibid.*
33 *Congressional Record,* 54th Cong., 1st Sess., 854, 965, 1016, 3240-42.

interest in naval expansion or extraterritorial acquisitions. As a congressman, McKinley had devoted himself to currency and tariff problems,
to the exclusion of foreign and naval affairs. And, as his inauguration
neared, he showed no inclination to take other than an isolationist
position. For these reasons, the Navy's immediate prospects seemed
dim.[34]

Amid the alarming developments in the Pacific and Caribbean, and
the excitement of the election, the climate within the Navy Department
remained one of business as usual. Perceiving the grave implications
of the Cuban struggle, Secretary Herbert had anticipated trouble by
ordering his squadrons to maintain a high degree of combat readiness.
In view of the distant operations required of the Asiatic Squadron,
which Herbert had reinforced as a security measure during the Sino-
Japanese War, he had instituted a rotation plan designed to keep the
squadron constantly at full strength. In accordance with the plan, the
department held in reserve on the Pacific coast certain units to be used
to relieve ships regularly attached to the Asiatic Station, which were
due for refitting at Mare Island. Prompted by the presence of a Spanish
force at Manila, the secretary had continued this policy after Japan
and China had made peace.[35]

By July, 1896, Secretary Herbert had become equally concerned for
the security of the Caribbean. As he said in consultation with Secretary
of State Olney, additional warships should be deployed in this area
which, if an international war evolved from the insurrection in Cuba,
would surely be a major zone of naval operations. On the other hand,
as both men realized, a conspicuous increase in the number of American
men-of-war stationed in the Caribbean might provoke rash Spanish
action to counter the move. This dilemma, which carried over to the
McKinley administration, compelled Herbert to weigh carefully every
assignment he contemplated for the sector in question.

Shortly after Herbert had discussed the matter with Olney, Cleveland's consul general in Havana, Fitzhugh Lee, dispatched to the State
Department a request for naval assistance in case mob violence threatened

34 Margaret Leech, *In the Days of McKinley* (New York, 1959), 144ff.; Sprout,
Naval Power, 224.
35 Herbert, "Grandfather's Talks," 342. Here Herbert adds a note: "Secretary
Long, my successor, in his history of the Navy . . . notices this act of mine and
gives me credit for foreseeing and providing against the war that then seemed to
be possible in the near future." See Long, *New Navy*, II, 152–61.

American interests in the capital city. He asked Olney "to have a man-of-war at Key West under a discreet officer, with a full complement of marines." Showing the message to Herbert, Olney expressed doubt as to the wisdom of complying. Since Lee wanted the commanding officer of this ship placed directly under his control and in readiness to proceed to Havana, and at his "request . . . drop anchor in this harbor," declared Olney, the proposition "does not at first blush strike me favorably." Herbert agreed and thus ended the first of several premature calls from Lee for naval protection.[36]

Later in the month, Assistant Secretary McAdoo brought up the question of departmental reorganization, to which the threat of war arising from the Cuban crisis had lent new urgency. In an address delivered at the War College, McAdoo referred to the "anomalous situation" of a civilian unfamiliar with the Navy having "unquestioned control of a military organization, hedged about with questions of the most technical . . . character." Recognizing the delicacy of the relationship between the uninformed civilian chief and his naval subordinates, the assistant secretary pointed out that all concerned must behave with the utmost tact—a quality which he advised his listeners to add to the list of attributes expected of naval officers.[37]

To better the lot of the civilian administrator, McAdoo recommended the establishment of a standing board of highly competent, experienced officers who would advise the secretary as necessary on military and technical matters. The board might in time, he observed, mature as an essential central agency, similar to the British Board of Admiralty. In conclusion, the assistant secretary proposed to complement this body by creating a "Board for the Military Defense of the United States," to be headed by the secretaries of the armed forces and staffed by military and naval officers who would coordinate strategic planning to insure the nation against aggression on land or sea.[38]

Meanwhile, the congressional committee which had investigated the system of officer promotion had submitted its report. Although hampered by testimony "having a very remote bearing if any on naval efficiency," the committee had produced a thorough appraisal of the subject. Its findings presented the department with three options: pro-

36 Navy Dept., *Annual Report*, 1896; Olney to Herbert (marked "personal"), July 14, 1896, in Herbert Papers.
37 Extracts from McAdoo's address appear in *NIP*, XXII (1896), 432ff.
38 *Ibid.*, 433.

motion by selection; retirement by selection; or retirement on the basis of age in grade.[39]

A contemporary student of naval administration judged any one of these choices workable if properly managed by the department. Whichever alternative was selected, he suggested, a fifth year should be added to the undergraduate course at the Naval Academy. This would have the dual advantage of allowing additional time for advanced instruction of midshipmen, and of easing the blockage of lower grades by retarding the commissioning of new ensigns.

As to the condition of enlisted personnel, the writer expressed mixed emotions. He accused officers of treating their men with unnecessary harshness in too many instances, even though by 1896 more than 70 per cent of the bluejackets were native-born Americans. He also denounced the employment of marines as shipboard police on the grounds that it injured morale and precluded the development of a sense of responsibility and self-respect among seamen.[40] Such complaints were probably justified, but it should be noted that the process of humanizing life aboard men-of-war was perforce a lengthy one. The lash had disappeared, but it would be a while yet before motion pictures and soda fountains boarded naval vessels to brighten the days of sailors at sea.[41]

Secretary Herbert arrived in Newport aboard the *Dolphin* on August 9 to deliver his final speech to the faculty and students of the War College. On this occasion, he reiterated his admiration for the work of the College, with special emphasis on the institution's vital role in the formulation of plans for offensive and defensive operations. Recalling Captain Taylor's closing address in 1894, the secretary concluded his remarks with the reminder that all weapons—however perfect—depended on skillful hands to operate them.[42]

As Herbert began drafting the last of his annual reports in the following month, he took great satisfaction in noting the rate of progress in delivery of new warships since Cleveland's inauguration in March, 1893. An impressive number of additions to the fleet, he announced, had entered active service or were nearing completion in various yards —public and private.[43]

The first of these to be commissioned, the armored cruiser *New*

39 W. F. Fullam, "The Organization of Naval Personnel," *NIP*, XXII (1896), 83; Navy Dept., *Annual Report*, 1896.
40 Fullam, "Naval Personnel," 84ff.
41 *Ibid.*, 94.
42 For Herbert's address of August 10, 1896, see *NIP*, XXII (1896), 574–75.
43 Navy Dept., *Annual Report*, 1896.

York, hoisted her colors in August, 1893.[44] The next year witnessed the commissioning of the four protected cruisers *Columbia, Cincinnati, Raleigh*, and *Minneapolis*, plus four monitors and an armored ram.[45] America's first battleships, the second-rates *Texas* and *Maine*, lit off boilers in 1895 for their shakedown cruises. The formidable *Olympia* headed for sea in the same year in company with three other light cruisers of the *Marblehead* class and three heavy gunboats.[46] By January, 1897, the first-rate battleships *Oregon, Massachusetts*, and *Indiana* would receive their orders to active duty. In the final phase of construction lay the experimental submarine *Plunger*, sixteen torpedo-boats, and six 1,000-ton gunboats of the *Wheeling* class. The combined tonnage displaced by the ships activated during the second Cleveland administration amounted to more than 117,000 tons.[47]

Of the vessels authorized during Herbert's term, the battleships *Kearsarge, Kentucky*, and *Illinois* were under construction in the yards of the Newport News Shipbuilding and Drydock Company. In Philadelphia, constructors at Cramps and Sons' yard worked on the unfinished hull of the *Alabama*. The Pacific Coast had claimed the *Wisconsin*, whose contract the secretary had awarded to the Union Iron Works in San Francisco. All five of the capital ships were scheduled for delivery between September and December, 1899. [48]

Four of the cruisers commissioned while Herbert held office crossed the Atlantic in the summer of 1895 to participate in an international review sponsored by the German Ministry of Marine at the Kaiser's instigation. Secretary Herbert had detailed the *New York, Columbia, San Francisco*, and *Marblehead* to represent the United States in this event, which commemorated the official opening of the Kiel Canal. Inasmuch as all of these cruisers had been laid down or launched during General Tracy's administration, Herbert invited the general to attend the review aboard one of them. As he wrote in a gracious note to Tracy, "Certainly you are entitled if anyone is, to be upon these ships when they are presented to the world." [49]

Secretary Herbert yielded his authority to John Davis Long in March,

44 *Ibid.*, 1893.
45 *Ibid.*, 1894.
46 *Ibid.*, 1895.
47 *Ibid.*, 1896. As recently as January, 1941, the *Wheeling* was berthed at the City of New York's Sanitation Department Pier on the East River, serving as a naval reserve center.
48 *Ibid.*, 1896; *NIP*, XXII (1896), 820; F. T. Jane, *The World's Fighting Ships, 1904, 1905* (London, 1905), "United States Navy," *passim*.
49 Herbert to Tracy, May 29, 1895, in Tracy Papers.

1897. In sum, the Alabaman's management of the Navy throughout the troubled years of depression, social unrest, and external crises that made up Cleveland's second term had demonstrated his energy, ability, and flexibility. The success of the construction program in 1895 and 1896 gave him ample reason for satisfaction. The fruits of that program had rendered the United States capable of standing up to the lesser of the traditional naval powers of Europe for the first time in history. The fleet had, since the spring of 1893, risen from ninth to sixth place among the navies of the world. For this advance, Hilary Herbert was in large measure responsible.

X

THE SEEDS OF WAR

PRESIDENT McKINLEY INHERITED GRAVE PROBLEMS FROM THE
second Cleveland administration. The depression at home persisted and, though business would revive in the summer of
1897, the economic outlook remained bleak in March as the
new President delivered his inaugural address. The nation's foreign trade
fared no better. In the Far East, American commerce had expanded
rapidly with the emergence of British cooperation in the wake of the
Guiana boundary settlement. Now businessmen were finding their prospects jeopardized by the ruthless drive of European powers for exclusive
concessions in China, in defiance of the open-door principle.[1] Even less
secure was the national investment in Cuba, which had risen to some
$33,000,000 since 1878. With the island in the throes of rebellion, the
value of this equity became more dubious every day. Yet McKinley
had come to office promising to restore prosperity and to take any step
short of war to terminate the Cuban conflict.[2]

Sharing his predecessor's desire, if not his resolution, to keep the
peace, President McKinley resisted the growing demand for armed intervention in Cuba, which the yellow press and the Cuban *junta* were
doing their best to nourish with propaganda. As public demonstrations
of sympathy for the Cuban nationalists increased, he tried to placate

1 La Feber, *New Empire*, 325-27; J. W. Pratt, "American Business and the
Spanish-American War," *HAHR*, XIV (May, 1934), 163ff.
2 Pratt, *Expansionists of 1898*, 212.

the jingoes on the one hand and reassure the Spanish government on the other.

In a sense, McKinley was more of an isolationist than Cleveland. Like the latter, he would countenance "no jingo nonsense . . . no plot to annex Hawaii," as he informed Carl Schurz. But, though Cleveland had opposed resuming the battleship program before 1896 as an economic safeguard, his successor opposed heavy naval construction as a matter of policy. A large battle fleet, declared McKinley, might involve the country in dangerous "foreign complications," which he hoped above all to avoid.[3]

The President's choice of John Davis Long as secretary of the navy reflected this opinion of naval expansion. Long, an amiable and scholarly politician, was the last man to favor costly construction for imperialist purposes. Fifty-nine at the time of his appointment, the new secretary had served three terms as governor of Massachusetts. A graduate of Harvard College and Harvard Law School, he had practiced law privately until he first moved to the State House. Long's biographer describes him as honest, efficient, and pedestrian, and "too wise to endeavor to master the intricacies" of his department. The ex-governor's readiness to delegate responsibility to his naval subordinates made him popular with the bureau chiefs and tended to reduce the tension that usually affected intradepartmental relations. But his administration marked a sharp departure from the pattern set by Tracy and followed by Herbert, both of whom had promoted as strenuously as possible a program aimed at providing the bases necessary to service the fleet.[4]

Forward-looking naval officers viewed the next four years with alarm. It appeared to them, at a crucial time for America, that the Navy would be operating under the auspices of men whose isolationist tendencies might usher in a new era of stagnation. When Secretary Long named the ultraconservative Captain A. S. Crowninshield chief of the Bureau of Navigation before the year was out, the progressives felt that their worst fears were confirmed.[5]

Seen in retrospect, the satisfaction of McKinley and Long with the state of the Navy seems reasonable. The fleet had grown substantially

3 McKinley is quoted in Pratt, *Foreign Policy*, 373. See also, Sprout, *Naval Power*, 224.

4 See sketch of Long in *DAB*, XI, 377–78. Another biographical sketch appears in the Boston *Transcript*, August 30, 1915. Among his scholarly accomplishments as an undergraduate at Harvard, Long translated the *Aeneid* into English blank verse.

5 *Messages and Papers*, XIII, 6268–69; Navy Dept., *Annual Report*, 1897, 1899; H. C. Lodge (ed.), *Selections from the Correspondence of Theodore Roosevelt and*

in size and quality since 1890, and five battleships were still under construction. Like many of their contemporaries, they thought the existing squadrons adequate to any mission the Navy would normally be expected to accomplish. Furthermore, in the unlikely event of a war with Spain, they had Herbert's assurance of the fleet's preparedness.[6]

The Republican-controlled Congress, though warlike in tone, concurred in the administration's aversion to spending money on additional battleships and authorized only three torpedo-boats and a training ship in 1897. During the special session late in the year, congressmen acted again in the interest of economy by voting to lower the contract price for armor plate, as Herbert had recommended in the preceding autumn. Instead of setting the price at $400 per ton, however, the House and Senate agreed on $300, which was $300 less than the figure specified in the contracts awarded by Whitney and Tracy, and $100 less than the unit price Herbert had proposed as the minimum acceptable to the contractors. Perhaps in anticipation of the armorers' rejection of this offer, Congress directed Secretary Long to draft plans for a naval forging plant, but did not appropriate funds to finance its construction.

Both Bethlehem and Carnegie refused to forge armor for the Navy at $300 a ton; and the stalemate continued until May 8, 1898, when the pressure of the war with Spain forced Congress to raise the figure to $413. This adjustment satisfied the contractors and enabled Long to order 37,000 tons of armor plate needed for the *Alabamas* and other unfinished men-of-war.[7]

Before the McKinley administration was fairly underway, congressional expansionists attacked the President's standpat attitude. In mid-March, Henry Cabot Lodge chided the government for failing to follow up Harrison's negotiations with Denmark for the purchase of the Danish West Indies and demanded an inquiry to ascertain the price and availability of the islands which he regarded as excellent sites for naval stations.[8] Other imperialists reopened the canal question, while a third bloc called on the President to renew overtures with Santo Domingo for a lease of Samaná Bay.[9]

Henry Cabot Lodge (New York, 1925), I, 263, 268; hereinafter cited as Lodge (ed.), *Selections*. Crowninshield was an old friend of Boss Platt; see Herrick, "Tracy's Navy," 157.

6 Herbert, "Grandfather's Talks," 342, in Herbert Papers; Navy Dept., *Annual Report*, 1897.

7 Allard, "Influence upon Steel Industry," 118ff.; Herbert, "Grandfather's Talks," 347, in Herbert Papers.

8 Tansill, *Danish West Indies*, 209; Pratt, *Expansionists of 1898*, 221.

9 S. Welles, *Naboth's Vineyard*, II, 528–29; Pratt, *Expansionists of 1898*, 222.

Of all the navalists in Congress, Lodge was the most active in the early months of the McKinley era. His belief in Mahan's theory of naval warfare, which he shared with Theodore Roosevelt, led him to doubt the capacity of Secretary Long for effective leadership of the Navy during a period of international tension which might well culminate in a war with a ranking maritime power. Accordingly, in December, 1896, he had visited the President-elect in Canton, Ohio, with the intention of persuading him to appoint Roosevelt assistant secretary. After a lengthy discussion, McKinley reluctantly promised to place one of the country's leading jingoes in what was to become a highly sensitive office.[10]

Roosevelt's brief stint in the department revealed him as an energetic administrator who combined an almost juvenile enthusiasm for the Navy with a flair for showmanship. The self-confident leader of an influential coterie of imperialists, Roosevelt possessed the headstrong traits of a militant patriot not content with pursuing a line of conduct other than one of his own choosing.

The benign magnetism of two uncles on his mother's side of the family accounted largely for his interest in sea power. Enchanted by tales of the Bullock brothers' exploits in the Confederate Navy, Roosevelt had begun work on *The Naval War of 1812* during his senior year at Harvard. This book, in which the author perceived the fallacies inherent in the naval policy of the past, was first published in 1883 and ran through four of its eight editions within two years! [11] Subsequently, Roosevelt wrote a review of Mahan's *magnum opus* for the *Atlantic Monthly* in which he endorsed the captain's ideas wholeheartedly. The young author's opinions were plainly those of an assertive imperialist determined to see his country attain the front rank of world powers.[12]

---

10 Roosevelt, *Autobiography*, 224; M. L. Storer, "How Theodore Roosevelt Was Appointed Assistant Secretary of the Navy," *Harper's Weekly*, LVI (June 11, 1912), 9. For a recent account, see H. K. Beale, *Theodore Roosevelt and the Rise of America to World Power* (Baltimore, 1956), 55; hereinafter cited as Beale, *Roosevelt and the Rise of America*. See also, New York *Sun*, December 6, 1896. Lodge had Tom Platt's support in his effort to have Roosevelt named assistant secretary.

11 Henry F. Pringle, *Theodore Roosevelt* (New York, 1956), 119ff. Roosevelt's book is considered authoritative today, despite the challenge of Mahan's *Sea Power in Its Relations to the War of 1812*, which appeared two years after the publication in New York of the eighth edition of Roosevelt's work.

12 Roosevelt, "Review of *The Influence of Sea Power upon History*," *Atlantic Monthly* (October, 1890), 567. See also, *Political Science Quarterly*, IX (March, 1894), 171.

Roosevelt's friendship with Mahan began in 1888, when the former came to the War College to deliver a lecture on the War of 1812. The two became frequent correspondents thereafter and before long found they had reached similar conclusions as to the means of raising national prestige to the level they desired. In April, 1897, Mahan, who had retired from active service two years earlier, was in London arranging for the publication of his biography of Lord Nelson when he learned about Roosevelt's appointment to the Navy Department. Delighted by the news, he wrote his friend at once, congratulating him and urging him to work vigorously for the annexation of Hawaii which, in the captain's view, the growth of Japan's naval power had rendered essential.[13]

Mahan's ideas concerning the direction of foreign and naval policy had long since won acceptance among Roosevelt's imperialist friends in Washington and New York, who supported the new assistant secretary's campaign to apply the captain's doctrine to current naval preparations. Among Roosevelt's cohorts were politicians, statesmen, prominent individuals in private life, and a generous sprinkling of naval officers—both active and retired. At the head of the list stood Mahan and Lodge, followed by two New England Republican veterans, Senators William E. Chandler and William Frye, and a trio of diplomatists, John Hay, Henry White, and William Rockhill. Representing the legal profession were General Tracy, now a partner of Coudert Brothers, a highly respected law firm in New York, and Judge William Howard Taft of the sixth federal circuit court. Historians Brooks and Henry Adams gave the circle an intellectual tone, while Charles Dana and Dr. Albert Shaw furnished outlets for its propagandizing in the editorial columns of the New York *Sun* and the *Review of Reviews*, respectively. The ranking naval member of the clique was retired Rear Admiral Luce; officers on active service included Commanders Richard Wainwright and Charles H. Davis. The latter had recently taken over the post of chief intelligence officer from Wainwright, who had been assigned to the *Maine* as Captain Charles D. Sigsbee's executive officer.

Probably because McKinley wanted to place the more outspoken

13 Puleston, *Mahan*, 182; Beale, *Roosevelt and the Rise of America*, 55–56, citing Mahan to Roosevelt, May 10, 1897, in Roosevelt Papers, Division of Manuscripts, Library of Congress; various letters of Roosevelt to Lodge, Luce, and Mahan, 1895–97, in E. E. Morison and J. H. Blum (eds.), *The Letters of Theodore Roosevelt* (Cambridge, Mass., 1951–54), I, *passim*. Mahan's *Life of Nelson: The Embodiment of the Sea Power of Great Britain* was published again by a Boston firm in 1899.

imperialists where they could do the least damage, he appointed several of the assistant secretary's friends to diplomatic positions overseas. Rockhill, for instance, became minister to Greece, while Hay and White went to London, the former as ambassador to the Court of St. James and the latter as legation secretary.[14]

Once established in the Navy Department, Roosevelt embarked on a campaign for additional battleships, in the course of which he startled his superiors with his forthright declarations of expansionist aims. Speaking before an audience at the Naval War College on June 2, 1897, the young administrator presented a forceful argument for building a large battle fleet. "It is certain," he maintained, "that we need a first-class navy, not merely a navy for defense." If the nation would—as it must —sustain the Monroe Doctrine, an offensive fleet was needed at once, for "we must trust to the ships whose business it is to fight and not to run. Diplomacy is utterly useless where there is no force behind it; the diplomat is the servant, not the master of the soldier." Admitting that he did not regard war as an unmitigated evil, Roosevelt assured his listeners that he favored sea power "not primarily to fight but to avert fighting." As a case in point, he referred to General Tracy's intensive naval preparations "six years ago," which had strongly influenced the peaceful outcome of the controversy with Chile.[15]

The assistant secretary's emphasis on force as a deterrent rather than an instrument of imperialism, did not wholly square with his personal convictions. In his reply to Mahan's exhortation concerning Hawaii, which he wrote prior to the address at Coasters' Harbor, Roosevelt expressed his desire to employ the fleet for the purpose of annexing Hawaii.

If I had my way, we would seize those islands tomorrow. . . . I have been getting matters in shape on the Pacific Coast just as fast as I have been allowed. My own belief is that we should act instantly before the two new Japanese warships leave England.

I would hoist our flag over the islands, leaving all details for after action. I believe we should build the Nicaraguan canal at once, and . . . build a dozen new battleships, half of them on the Pacific Coast. . . . I am fully alive to the danger from Japan.[16]

14 E. R. May, *Imperial Democracy* (New York, 1961), 122; Beale, *Roosevelt and the Rise of America*, 55; Tyler Dennett, *John Hay: From Poetry to Politics* (New York, 1933), 179; Allan Nevins, *Henry White* (New York, 1930), 120.

15 The June address at Newport appears in *NIP*, XXIII (1897).

16 Roosevelt to Mahan, May 3, 1897, in Morison and Blum (eds.), *Letters of*

Roosevelt was not alone in his concern for the future of Hawaii. The Dole regime's immigration policy had, by the summer of 1897, created an inflammatory situation which Japan might attempt to resolve momentarily by sending men-of-war to Honolulu. The Hawaiian government, alarmed by the rapid growth of Japanese immigration and commerce in the islands, had not only barred further immigration but had returned about a thousand Japanese coolies to their homeland. At this, the government in Tokyo lodged an official protest and thereby unwittingly handed American imperialists an excuse for reopening the question of annexation.

Thus armed, Roosevelt and Lodge moved to bring the Republic of Hawaii under the eagle's wing. Finding Secretary of State John Sherman cool to their proposal, they appealed directly to the President. To their surprise, McKinley seemed receptive to annexation. He had concluded privately that a gesture in this direction would appease the imperialists and at the same time distract public attention from the Cuban crisis. Apparently secure in the belief that the Senate would not ratify, the President sent a signed treaty of annexation to that body on June 16. The elderly secretary of state, who remained unaware of his chief's reversal even after the administration had commenced negotiation with the Hawaiian government, assured the Japanese minister of America's intention to respect the sovereignty of the island republic.

As McKinley had expected, the Senate took no action on the treaty. The administration then placed the matter before the public and notified the Japanese government of the pending agreement. Japan protested again, in a note to which the State Department replied that the decision to annex Hawaii implied no threat of aggression or further American territorial aspirations in the Pacific.[17]

While Sherman sought to soothe the Japanese through diplomatic channels, the Navy Department prepared warships in the Pacific to apply more forceful persuasion if necessary. Secretary Long issued secret orders to his squadron commander at Pearl Harbor, instructing him to promote amicable relations with the Japanese in Honolulu, if possible. If not, the commander was to hoist the Stars and Stripes and proclaim a protectorate. In addition, Long warned his attaché at Yoka-

---

Theodore Roosevelt, I. The assistant secretary made a second appeal for naval expansion in the same vein in an address he delivered late in July to the Ohio Naval Militia. The speech is reprinted in New York *Herald*, July 24, 1897.

17 Pratt, *Expansionists of 1898*, p. 57; Bemis, *Secretaries of State*, IX, 34.

hama to keep the department informed of Japanese naval movements and directed the commanding officer of the *Oregon*—then in Puget Sound—to prepare his ship for a speedy passage to Pearl Harbor on short notice.[18]

Long's precautions in this instance proved unnecessary. Sherman's diplomacy, abetted by the progressive exclusion of Japan from the China trade at the hands of Russia and Germany, served to dissipate the crisis as June ended. When three units of the Pacific Squadron entered Pearl Harbor a month later, the Japanese cruiser on station merely exchanged routine courtesies with the Americans.[19]

Was the Japanese Navy as much of a threat in 1897 as Mahan and Roosevelt believed? At the time, Japan had only two battleships in commission: the second-rate, 7,300-ton *Chin Yen*, which had been captured in the recent war with China, and the third-rate *Fuso* of 3,800 tons displacement. Neither ship possessed significant firepower or speed. Two new semiarmored cruisers, the *Suma* and *Akashi*, of Japanese design and construction, offered a slightly greater challenge. Displacing 2,700 tons, each of these warships mounted two 6-inch rifles and could sustain speeds up to 19 knots. Six older light cruisers, of from 2,400 to 3,700 tons, completed the list of battle-worthy units. They accounted for the international character of the Japanese fleet; two came from Britain, two from France, one from Japan, and the sixth—formerly the *Esmeralda*—had been purchased from Chile.[20]

What bothered Mahan and Roosevelt was the Japanese naval potential as measured by the battleships on order in British shipyards. The 12,300-ton *Fuji* which, with her sister ship the *Yashima*, was scheduled for delivery within a year, had a designed speed of 15 knots and mounted four 12-inch guns. Two additional capital ships also on order but not as near completion, the *Shikishima* and *Asahi*, carried equivalent armament on a displacement of 15,000 tons and would travel at 18 knots at flank speed. Last on the roster of warships under construction were

18 Navy Dept., Ciphers Sent, I, 461, Navy Arch; Long to Commander, Pacific Station, July 12, 1897, in Confidential Correspondence, II, 314–317, Navy Arch.

19 Navy Dept., *Annual Report*, 1897; Leech, *McKinley*, 146–47; John A. Garraty, *Henry Cabot Lodge: A Biography* (New York, 1953), 199; La Feber, *New Empire*, 364; Philadelphia *Press*, January 10, 1898. The Japanese cruiser at Pearl Harbor was commanded by the redoubtable Captain—later Admiral—Togo.

20 R. N. Ballard, *The Influence of the Sea on the Political History of Japan* (New York, 1921), Tables I and II.

two 4,700-ton cruisers of the *Asama* class, which would soon be launched by yards in the United States! [21]

Hence, though Japan had in the summer of 1897 no vessel to match the *Maine* or *Texas*—not to mention the *Oregons*—the ambitious plans of Tokyo's Ministry of Marine could not be ignored by the Navy Department. When commissioned and manned by seamen whose high degree of training and morale had helped overcome the numerically superior Chinese at the Yalu and at Wei-hei-Wei, units of the Japanese Navy of the future would pose a challenge to every naval force in the Pacific. [22]

As soon as Americans realized that the Hawaiian crisis had evaporated, they turned their attention back to Cuba. Pleased as he was by the outcome of the diplomatic exchange with Tokyo, McKinley now felt it wise to encourage the imperialists in Congress to debate such old issues as the isthmian canal and naval expansion in order to divert the public and thus gain time to find a way out of the Cuban maze. [23]

Despite the outbreak of anti-American riots on the streets of Madrid, the Queen Regent and her principal ministers were as eager as President McKinley was to avoid war over Cuba. [24] In May, eight weeks before he was murdered by an anarchist at San Sebastian, Conservative Premier Antonio Canovas made his position clear to newsmen. "If, over and above what exists, we were to add 30,000 . . . Americans on that island, the great fleet, and all the power of that republic, what would be our fate?" [25]

Canovas' successor, the Liberal Praxedes Mateo Sagasta, risked civil war in Spain to meet the demands of the United States and several European powers for reform of the colonial regime in Cuba. [26] Replacing the unpopular author of the reconcentration system, Governor Valeriano Weyler, with Captain-General Ramon Blanco y Erenas, Sagasta promised to liberate American captives on the island and to

21 *Ibid.* When originally ordered, the *Asamas* were classified as battleships. E. A. Falk, biographer of Robley Evans, presents an interesting study of Japan's naval development up to the termination of the final naval disarmament conference prior to World War II in *Togo and the Rise of Japanese Sea Power* (New York, 1936).
22 For a reliable British evaluation, see H. W. Wilson, *Battleships in Action* (New York, 1928), I, 114–15.
23 May, *Imperial Democracy*, 122–23.
24 *Ibid.*, 106.
25 *Ibid.*, citing Madrid *Heraldo*, May 21, 1897; La Feber, *New Empire*, 336–37.
26 May, *Imperial Democracy*, 102–103 Cf. La Feber, *New Empire*, 335

improve conditions in the reconcentration camps.[27] The premier then
announced the decision of the Queen Regent to grant Cuba limited
autonomy in the near future.[28]

Sagasta's conciliatory program allowed McKinley a breathing spell.
Realizing that time alone would tell whether Madrid had sufficient
control over the military in Cuba to establish a degree of self-rule and
effect a workable peace, he counseled patience in his annual message
to Congress and assured the world that the administration would under
no circumstances annex the island.[29]

For three years the Navy had experienced difficulties arising from the
insurrection. Cuban nationalists—many of them United States citizens—
were constantly embarking on filibustering expeditions from American
ports in violation of neutrality laws. To enforce the laws, Secretary
Long ordered naval vessels to intercept seaborne rebels en route from
Florida to their homeland. In cases where those apprehended by the
patrol claimed American citizenship, they were turned over to civil
authorities. The net result of this necessary procedure was a series of
court actions so distasteful as to produce new converts to interventionism.[30]

Neutrality enforcement was only one of the complications facing
the Navy at this time. In his determination to avoid provocation, Cleveland had directed Herbert to hold the routine maneuvers scheduled for
the North Atlantic Squadron in December, 1896, in northern waters
rather than in the Gulf of Florida as usual. Hoping that relations with
Sagasta's ministry would improve to the extent of permitting the squadron to operate in the south again without incurring suspicion in Madrid, Long had deferred his decision as to the location of exercises for
the coming winter.[31]

Like Cleveland, McKinley wished to prevent any naval movement
that might anger Spain. With this in mind, he warned Long against
deploying an abnormally large number of men-of-war in the vicinity
of Cuba. The secretary was unable, therefore, to concentrate as much
strength as he desired in dispositions likely to facilitate interception of
Spanish forces in the event Madrid elected to strike.[32]

27 Chadwick, *Spanish War*, I, 89. A provocative interpretation of the diplomatic
maneuvering behind this move appears in La Feber, *New Empire*, 336–37.
28 Pratt, *Foreign Policy*, 377; May, *Imperial Democracy*, 125–26.
29 *Messages and Papers*, X, 130–38; New York *World*, December 8, 1897.
30 Navy Dept., *Annual Report*, 1895–98; Mitchell, *Modern Navy*, 48.
31 Navy Dept., *Annual Report*, 1896–98; Chadwick, *Spanish War*, I, 4.
32 Chadwick, *Spanish War*, I, 3; Navy Dept., *Annual Report*, 1897, Appendix A;
May, *Imperial Democracy*, 127–28.

During the fall, while Long and his assistant were pondering the question of ship deployment, Germany abruptly challenged American policy in two areas. The first thrust occurred in retaliation for the imprisonment of a German national by Haitian officials at Port-au-Prince. The Kaiser dispatched two gunboats with an ultimatum demanding the release of the prisoner and the payment of an indemnity within eight hours.[33] Fearful of the gunboats anchored off the Môle St. Nicolas, the Haitian government complied with alacrity. Then the Germans struck again—across the Pacific. News reached the United States in mid-November that Germany had seized Kiaochow, the foremost port on the Shantung Peninsula. Meanwhile, the Berlin press had taken both the Monroe Doctrine and the open-door policy under fire, while playing up the enactment of an unprecedented naval budget for 1898 which, among other things, would provide four new cruisers designed for service in the South Atlantic and Caribbean.[34]

In view of the administration's preoccupation with Cuba, the President felt constrained to accept Germany's actions without protest, despite the deep resentment of Americans who believed their interests warranted naval protection. Roosevelt expressed the sentiment of extremists when he confided to Mahan that, given his way, he would have driven the Spanish from Cuba by force and then admonished Germany to stay out of the western hemisphere. In the opinion of the assistant secretary, McKinley's passive acceptance of the gunboat mission especially, which Roosevelt interpreted as an outrageous offense against the Monroe Doctrine, was nothing short of deplorable. What he failed to perceive was the President's reluctance to antagonize the Germans for fear they would conclude an alliance with Spain.[35]

Anti-German sentiment in the United States faded into the background as the Cuban junta and the yellow press redoubled their efforts to shame the government into war with Spain. Sensational accounts of Spanish atrocities elicited fresh support for the Cuban nationalists, particularly in New York where more than 30 per cent of all such articles printed in the domestic press from 1895 to 1898 appeared. Joseph Pulitzer's *World* and William Randolph Hearst's *Journal* vied with each other for the honor of publishing the most lurid reports of Cuban

33 New York *World*, November 30, 1897; La Feber, *New Empire*, 323.
34 Baltimore *Sun*, January 18, 1898; New York *Journal of Commerce*, December 31, 1897. German naval appropriations rose from $33,000,000 in 1897 to $56,100,000 in 1898.
35 Roosevelt to Mahan, May 3, 1897, in Morison and Blum (eds.), *Letters of Theodore Roosevelt*, I. See also, Puleston, *Mahan*, 182; May, *Imperial Democracy*, 128.

suffering, in the apparently justified belief that New Yorkers bought
newspapers for their shock value. The circulation of both papers rose
to unheard-of heights before war was declared.[36]

The new nationalism, engendered by the country's phenomenal
material growth since the Civil War and made militant by the rapid
development of the modern Navy, had conditioned the reading public
to jingoist journalism. Consequently, circulation-hungry editors calling
on the government to give positive aid to the suffering Cuban under-
dogs evoked a resounding echo among a sympathetic people already
spoiling for a fight with oppressors. Imperialist spokesmen responded to
the rising demand for action by urging the administration to grant the
insurgent regime immediate recognition—regardless of the repercussions
in Madrid. But the President stood firm against the tide; recognition
would mean intervention which, in turn, would lead to war, and war
was precisely what he hoped to avoid.[37]

Theodore Roosevelt, whose primary goal was naval preparedness for
a war he deemed inevitable, found his sphere of activity limited by the
caution of his superiors and the burden of his administrative chores.[38]
He was obliged to suspend his frantic efforts to place the department
on a war footing long enough to attend to the prosaic business of promotion and recruitment. Having studied the current systems hurriedly,
he proposed to remove unfit officers from the promotion ladder and to
promise enlisted recruits pensions on a par with those granted soldiers.
Although the memorandum on these subjects he drafted for Long
touched on some of the sorest spots in naval administration, his ideas
were ultimately adopted.[39]

The necessity of coping with departmental routine did not deflect the
assistant secretary's principal aim. He worked tirelessly to convert Long
to the offensive doctrine preached by Mahan and succeeded to the
extent of persuading the secretary to recommend the construction of
one battleship before the year ended. But Congress denied him this
triumph by voting down Long's recommendation.[40]

36 J. E. Wisan, *The Cuban Crisis as Reflected in the New York Press* (New
York, 1934), 21–26, 33–34, 187–90. Wisan maintains that the yellow press was the
primary instrument in bringing to pass the Spanish–American War.
37 *Ibid.,* 455–60.
38 Pratt, *Expansionists of 1898,* p. 210ff.
39 Navy Dept., *Annual Report,* 1898; Roosevelt to Long, December 9, 1897,
in Morison and Blum (eds.), *Letters of Theodore Roosevelt,* I.
40 Roosevelt to Mahan, May 1, 1897, in Mahan Papers, Puleston Collection; Navy
Dept., *Annual Report,* 1897, 1898.

As 1898 began, Roosevelt plagued his superior relentlessly with renewed arguments for more battleships and supporting vessels and for the concentration of existing men-of-war in positions of tactical advantage. Convinced now that war with Spain was not only inevitable but advisable as well, he directed his energies to gearing the Navy for victory. His conviction had at base three elements which, he insisted, were bound to determine the course of the United States during the next twelve months: humanitarianism, economic interest, and strategic necessity. As far as Roosevelt was concerned, the three factors added up to one quantity—war.[41]

Aware of his chief's opposition to warlike measures, the assistant secretary sought the cooperation of his friends in the service. His close association with such "natural allies" as Robley Evans, William T. Sampson, and H. C. Taylor, in addition to Wainwright and Davis, made the task of forearming the Navy easier to accomplish. Roosevelt's machiavellian methods in this instance also stood him in good stead; he had no hesitation in exploiting personal friendships to further his cause.[42]

Since September, 1897, the question of the strategy to be followed in a naval war with Spain had occupied the thoughts of the assistant secretary's imperialist friends. At one of their meetings, Captain Mahan recalled the pattern set by British empire-builders in the seventeenth century which attested to the wisdom of attacking Spanish colonies as the surest means of defeating the mother country. Since the Philippines represented the most vulnerable—and to America the most valuable—of Spain's possessions, declared the captain, they should be seized as soon as hostilities opened. Mahan's reasoning appealed to Roosevelt, who had already drafted a rough plan for operations against the Spanish at Manila.[43]

Thus, with Long's grudging consent, Manila became the primary target of the Asiatic Squadron. Roosevelt's plan required the squadron to blockade the port when notified of a declaration of war and to destroy the Spanish forces stationed there with all possible speed. In order to carry out its mission, as the assistant secretary knew, the squadron would need a more daring tactician than its current commander, as well as greater firepower than it possessed at the time. In early

41 Herrick, "Naval Policy under Theodore Roosevelt," 33–35.
42 *Ibid.;* Roosevelt, *Autobiography,* 227.
43 Puleston, *Mahan,* 184; Beale, *Roosevelt and the Rise of America,* 62, citing Roosevelt to Lodge, September 21, 1897, and J. Brye to Roosevelt, September 12, 1898, in Roosevelt Papers.

January, 1898, Roosevelt set out to correct these deficiencies. Finding the right man presented no problem, but getting him the assignment was another matter. The officer he selected, Commodore George Dewey, lacked the necessary seniority and would have to be maneuvered into the command over the heads of politically influential seniors. Roosevelt proved equal to the task; he prevailed upon Senator Redfield Proctor of Vermont, one of McKinley's intimates, to convince the President of Dewey's unique fitness for the Asiatic command. Before the month ended, the commodore had departed for Nagasaki.

This accomplished, the assistant secretary turned to the job of finding an additional cruiser to reinforce the Asiatic Squadron. But Long, unwilling to disperse his strength further, blocked Roosevelt's efforts to transfer a heavily armed unit to the Far East. Not until March did the secretary agree to order the *Baltimore* detached from the Pacific Station for duty with Dewey's command.[44]

Part of Roosevelt's blueprint for operations in the Philippines contemplated the destruction of the Manila-based squadron commanded by Rear Admiral Don Patricio Montojo y Pasaron. Consequently, when Dewey sent a dispatch in January complaining of the shortage of supply ships and coal required for the Philippines mission, the assistant secretary pleaded with his chief to transfer auxiliary vessels from the South Atlantic and European stations to the Far East. At the same time, he urged Long to arrange for the delivery of large shipments of coal to the Asiatic Squadron, while privately resolving to see to these preparations himself if Long failed to do so.[45]

The secretary's reluctance to cooperate with his assistant's desire to satisfy Dewey's needs derived largely from his concern for the security of the Gulf and western Atlantic coastal approaches. Shortly after New Year's Day, the President relieved Long's mind by granting him permission to base the North Atlantic Squadron on Key West for the remainder of the winter and to hold maneuvers off the west coast of Florida. Anticipating an adverse Spanish reaction to the move, McKinley

---

44 Roosevelt, *Autobiography*, 231–32; Herrick, "Naval Policy of Roosevelt," 34; Navy Dept., *Annual Report*, 1898. Dewey had an impressive record: he had graduated at the top of his class from Naval Academy and had been commended for meritorious service under Farragut during the Civil War. Regarding the *Baltimore*, Long decided in February to send the cruiser to the Far East, but only as a replacement for the *Olympia* which, in accordance with the rotation plan Herbert had originated, would then return to the west coast.

45 Roosevelt to Lodge, January 14, 1898, in Morison and Blum (eds.), *Letters of Theodore Roosevelt*, I.

had consulted Minister Dupuy de Lôme in December. De Lôme had at first balked at the prospect of such a large concentration of warships in the vicinity of Cuba, but yielded when the President reassured him of the routine nature of the squadron's schedule.[46]

Accordingly, the armored elements of the North Atlantic force, the *New York, Iowa, Massachusetts, Indiana,* and *Texas,* prepared to steam southward in mid-January. McKinley's decision to send the squadron to Key West has been interpreted as a gesture of appeasement to the jingoes and as a means of applying pressure on Spain for a swift settlement of the Cuban controversy.[47] Naval historian French E. Chadwick, who was in command of the *Iowa* at the time, discounted the international implications of the movement. After all, the squadron had for the past two years suspended exercises in Florida's "genial winter climate" in deference to Spanish sensitivity, even though the area west of the Florida keys was clearly within the territorial jurisdiction of the United States. Besides, declared Chadwick, the run from Hampton Roads to Florida Bay, which required only sixty hours to complete at twelve knots, had little or no meaning in terms of strategic disadvantage.[48]

De Lôme's acceptance of the squadron's transfer to Key West, coupled with evidence of Governor Blanco's determination to carry forward the Sagasta reform program, strengthened McKinley's hope for a settlement in Cuba without American intervention. With this in mind, he followed up his announcement of the forthcoming maneuvers in Florida waters with the promise that ships of the North Atlantic Squadron would soon begin to deliver funds, food, and medical supplies to the innocent victims of the island's plight. His assurance of aid to the needy drew hearty applause from humanitarians everywhere and temporarily dampened the ardor of interventionists.[49]

Suddenly the atmosphere changed. On January 12, Consul-General

46 Navy Dept., *Annual Report,* 1898; Chadwick, *Spanish War,* I, 3–5.
47 F. E. Chadwick, *The Relations of the United States and Spain: Diplomacy* (New York, 1911), 532; hereinafter cited as Chadwick, *Diplomacy.* Navy Dept., *Annual Report,* 1898. May, *Imperial Democracy,* 134–35.
48 Chadwick, *Spanish War,* I, 4. Captain Chadwick remained in command of the *Iowa* until Admiral Sicard was replaced by William T. Sampson as commander of the North Atlantic Squadron. He then took command of Sampson's flagship, the armored cruiser *New York.*
49 *House Executive Documents,* 55th Cong., 2nd Sess., No. 405; Navy Dept., *Annual Report,* 1898, 1899; New York *Tribune,* January 17, 1898; New York *Evening Post,* January 16, 1898; La Feber, *New Empire,* 343–44.

Lee notified the State Department of the outbreak of rioting in Havana which he feared might endanger the lives and property of American residents. Lee exaggerated the danger; the rioters, most of whom were junior officers from the Spanish garrison, were bent on nothing more drastic than smashing the presses of an anti-Weyler newspaper. The disturbance ended quickly, but not quickly enough to prevent Lee from warning the President that anarchy was on the march in Havana. Horrified at the thought of Americans falling prey to wanton attacks on the city's streets, McKinley served notice on De Lôme that a recurrence of violence in the capital would necessitate the prompt dispatch of United States forces to the scene.

Although the short-lived riots proved harmless, they influenced the administration's subsequent course of action. In the next ten days, as congressmen and editors debated Blanco's ability to administer a quasi-autonomous regime without the full support of the Spanish military, interventionist spokesmen pointed to the riots as proof of the governor's lack of control and urged the President to take whatever steps were necessary to free Cuba from Spanish oppression. To McKinley, the rising in Havana meant that unruly Spanish troops could defy Blanco at will and endanger the entire reform movement, not to mention the lives of Americans residing in Cuba. For this reason, he authorized Secretary Long to redeploy naval units in the Atlantic immediately.[50]

Long wasted no time. Within hours, he dispatched orders to Rear Admiral Thomas Selfridge, commander of the European Station, and to Commodore Dewey to retain all seamen whose enlistments were about to expire. On January 17 he instructed Captain C. M. Chester, who had command of the South Atlantic Squadron, to start a rumor of his intention to take the cruiser *Cincinnati* and the gunboat *Castine* to the northern limit of his station, while actually steaming to Pará, Brazil, where he was to await further orders. On the same date, Long diverted the *Wilmington* from her course to the South Atlantic Station and sent her instead to La Guayra on the northern coast of Venezuela. Before the day ended, he had also directed the *Helena* to proceed to Lisbon rather than Hong Kong, her original destination, and had moved Self-

50 Walter Millis, *The Martial Spirit* (Cambridge, Mass., 1931), 95; May, *Imperial Democracy*, 137; La Feber, *New Empire*, 344. These accounts vary in detail only. For additional comment, see L. S. Mayo (ed.) *America of Yesterday, As Reflected in the Journal of John Davis Long* (Boston, 1923), 153–55; hereinafter cited as Mayo (ed.), *Journal of Long*. See also, Navy Dept., *Annual Report*, 1898; Millis, *Martial Spirit*, 94–96; New York *Evening Post*, January 14, 1898.

ridge's small European force—led by the *San Francisco*—from the Mediterranean to Lisbon where Spanish naval movements might be observed and, if necessary, intercepted.[51] This completed the routing of ships to points of vantage near Cuba in the west and Spain in the east.

Meanwhile the units of Rear Admiral Montgomery Sicard's large North Atlantic Squadron were assembling at Key West. The first to arrive, the *Maine*, had been assigned in December to special duty as a guard ship at the disposal of the consul-general at Havana, with whom Captain Sigsbee kept in telegraphic contact from Key West. The five armored men-of-war from Hampton Roads dropped anchor on January 23. On the following day, the light cruisers *Detroit* and *Montgomery* returned from patrol stations to rejoin the squadron. Counting the torpedo-boats *Cushing* and *Ericsson*, which moored in the inner harbor nightly after searching for filibusters, Sicard's command numbered ten ships in all by January 25.

That morning witnessed the departure of eight of his vessels for Dry Tortugas, which the admiral had chosen as a coaling station for the deeper-draft warships unable to fuel at the pier in Key West. This left the *Cushing, Ericsson,* and the newly arrived supply ship *Fern,* which Sicard directed to remain at Key West and ferry messages and supplies to Tortugas.[52]

The rapid shifting of naval vessels in the Atlantic and Caribbean reflected the renewed tension in the White House, where President McKinley anxiously awaited further word from Havana. Although Lee had reported within forty-eight hours of the dispatch of his riot warning that order had been restored, he had failed to elaborate. As time passed with no evaluation of conditions forthcoming, McKinley's anxiety increased. On January 24 his concern for Americans in Havana induced him to take a step which, though peaceable in intent, set the stage for war.

At the President's request, William R. Day, who had succeeded Sherman as secretary of state, sounded out the Spanish minister's reaction to a proposal to send an American warship to Havana on a courtesy call. This idea had occurred to McKinley during a conference with Long, who remarked that the *Maine* might better be posted to Havana osten-

---

51 Long to Chester, January 17, 1898, Ciphers Sent, 1898, in Navy Arch.; Navy Dept., *Annual Report,* 1898; Chadwick, *Spanish War,* I, 3–5. Pará is now known as Belem; La Guayra is now spelled La Guaira.
52 Navy Dept., *Annual Report,* 1898; Chadwick, *Spanish War,* I, 5. Cf. J. E. Weems, *The Fate of the Maine* (New York, 1958).

sibly as a gesture of good will than dispatched there hastily in response to a call for help from Lee. Realizing that he could not prevent the administration from sending the ship, De Lôme made no objection but tried to save face by announcing his government's decision to return the compliment. The armored cruiser *Vizcaya* would in the near future make a similar visit to New York!

Opinions differed as to the wisdom of ordering a battleship to Havana on the heels of the January riots. Even the alarmist Fitzhugh Lee belatedly suggested delaying the *Maine's* departure, only to learn that the ship had already sailed from Dry Tortugas for Havana. Editors of some newspapers suspected that the *Maine's* movement foreshadowed intervention, while others hailed it as an enlightened display of the nation's determination to protect American citizens wherever they might be. Secretary Long felt sure the presence of the *Maine* at Havana would have a salutary effect.[53]

The crew of the *Maine* did not share the secretary's confidence in the outcome of the mission. Many a seaman wrote home of his forebodings of violence occurring after the ship had reached her destination. Mrs. Richard Wainwright, the wife of the ship's executive officer, on hearing of the *Maine's* departure, expressed her misgivings bluntly: "You might as well send a lighted candle on a visit to an open cask of gunpowder!" [54]

On January 25, when the *Maine* dropped anchor in Havana harbor, the nationalist rebellion had just passed its third anniversary with insurgents still in the field and fighting hard, though Spain had sent more than 200,000 troops against them. The appearance of the *Maine* reminded disheartened Spanish officials of the substantial assistance America had given their country's enemies. Predictably, their attitude toward the ship's company was correct but far from friendly.[55]

Determined to avoid a second *Baltimore* incident, Captain Sigsbee refused to grant his crew liberty in Havana, though he and his officers moved freely through the city on official or personal errands. Some of them attended a bullfight at the invitation of the acting governor, who boarded the *Maine* to welcome Sigsbee.

Both the captain and Wainwright appreciated the vulnerability of their position. They realized that many of the Spaniards they encountered regarded the *Maine's* presence as a provocative insult. Consequently,

53 Mayo (ed.), *Journal of Long*, 153–55; Pittsburgh *Press*, January 25, 1898; New York *Journal of Commerce*, January 25, 1898; New York *Herald*, January 26, 1898.
54 Cummings, *Wainwright*, 83, citing Wainwright Scrapbook, 1898; Weems, *Fate of the Maine*, 47–51.
55 Wilson, *Battleships in Action*, I, 116ff.

Sigsbee directed his executive officer to tighten security measures generally.

Wainwright's adjustment of daily routine to meet the captain's requirements was thorough. Setting an unusually numerous anchor watch, he had the deck batteries manned day and night by a fourth of the crew and saw to it that a supply of ammunition was shifted to the ready boxes around the rapid-fire guns. Small arms were issued to all officers and petty officers on watch, and two of the main boilers were lit off instead of the usual one for port routine.

In the course of frequent security inspections, the executive officer reminded lookouts to watch carefully all craft moving in the vicinity of the *Maine's* anchorage. Taking no chances, he instructed the gangway watch to warn off all unofficial visitors—a precaution which even Captain Sigsbee thought "rather severe." [56]

During the first two weeks of the Maine's stay in Havana, the New York *Journal* printed a translation of a letter allegedly written by De Lôme and stolen by an agent of the junta. The letter, which the minister admitted he had writtten in the preceding month to a friend in Cuba, described McKinley as "weak and a bidder for the admiration of the crowd . . . who tries to keep the door open behind him . . . while keeping on good terms with the jingoes of the party." De Lôme then attacked the "newspaper rabble" reporting from Havana and concluded with the suggestion that Madrid send a prominent Spaniard to Washington to negotiate a commercial agreement with the administration, "if only for effect."

Facsimiles of the minister's letter appeared on front pages of newspapers in all parts of the country within a few days of its publication by the *Journal*, inflaming tempers and creating a fresh demand for assertive action. But the Spanish government moved so swiftly to recall De Lôme and convey regrets that the President declared the matter closed before the State Department could avail itself of the diplomatic leverage presented by the minister's indiscretion. As popular indignation subsided, editors again focused their attention on Havana and the *Maine*.[57]

---

56 Weems, *Fate of the Maine*, 48–59; Millis, *Martial Spirit*, 96–97; Cummings, *Wainwright*, 86; Navy Dept., *Annual Report*, 1898.

57 The notorious De Lôme letter first appeared in print in Hearst's New York *Journal*, whose editor had apparently bargained for the original with the junta agent who stole it. The *Journal* published the translation on February 9, 1898. Extracts from the letter are quoted in May, *Imperial Democracy*, 137; and in Millis, *Martial Spirit*, 98.

Conditions aboard the battleship remained serene, despite the loss of liberty and the extra duties imposed on the crew by Wainwright's security measures. In view of the circumstances, the executive officer attempted to keep his men fully occupied during the daylight hours by scheduling frequent exercises for each division. But these diversions had to be curtailed when the captain warned the officers to make sure nothing occurred aboard ship that might be misinterpreted by Spanish authorities. On Tuesday, February 15, Wainwright was supervising gunnery drills when the *Maine* swung on her anchor so as to bring the Spanish cruiser *Alfonso XII* directly in the simulated line of fire. Mindful of his superior's admonition, he canceled the drills and ordered the guns secured.

Later in the day, the Ward liner *City of Washington* came to anchor about four hundred feet from the Maine's port quarter. Passengers aboard the American steamer gazed with admiration at the warship's gleaming white hull and ochre superstructure, while they listened to the strains of accordion music coming from her main deck.[58] At 9:40 that evening, what sounded like heavy gunfire brought the *Washington's* passengers topside on the run. Crowding the rail, they saw a rush of fire and smoke shoot up from the *Maine*, followed by the prolonged roar of a violent explosion.[59] Officers and men aboard the flaming vessel worked heroically to extricate shipmates trapped in compartments below. As boats were being lowered to ferry the wounded to shore, other lifeboats pulled away from the *Washington* and the *Alfonso XII* to assist in the rescue work.

Throughout the ordeal, Sigsbee and Wainwright maintained, in the words of a British authority, "the highest standards of discipline." Despite their efforts, 254 men lost their lives in the holocaust; 88 others survived only to die afterwards in hospitals ashore. Since the explosion shattered the forecastle, killing everyone in it, proportionately more officers than men lived to tell the tale.[60]

After lifeboat crews had taken off the last of the survivors, the captain stepped into his gig and directed the coxswain to head for the

58 Cummings, *Wainwright*, 86. Cf., Weems, *Fate of the Maine*, 62.
59 Wilson, *Battleships in Action*, I, 116–17.
60 *Ibid.* The British authority mentioned, H. W. Wilson, devotes a section of his two-volume work to the *Maine* disaster. Other accounts of the explosion may be found in Navy Dept., *Annual Report*, 1898; Weems, *Fate of the Maine*, 92–93. The preliminary report drafted by Sigsbee is reprinted in the secretary's report for 1899; a facsimile appears in Weems, *Fate of the Maine*, pictorial section.

Ward liner. There he was welcomed by the merchant captain and introduced to Blanco's chief of staff, who had come aboard the *Washington* to extend his sympathy. Excusing himself, Sigsbee went to the cabin assigned him and drafted a preliminary report to Secretary Long: "*Maine* blown up . . . and destroyed. Send light-house tenders from Key West. . . . Public opinion should be suspended until further report." [61]

---

61 Weems, *Fate of the Maine,* pictorial section.

XI
ON THE BRINK

THE *Maine* INQUIRY BEGAN IN HAVANA ON FEBRUARY 19, 1898, upon the arrival of the U.S.S. *Fern* with a crew of divers from squadron headquarters at Key West. Under the supervision of Commander Wainwright, who had stayed in the city to take charge of the wrecked hull, the divers submerged daily to search for clues to the source of the fatal explosion. On the basis of incomplete evidence, Wainwright concluded that a mine, located on the port side below the waterline, had probably blown up the battleship.[1]

On February 21 the lighthouse tender *Mangrove* anchored near the *Fern* and disembarked the members of the court of inquiry detailed to determine the cause of the disaster. The court consisted of Captain Sampson, senior member, Captain Chadwick, and Lieutenant Commander William Potter, members, and Lieutenant Commander Adolph Marix, judge advocate. After a thorough scrutiny of the wreckage and close questioning of survivors, eyewitnesses, and divers, the court decided that the *Maine* had been mined.

Specifically, Sampson's final report, which was not publicized until March 28, stated that "the *Maine* was destroyed by a submarine mine, which caused the explosion of two or more magazines." The impact of the external blast, occurring near frame number 18 in the forepart of the hull had, according to the report, thrust the keel upward in the form of an inverted "V" whose apex reached the level of the bridge

---

1 Cummings, *Wainwright*, 90.

deck. The court's intensive probing failed to unearth a single act of sabotage or neglect on the part of the ship's company which might have caused a fire to ignite in the *Maine's* electrical circuits, boiler rooms, or magazines. The absence of such an indication, together with the shape of the twisted keel, convinced Sampson and his colleagues that persons unknown had planted an underwater device for the purpose of destroying the vessel.[2]

Subsequent interpretations of the battleship's destruction expressed confidence in the integrity of the American court, but disputed its verdict. An official Spanish board of inquiry which convened in March attributed the disaster to an accidental explosion in one of the forward magazines, an opinion held by British ordnance experts and a small minority of American officers, including the current chief of the Bureau of Steam Engineering, Commodore George W. Melville.[3]

A British account of the sinking, published thirty years after the event, concurred in the findings of the Spanish board. Basing his conclusion on data derived from experiments as well as actual accidents at sea, the author discarded the principal prop of the American theory. Recent experience had, he argued, invalidated the explanation suggested by the upthrust keel. Since 1898, several shipboard explosions had produced much the same effect.[4]

Some of the testimony recorded by Sampson's court tends to corroborate this argument. For one thing, the divers had found not a trace of a mine in the harbor's soft bottom mud. For another, members of Wainwright's salvage crew testified that they had seen no dead fish floating near the wreck on the morning after the explosion. Nor did eyewitnesses aboard the *City of Washington* recall noticing an upheaval

2 *Senate Executive Documents,* 55th Cong., 2nd Sess., No. 207. For the report of the court convened in 1911, which raised the wreck and reexamined it, see "U.S.S. *Maine* Court of Inquiry," in *House Executive Documents,* 62nd Cong., 2nd Sess., No. 310. Influenced by the condition of the keel, the second court upheld the judgment of the first. The opinions of Captain Chadwick appear in his *Diplomacy,* 559–63.

3 For the official findings of the Spanish inquiry, see *Senate Executive Documents* 55th Cong., 2nd Sess., No. 885. The American officers who believed the explosion accidental kept their thoughts to themselves. Of the relatively few to express this unpopular interpretation of the sinking, Commodore Melville spoke out at the time of the second court's investigation. See G. W. Melville, "The Destruction of the Maine," *North American Review* (June, 1911), 43ff; "Melville, George Wallace," in *DAB,* XII, 521–22. In 1898, Melville was completing fifteen years of service as chief of the Bureau of Steam Engineering.

4 Wilson, *Battleships in Action,* I ,118–19.

of water of the kind that normally follows the detonation of a submerged mine.[5]

Another weakness of the American explanation lies in the unanswered question of who had the motive and opportunity for planting the device. Spanish officials would hardly have invited American intervention by doing so, especially at a time when one of their few effective cruisers, the *Vizcaya*, was approaching New York on a courtesy call. Besides, neither they nor anyone else in Havana—including the consul-general—knew where the *Maine* would anchor before she entered the harbor.

If the court of inquiry had been able to prove the mine theory, then suspicion might more logically have fallen on agents of the Cuban nationalists, for this camp alone stood to gain from the consequences of provoking the United States. The nationalists' desire for American military aid might have motivated their leaders to mine the battleship —given the opportunity—with the expectation that the Spanish would seem guilty of an unpardonable provocation to war. Inasmuch as no deathbed confession or drunken disclosure of Cuban complicity has come to light so far, however, the probability of an internal cause is difficult to deny.[6]

A naval officer brought word of the *Maine* disaster to the White House at dawn on February 16; by nightfall, the press had informed the nation. Hoping to forestall the rise of hysteria which he feared might develop in the aftermath of the initial shock, McKinley appealed for calm and objectivity pending publication of the court's findings. Moderates in Congress, such as Hale, Reed, and Boutelle, rallied to the President's side; even Senator Lodge urged his colleagues to suspend judgment until all the facts were known. Business journals, which had consistently opposed forcible intervention in Cuba, also endorsed McKinley's appeal, as did prominent clerics of all faiths and leaders of various minority groups. For more than a month after the *Maine* went down, responsible men of peace held out the possibility of an accidental cause having no bearing on relations with Spain.[7]

5 *Ibid*. Cf. Weems, *Maine*, 126–28; Mitchell, *Modern Navy*, 50–55. See also, *Army and Navy Journal* (New York), February 19, 1898; *Senate Executive Documents*, 55th Cong., 2nd Sess., No. 207.

6 According to John Weems's unofficial account, published in 1958, President Franklin Roosevelt obtained from Naval Academy officials a statement absolving Spain of guilt for the *Maine* disaster, which Roosevelt sent in 1935 to Ambassador Claude Bowers for delivery to the Spanish government.

7 For the reaction of McKinley to the news of the explosion, see Mayo (ed.), *Journal of Long*, 160–65. Representative editorial comment directed at businessmen

Predictably, the voices of calm failed to dampen the sensationalism of the yellow press. Hearst's New York *Journal*, which devoted eight pages daily to the *Maine* for a full week and chartered dispatch boats to facilitate the flow of uncensored news from Cuba, offered a reward of $50,000 "for the conviction of the criminals who sent 258 American sailors to their death." Pulitzer's *World* dwelt on the cause of the tragedy, alleging inaccurately that divers had discovered positive proof of the mine theory.[8]

So effective were the insinuations circulated by the yellow press that, despite the President's plea for patience, they convinced a large segment of the public that the *Maine* had been blown up deliberately. And although Sampson's report would not reach Washington until March 28, the implications of Spanish guilt proved too strong for the uninformed nation to ignore.

Heralded by the junta's frenzied warnings of her hostile purpose, the armored cruiser *Vizcaya* slipped artlessly through New York's Narrows on February 19. A lieutenant representing the commandant of the Brooklyn Navy Yard boarded the cruiser, exchanged civilities with Captain Antonio Eulate, and apprised him of the tragedy in Havana. Appalled by the news, Eulate expressed his sympathy and promptly ordered the *Vizcaya's* colors half-masted.[9]

Throughout the eventful period following the outbreak of the January riots, Secretary Long found himself the object of national attention. As McKinley's closest friend in the cabinet, he had ever since the inauguration enjoyed the President's confidence. Now, upon the loss of one of the Navy's eight combat-worthy armored ships, Long had to face not only the limelight but also the prospect of daily, time-consuming conferences at the White House. These sessions centered on the sinking of the *Maine*, its effects on the delicate relations with Madrid, and its significance in terms of current naval dispositions.

---

appears in New York *Journal of Commerce*, February 16, 1898; Boston *Herald*, February 18, 19, 1898; New York *Tribune*, February 17, 1898. The public reaction is reflected in editorials printed in New York *Sun*, February 17, 1898; New York *Times*, February 20, March 30, 1898; St. Louis *Republic*, February 18, 1898; New York *Tribune*, March 30, 1898; Washington *Post*, February 19, 1898. For a recent analysis, see La Feber, *New Empire*, 348–49. For an earlier version of the general reaction and its causes, see Wisan, *The Cuban Crisis*, 390–95.

8 New York *Journal*, February 17, 19, 1898; New York *World*, February 20, 22, 1898. See Wisan's *The Cuban Crisis* for the extensive coverage given the *Maine* sinking in the Hearst and Pulitzer papers and their subsequent rise in circulation, especially pp. 390–95, and pp. 455–60.

9 Weems, *Maine*, 99–100; Wisan, *The Cuban Crisis*, 391–92.

The secretary, alarmed at first by the possibility of official Spanish involvement in the outrage, drew a breath of relief when McKinley expressed his confidence in the innocence of Governor Blanco's regime. A message from Fitzhugh Lee had presented a fresh version of the mine theory. According to the consul-general, unidentified agents had—unknown to Spanish officials—anchored a submerged device at a point where the *Maine* would probably strike it while swinging with the wind or tide. The collison took place on the night of February 15, and set off an explosion which caused a second blast in the forward magazine containing saluting powder.

Perhaps because Lee's interpretation offered an escape from the consequences of indicting Spain for a blacker crime, McKinley accepted it. With the approval of the secretaries of state and navy, and the chief of the Bureau of Ordnance, all of whom admitted the plausibility of the new theory, McKinley concluded that the gravest offense chargeable to Spain was negligence. Thus reassured, the President and Long continued to hope for peace.[10]

Nevertheless, the loss of the *Maine* induced Secretary Long to implement numerous changes of assignment during the remainder of the month and in March. Captains Sampson of the *New York* and Chadwick of the *Iowa* were directed on February 16 to return in their ships to Key West, where both men were detached for service on the court of inquiry. The *Massachusetts* and *Indiana* remained temporarily at Dry Tortugas, while the *Montgomery* departed for Havana in response to orders placing her at the disposal of Captain Sampson. Long had in the meantime instructed Captain Chester in the *Cincinnati* to leave Pará in company with the *Castine* and steam slowly northward to Barbados.[11]

To Roosevelt, these operations seemed tame. Outraged at the administration's failure to avenge the *Maine*, he had decided that McKinley had "no more backbone than a chocolate éclair" and that Long would never of his own initiative condition the fleet adequately for war. The assistant secretary yearned for the opportunity to insure the readiness of the North Atlantic and Asiatic Squadrons. He had kept in close

10 Leech, *McKinley*, 170–78; Mayo (ed.), *Journal of Long*, 171–72. Cf. H. W. Morgan, *William McKinley and His America* (Syracuse, N.Y., 1963), 362. This work, the most recently published biography of McKinley, maintains that both Lee and Sigsbee considered the explosion accidental. In Lee's case, certain sources which Morgan has apparently overlooked, including Captain Chadwick's authoritative *Spanish War*, indicate the consul's belief that persons unknown had set a "submerged device" to destroy the *Maine*.

11 Chadwick, *Spanish War*, I, 9–11; Navy Dept., *Annual Report*, 1898.

touch with Dewey since the latter had moved his flagship from Nagasaki to Hong Kong where, the commodore informed him, the harbor was filled with ships of many nations and the atmosphere tense with the expectancy of war.[12]

Roosevelt's chance came on Saturday, February 25. Thinking it safe to leave the department in his assistant's hands for a weekend afternoon, the weary Long departed at lunchtime for home and a rest. No sooner was he out of the way than Roosevelt set sparks flying. In the few hours given him as acting secretary, the young man bombarded bureau chiefs, squadron commanders, and even congressmen with demands for measures he deemed essential to the Navy's preparedness. Perhaps the most significant of his actions on this occasion was the famous dispatch to Commodore Dewey: "Order the squadron, except the *Monocacy*, to Hong Kong. Keep full of coal. In the event declaration of war Spain, your duty will be to see that the Spanish squadron does not leave the Asiatic coast and then offensive operations in the Philippines. Keep *Olympia* until further orders." [13]

The reference to the *Monocacy*, an antiquated paddle-wheeler, reflected Roosevelt's opinion that she would hinder rather than help the squadron's performance in Philippine waters and might better be left behind. Regarding the *Olympia*, the acting secretary explained later that he did not wish to deprive Dewey of his strongest asset, though he "had been notified that she would soon be recalled to the United States." [14] The truth was that he had no intention of allowing this to happen.

Secretary Long's journal presents a full—if somewhat sardonic—account of his assistant's conduct on the afternoon of February 25. Roosevelt took it upon himself to follow up the message to Dewey with a cable to agents in Hong Kong instructing them to buy as much coal as they could find in the colony. He then had orders transmitted to the commanders of the European and South Atlantic forces, designating their mobilization stations and alerting them to the imminence of war. Ad-

12 Roosevelt quoted in Leech, *McKinley*, 169, citing a "variety of sources." See also, Sprout, *Naval Power*, 228–30; Long, *New Navy*, II, 162; Dewey, *Autobiography*, 181; Falk, *Togo*, 250.

13 Quoted from Roosevelt, *Autobiography*, 234. The text also appears in Pratt, *Expansionists of 1898*, 12–13, and in a number of other works, including Chadwick, *Spanish War*, I, 10; Millis, *Martial Spirit*, 112. For comment, see Leech, *McKinley*, 169; Beale, *Roosevelt and the Rise of America*, 61–63.

14 Roosevelt, *Autobiography*, 234; Sprout, *Naval Power*, 230; Herrick, "Naval Policy of Roosevelt," 35–36; Dewey, *Autobiography*, 181–85. The cruiser *Olympia* served as Dewey's flagship at Manila Bay.

miral Selfridge was to coal the ships of his European Squadron and to stand by at Lisbon for reassignment. Captain Chester was notified that the *Wilmington* would join the *Cincinnati* and *Castine* at Barbados, where all three would fuel and await further orders.[15]

The energetic Roosevelt did not stop there. He requisitioned ammunition, according to Long, "without the ships to move it," plagued the Bureau of Ordnance with questions about the condition of shipboard armament, and bedeviled Congress with pleas for approval of unlimited recruitment of seamen. "He has gone at things like a bull in a China shop," lamented the secretary, causing "more of an explosion than happened to the *Maine!*" Consequently, in Long's judgment, Roosevelt was "hardly fit to be entrusted with the responsibilities of the department at this crucial time, . . . the very devil seemed to possess him yesterday afternoon." [16]

A number of scholars take issue with Long's analysis of his assistant's behavior. Rejecting the assumption that Roosevelt's newfound authority had gone to his head and prompted him to act impulsively, these writers attribute his handiwork to a deliberate plan formulated over a period of months by Mahan and others of the imperialist clan. Long's absence had simply provided the opportunity for setting in motion a prearranged procedure.[17]

Secretary Long was thunderstruck on his return to the department Sunday morning. A copy of Roosevelt's message to Dewey gave him the first indication of what had transpired. As further evidence of his assistant's audacity became apparent during the day, the secretary's indignation increased in direct proportion. Despite his anger, Long made no attempt to nullify Roosevelt's actions. To the latter's amazement, he even allowed Dewey to retain the *Olympia*, which the secretary had scheduled for recall when relieved in March by the *Baltimore*. Perhaps Long, overworked as he was, felt less chagrin at the results of his assistant's brief reign of terror than at the means taken to produce them.[18]

Commodore Dewey had nothing but praise for Roosevelt's exercise of authority. He wrote subsequently that his young friend's timely assis-

---

15 Mayo (ed.), *Journal of Long*, 168–69; Chadwick, *Spanish War*, I, 10.
16 Mayo (ed.), *Journal of Long*, 168–70. Also quoted in full or in part in a number of the works cited above in notes 12–14.
17 Pringle, *Theodore Roosevelt*, 119–32; Beale, *Roosevelt and the Rise of America*, 62–65. Puleston, *Mahan*, 185; Fletcher Pratt, *The Compact History of the United States Navy* (New York, 1957), 182–85.
18 F. Pratt, *Compact History of USN*, 182–85; Mayo (ed.), *Journal of Long*, 169–71; Sprout, *Naval Power*, 230.

tance had made possible the victory at Manila Bay. Indeed, he credited Roosevelt with initiating the entire preparedness program.

The first step was taken on February 25, when . . . instructions were sent to the Asiatic, European, and South Atlantic squadrons to *rendezvous* at . . . points where, should war break out, they would be most available. The message to the Asiatic Squadron bore the signature of that Assistant Secretary who had seized the opportunity while Acting Secretary to hasten preparations for a conflict which was inevitable.[19]

Not all recent historians share Dewey's high opinion of Roosevelt's cyclonic performance. Margaret Leech, for one, considers his "gestures" wasted and believes they merely convinced Long that his assistant was "too nervous to remain in a position of serious responsibility." [20]

Wasted or not, the measures initiated by Roosevelt marked the beginning of a period of intensified activity in the Navy Department. During the first two weeks of March, the cruisers *Columbia* and *Minneapolis*, which had been lying in reduced commission at Philadelphia, were reactivated and manned with complements in excess of their legal quotas. The *Brooklyn* was moved from La Guayra to Hampton Roads, where the *Bancroft* was ordered to meet her on the torpedo-boat's arrival from Lisbon. The commander of the European Squadron, still standing by at the Portugese capital, received with the order detaching the *Bancroft* instructions to send the *Helena* to Key West. He himself was to steam in the *San Francisco* to Newcastle, England, for the purpose of commissioning two newly acquired light cruisers which he would subsequently escort to New York. The same period witnessed stepped-up preparations on the west coast. At Mare Island a supply of ammunition earmarked for the Asiatic Squadron was put aboard the old wooden corvette *Mohican*, whose captain had orders to proceed to Pearl Harbor and deliver the shipment to the *Baltimore*, then flagship of Rear Admiral J. N. Miller's Pacific Squadron. Long had already directed Miller to detach his flagship for service with Dewey as soon as she had received the ammunition, and to return with his staff to California. Miller's recall completed the dissolution of three of the Navy's traditional squadrons, leaving intact only the North Atlantic and Asiatic forces.[21]

19 Dewey is quoted in Roosevelt, *Autobiography*, 234. See also, Dewey, *Autobiography*, 170–72.
20 Leech, *McKinley*, 169.
21 Navy Dept., *Annual Report*, 1898; Chadwick, *Spanish War*, I, 9-11. The North Atlantic Squadron was not allowed to remain intact long, as the following pages indicate.

The dramatic voyage of the *Oregon* highlighted the naval mobilization of 1898. Believing that Spain would, in the event of war, dispose its heaviest units in Cuban waters, the secretary decided to reinforce the North Atlantic Squadron by bringing the battleship as quickly as possible from her station in Puget Sound to Key West. Accordingly, on March 1, Long ordered her commanding officer, Captain A. H. McCormick, to get under way at once for San Francisco where the ship would be prepared for the arduous cruise around Cape Horn.

The *Oregon* arrived at Mare Island on March 9 for a hectic week of coaling, provisioning, and loading ammunition. Meanwhile, Captain Mc-Cormick's failing health compelled Long to transfer him to shore duty, whereupon Captain Charles E. Clark assumed command. On March 19, Clark conned the battleship through the Golden Gate and, in compliance with a message from the secretary, set course for Callao, Peru.

While the *Oregon* steamed southward at an average rate of 10.7 knots, the gunboat *Marietta* put out from Panama Bay and headed for Callao to contract in advance for lighterage of coal to the battleship. This accomplished, the gunboat departed for Sandy Point, Patagonia, to make similar arrangements and await the *Oregon's* arrival. Thence the two ships would make the remainder of the voyage in company.

Anchoring off Callao on April 6, Clark's crew transferred from lighters 1,100 tons of coal, much of which had to be deck-loaded. The next morning found the *Oregon* at sea again, heading for Cape Horn and the awesome Strait of Magellan. Delayed by foul weather as she passed through the narrow channel, the battleship finally reached Sandy Point on April 17. [22]

Having coaled again, the *Oregon* and her gunboat escort took leave of Sandy Point and entered the South Atlantic on course to Rio de Janeiro. Head seas and the *Marietta's* low speed prolonged the run to Rio until the end of the month. Once there, Clark received a telegram from Long advising him of the existence of war with Spain and of the recent sailing of an enemy squadron of four armored cruisers and three fast destroyers westbound from the Cape Verde Islands. The message warned Clark to avoid this force on the final leg of his cruise by whatever means he chose. As an added precaution, stated Long, the ex-

22   Chadwick, *Spanish War*, I, 13–14. Other similar accounts of the voyage appear in F. Pratt, *Compact History of USN*, 185–86; Mitchell, *Modern Navy*, 60–61. For the official version, see Navy Dept., *Annual Report*, 1898. Sandy Point, Patagonia, is now Puenta Arenas, Argentina; since 1881, western and eastern Patagonia have belonged to Chile and Argentina, respectively.

Brazilian auxiliary cruiser *Nictheroy*, recently purchased by the department, would augment the Oregon's escort during the passage to Florida. May 3 brought news of Dewey's success at Manila, and the following morning witnessed the departure of Clark and his charges from Rio.[23]

Touching at Bahia on May 9, Captain Clark found new orders awaiting him. In the absence of further reports of the position of the Spanish squadron, Long wanted him to steam directly to the British West Indies. To allow the *Oregon* to steam at flank speed if necessary, the secretary directed Clark to abandon his slow escorts, which would thereafter proceed independently to Key West.

The battleship completed the 2,500-mile leg to Barbados on May 18, having logged an average speed of 11.7 knots. British port authorities, mindful of neutrality regulations, permitted Clark to purchase four hundred tons of coal but refused his request to communicate with Washington. Underway once more that evening, the *Oregon* followed a circuitous course to Jupiter Inlet, Florida, keeping east and north of the Bahamas. Arriving at her destination on May 24, "in a thoroughly efficient condition," the battleship had averaged 11.6 knots for the 14,700 miles covered from Bremerton to Jupiter at a total coal consumption of 4,100 tons. By completing the voyage in seventy-one days, the *Oregon* accomplished a feat unparalleled in naval history. And, by calling the nation's attention to the time and risk involved in such a voyage, her achievement undoubtedly influenced the subsequent decision to build the Panama Canal.[24]

In early March, as the *Oregon* set out on her long journey, America moved closer to war. Three developments accounted for this trend, which gathered momentum in the course of the month. The first occurred on March 8, midway between the destruction of the *Maine* and the publication of the court's report. Congress appropriated on that date $50,000,000 for security measures, the lion's share of which sum was to pay for a crash program of naval construction and ship-procurement. The men-of-war authorized in the act included three 12,500-ton battleships, the *Missouri, Ohio,* and second *Maine*. Each was designed to mount four 12-inch and four 8-inch rifles and to sustain speeds of up to 18 knots. Supplementing the *Missouris* in the program were sixteen destroyers, fourteen torpedo-boats, and four monitors. The appearance

23 Chadwick, *Spanish War*, I, 13–14; F. Pratt, *Compact History of USN*. 185–86; Mitchell, *Modern Navy*, 60–61; Navy Dept., *Annual Report*, 1898. The *Nictheroy* was renamed U.S.S. *Buffalo*.
24 Chadwick, *Spanish War*, I, 14–16; Navy Dept., *Annual Report*, 1898.

of destroyers on the list marked the United States Navy's belated acceptance of a type already popular abroad.[25]

To bolster the strength of a fleet facing the threat of war with a ranking naval power, Secretary Long embarked on a procurement drive reminiscent of Gideon Welles's effort in the Civil War. The secretary ordered agents in the United States and South America to buy suitable vessels of various types for the Navy. To negotiate similar transactions in continental Europe and the British Isles, Long authorized Commander W. H. Brownson and Lieutenant J. C. Caldwell, the attaché in London, to act for the department.[26]

The Brazilian government was persuaded to sell two protected cruisers nearing completion in a British yard on the River Tyne, as well as the auxiliary cruiser *Nictheroy*. The *San Francisco* would escort the British-built vessels to New York, as the *Nictheroy* steamed to Key West in the wake of the *Marietta*.[27] Commander Brownson's efforts to buy ships in European countries netted the Navy an additional light cruiser and a pair of torpedo-boats.[28]

The department purchased or chartered from domestic lines eleven merchantmen displacing from 4,000 to 15,000 tons. The heavier vessels of this lot, the *St. Louis*, *St. Paul*, *Harvard*, and *Yale*, could attain speeds of up to twenty-two knots and remain at sea for three weeks without refueling. From the Treasury Department, Long borrowed nine revenue cutters for the duration of the crisis; and from other sources he commandeered numerous craft for service as tenders, tugs, colliers, and hospital ships. A total of twenty-eight yachts completed the improvised auxiliary fleet, some of which were lent or donated by their owners. J. P. Morgan, for instance, offered the Navy his steam yacht, the *Corsair*; as the gunboat *Gloucester*, she would perform creditably in the line at Santiago under the command of Wainwright, formerly the *Maine's* executive officer. In all, 128 vessels joined the Navy in 1898, at a cost of about $18,000,000. [29]

25 Navy Dept., *Annual Report*, 1898. See also, New York *Times*, March 9, 1898; Mitchell, *Modern Navy*, Table V, 131; Wilson, *Battleships in Action*, I, 119ff.
26 Chadwick, *Spanish War*, I, Appendix, 402–403.
27 An unnamed torpedo-boat was christened *Somers* when purchased from the Schichau Works, Elbing, Germany. The *Diogenes*, which the department bought from the Thames Iron Works, London, became the U.S.S. *Topeka*. Other acquisitions included two additional ex-Brazilian cruisers, the *Almirante Abrouall* and the *Amazonas*, subsequently renamed *New Orleans* and *Albany*, respectively.
28 Navy Dept., *Annual Report*, 1898; Mitchell, *Modern Navy*, 48.
29 Mitchell, *Modern Navy*, 48. The *St. Louis* and *St. Paul*, each displacing 14,910 tons, and the 13,000-ton *New York* (renamed *Harvard*) and *Paris* (renamed

The passage of the Act of 1898, which enabled Long to procure private ships besides resuming the battleship program, provoked unexpected reactions in the United States and Spain. With naval expansion assured, chauvinism at home increased, while reports from Madrid indicated that word of the appropriation had stunned the ministry and dampened the ardor of warmongers.[30]

Within a week of the enactment, the conservative Senator Redfield Proctor, an intimate friend of the President and a trusted champion of the business community, unwittingly struck the second blow for war. In a speech delivered on March 17, Proctor described the appalling sights he had witnessed during his recent tour of Cuba. While there, he had discussed the island's plight with certain merchants and planters whose opinions he respected. These men, declared the senator, had convinced him of the hopelessness of a peaceful settlement with Spain; Cuba must either be freed at once or placed under American protection. The first major break in the ranks of businessmen for peace followed this address —a break reflected in the editorial columns of papers catering to commercial interests.[31]

When the public read the verdict of the *Maine* court of inquiry, the die was cast. The furious response to the official report of the deliberate destruction of the battleship overwhelmed the moderates and virtually extinguished the peace camp. "Remember the *Maine*" became the interventionists' war cry, and "Cuba Libre" the slogan of liberal humanitarians. That Sampson's court had advanced no evidence of Spanish complicity in the sinking made no difference; to most Americans, the inference of guilt was plain. Now responsible editors joined the yellow press in demanding revenge, while formerly moderate congressmen, businessmen, and clerics flocked to the standard of interventionism.[32]

Yale) were chartered "for the duration" from the International Navigation Company, an American line.

30 Mayo (ed.), *Journal of Long*, 172; Leech, *McKinley*, 171. See also, Boston *Evening Transcript*, March 8, 1898; New York *Tribune*, March 27, 1898; New York *World*, March 11, 1898; New York *Commercial Advertiser*, March 11, 1898; Philadelphia *Press*, March 21, 1898.

31 *Congressional Record*, 55th Cong., 2nd Sess., 2916-19. Cf. La Feber, *New Empire*, 391; New York *Commercial Advertiser*, April 2, 1898; New York *Times*, March 18, 1898.

32 Millis, *Martial Spirit*, 129; Mayo (ed.), *Journal of Long*, 175-76. See also, New York *Times*, March 25, 30, 1898; New York *Tribune*, March 24, 30, 1898; Washington *Evening Star*, March 25, 1898. McKinley's proposal of "neutral intervention," which he made on April 11 in his message to Congress, appears in *Messages and Papers*, X, 139-50; and in Norman Graebner, *Ideas and Diplomacy* (New York, 1964), 350-56.

Before the month ended, moderate administration spokesmen in Congress found themselves facing a revolt that threatened the authority of even veteran Speaker of the House Tom Reed. Convinced that the show of interventionist strength on Capitol Hill had deprived him of an alternative to positive action, McKinley reluctantly drafted a three-point ultimatum for delivery to Premier Sagasta.

The President's message opened with a demand for an armistice in Cuba to be effective from April 1 to October 1, during which time he would mediate negotiations between the belligerents for a permanent peace. The second point stipulated liberation of Cubans from reconcentration camps and Madrid's consent to American relief measures on behalf of the island's sufferers. The third and—as it proved—critical point spelled out the consequences of failure to negotiate a lasting settlement by October 1. If no peace treaty materialized by then, the President of the United States would assume the role of final arbiter.

Too little and too late, Sagasta's reply rejected the demand for a truce and denied the President the right to establish a fully autonomous regime in Cuba even if, as arbiter, he considered such action essential to peace. Although the premier signified his acceptance of the other conditions set forth in the ultimatum, he remained adamant in his refusal to concede this point.[33]

Despite international appeals for peace, to which Spain responded by belatedly offering an armistice and the United States by proposing neutral intervention, neither government would retreat from its stand on the issue of a free Cuba. Suddenly—on April 19—Congress brought matters to a head; both houses adopted a resolution for Cuban independence, authorizing the President to use force if necessary to bring this to pass. Bowing to the will of the majority, McKinley signed the resolution and framed a second ultimatum requiring Spain to accede to point three of the first within seventy-two hours. On April 21, the State Department learned that Spain had already severed relations with the United States.[34]

33 May, *Imperial Democracy*, 152–56; Millis, *Martial Spirit*, 129–31. New York *Tribune*, April 1, 1898.
34 For detailed accounts of the final phase of peacetime diplomacy, see Mayo (ed.), *Journal of Long*, 176–79; Chadwick, *Diplomacy*, 550–63. Editorial analyses appear in Washington *Evening Star*, April 11, 1898; New York *Times*, April 7, 1898; *The Nation* (New York), April 21, 1898. Margaret Leech recounts the dismissal of the United States minister to Spain, Stuart L. Woodford, a friend and correspondent of Benjamin Tracy's in Brooklyn Republican days. See Leech, *McKinley*, 191.

For more than a month, the Navy Department had known of Spanish naval movements which indicated a possible redeployment for the purpose of defending Cuba and Puerto Rico. In mid-March, the destroyers *Terror*, *Pluton*, and *Fury*, accompanied by three torpedo-boats, had steamed from Cadíz to a base in the Canary Islands. At about the same time, the armored cruiser *Almirante Oquendo* had joined the *Vizcaya* at Havana, where the latter had anchored after completing her courtesy call at New York. The two cruisers stood out of Havana on April 1 and reportedly headed for a point three hundred miles east of St. Thomas, Danish West Indies, at which they were expected to meet the six lighter men-of-war en route from the Canaries.

News of this plan reached Commodore Sampson, who had received his promotion on March 26, together with orders to relieve the ailing Admiral Sicard of command of the North Atlantic Squadron. Notifying naval vessels in the vicinity of St. Thomas of the probable location of the rendezvous, Sampson urged the department to take action if the Spanish warships were sighted in the area. His precautions proved needless inasmuch as breakdowns and shortages compelled the destroyers and torpedo-boats to turn back to the Cape Verde Islands base. The eastbound cruisers were directed to follow suit. Arriving at this base on April 19, their commanders were happy to see that the armored cruisers *Infanta Maria Teresa* and *Cristobal Colón* had, in addition to the lighter ships, preceded them. The concentration of strength off Cape Verde resulted from the Ministry of Marine's decision to form a squadron under the command of Admiral Pascual Cervera y Topete for possible combat operations in the Cuban zone.[35]

Meanwhile, the threat of war had induced Secretary Long to attempt to solve the old problem of creating an appropriate agency for making military and technical decisions without endangering the prerogative of the department's civilian head. Under pressure from Roosevelt and the latter's naval allies, Long instituted the Naval Board of 1898, which he hoped would relieve him of certain responsibilities while leaving his authority unchallenged. The membership of the board, which changed from time to time, consisted originally of the assistant secretary, Admiral

35 Navy Dept., *Annual Report*, 1898. Sampson and Dewey received promotions to rear admiral on April 21 and May 7, respectively. For the details of Sampson's appointment to command of the North Atlantic Squadron, see Long, *New Navy*, I, 211; Chadwick, *Spanish War*, I, 18–21. Captain Chadwick continued to serve as commanding officer of Sampson's flagship *New York* throughout the war, with the exception of the interlude caused by the *Maine* inquiry, and occasionally acted as his chief of staff.

Crowninshield, Captain B. F. Barker, and Commander Richardson Clover. Only Crowninshield held his place for the duration of the war. Roosevelt, Barker, and Clover, who departed in May, were replaced by Admiral Sicard, former commander of the North Atlantic Squadron, and Captain Mahan. Long had recalled Mahan from retirement in Italy to serve on the board; he arrived in Washington a day after Roosevelt had left for service with the Rough Riders.[36]

Captain Mahan subsequently described the functions of the war board in a letter to Dewey:

> The Naval Board . . . was simply a meeting of officers whose other . . . duties indicated them to be proper persons for fruitful consultation and for coordination of the many and speedy steps which had to be taken outside and beyond bureau action. . . . As such steps would need the Secretary's sanction, the Board fell naturally into the position of an advisory body.[37]

Despite the limitations pointed out by Mahan, the war board filled a gap in naval administration and would be missed when disbanded at the end of the war. Thereafter, a demand arose for the establishment of a similar agency, which came into being in March, 1900, as the general board.[38]

Long followed up this administrative measure with a thorough reorganization of the North Atlantic Squadron in response to political pressure for naval protection of east coast interests. He divided his main strategic force into four elements, three of which he planned to employ as instruments of coastal defense. The fourth, the remnant of Sampson's fleet, would remain at Key West on the alert for operations against the Spanish Navy.

One of the newly formed squadrons, the Auxiliary Naval Force or "Mosquito Fleet," can best be described as the combined local defense forces of the eastern seaboard. Commanded by Rear Admiral Henry Erben and manned by naval militia, this armada consisted of forty-one decrepit monitors and a collection of yachts and tugs, none of which were considered fit for sea duty.

To protect coastal shipping and to insure the serenity of seashore com-

---

36 Eure, "Military Colleges," *passim*, in NWC; J. Butler, "General Board of the Navy," *NIP*, LXVI (1930); Navy Dept., *Annual Report*, 1898–1902; Mayo (ed.), *Journal of Long*, 156.

37 Mahan to Dewey, March 1, 1900, in NWC. This letter is reprinted in full in Butler, "General Board of the Navy," and is cited in Eure, "Military Colleges," 38–39. Admiral Dewey became head of the General Board in 1900.

38 H. C. Taylor to Long (memorandum), March 10, 1900, in NWC. Taylor then headed the Bureau of Navigation.

munities, the secretary organized the Northern Patrol Squadron, which would operate from Norfolk under the command of Commodore John A. Howell. This force, though weak in firepower, boasted considerable speed; it consisted of the protected cruisers *San Francisco, Columbia,* and *Minneapolis,* and four ex-merchantmen converted to auxiliary cruisers.

Since neither of the aforementioned squadrons possessed appreciable capability for engaging heavy armored cruisers, their separation from the main Atlantic fleet would of itself have barely affected the strategic situation. But, when Long tried to resolve once and for all the conflict between strategy and politics by bringing north two battleships and an armored cruiser, he committed a blunder harking back to Gideon Welles's dilution of the Union blockade.

The most formidable of the warships originally detached from Key West for service with the so-called Flying Squadron were the battleship *Massachusetts,* the second-rate *Texas,* and the armored cruiser *Brooklyn,* which became the flagship of the squadron commander, Commodore Schley. Subsequently, Schley's command was augmented by the auxiliary cruiser *New Orleans* and two former components of Howell's force, the *Columbia* and *Minneapolis.*

Secretary Long directed Schley to patrol the seaboard at high speed, striking at enemy raiders wherever he encountered them. The commodore's overall mission was to supplement Howell's patrol and to provide a link between the latter's southern operating limit—the Delaware Capes —and Sampson's base at Key West.

The nation's chief reliance in the west, the North Atlantic Squadron, retained considerable striking power in spite of the reductions effected by Long. As if to compensate Sampson for the losses he had sustained, the department added a number of light units to the warships assembled at Key West. Recent arrivals included the unarmored cruisers *Marblehead* and *Cincinnati,* six gunboats, four torpedo-boats, four virtually useless monitors, and the dispatch-boat *Dolphin.* The gunboat *Gloucester* and the long-awaited *Oregon* would join the squadron in April and May, respectively, bringing the total to twenty-three.[39]

By placing Sampson in broad command of all Atlantic forces, Long

39 Navy Dept., *Annual Report,* 1898; Chadwick, *Spanish War,* 16–17. Sampson's first action, on relieving Admiral Sicard, was to detach Chadwick from command of the *Iowa* and, upon completion of the *Maine* investigation in Havana, to give him command of the *New York.* For critical comment concerning the appointment and promotion of Sampson, see Mitchell, *Modern Navy,* 61ff.; Wilson, *Battleships in Action,* I, 128–29; Potter and Nimitz (eds.), *Sea Power,* 368ff.; Cummings, *Wainwright,* 95; Sprout, *Naval Power,* 234–36. Long defends the assignment in *New Navy,* II, 210ff.

had ignored the niceties of naval protocol. Roosevelt's maneuvering on behalf of Dewey had violated the principle of seniority, but only seven officers were senior to Dewey; on the other hand, seventeen outranked Sampson. The hierarchy looked askance at Sampson's sudden rise to prominence, not only because the secretary had awarded the Navy's most prestigious command to a junior captain, but also because he promoted him to rear admiral over the heads of sixteen seniors.

For these transgressions, Secretary Long assumed full responsibility. He had ordered Sampson to relieve Sicard, declared Long with embarrassing candor, simply because he judged him the most competent man for the task at hand. Pointing out that Commodore Sampson enjoyed no political influence whatever, the secretary defended the appointment as a move made "in the interests of the country, to which the eye of the Department was single." President McKinley, Long announced, "gave his cordial approval, and Sampson was to give ample evidence that the assignment was right." [40]

Two days before his elevation to squadron commander became official, the commodore received the department's first detailed operation plan for the Cuban area. "Based largely on certain suggestions of Captain Mahan," the document specified a close blockade of the island's coast as the preliminary to an offensive strike which, because of the dispersal of warships along the eastern seaboard, would have to await reconcentration at Key West.

This blueprint contemplated a blockading force of ships deployed in three lines. The inner line, consisting of torpedo-boats and revenue cutters—"improvised to act as . . . destroyers"—was to take station near the harbor mouths of Havana and Matanzas, in order to prevent sorties by swift Spanish torpedo-craft. The second or middle line, to be composed of protected cruisers, would serve as backstop to the inner blockaders; the cruisers were to move in to help the smaller craft as needed. To satisfy the requirements of international law, an outer force of battleships "must keep the sea," well offshore of the second line.

On the same day—March 24—the department directed squadron commanders to paint their white-and-ochre warships lead gray. Shortly thereafter, Long warned Sampson to land all ship's boats and other disposable

40 Chadwick, *Spanish War*, I, 20–21; Long, *New Navy*, I, 212. According to these sources, Sampson had graduated first in his class from the Naval Academy, had maintained his "professional superiority," and had the experience of acting as the commander of the North Atlantic Squadron during Sicard's illness before he officially relieved the admiral.

gear at Key West. Similar instructions reached Dewey on April 7.
The message that relayed Madrid's decision for war to Washington on
April 21 was followed by contradictory reports of Spanish naval activity.
One such report informed Secretary Long of Admiral Cervera's de-
parture from Cape Verde for an unknown destination; another placed
his squadron in the vicinity of Port-au-Prince. Reliable or not, the information prompted McKinley to avail himself of emergency powers.
He approved Sampson's promotion and then ordered Long to establish
a blockade of Cuba. Before dawn, April 22, the gray warships of the
North Atlantic Squadron weighed anchor and headed for prearranged
blockading stations off the Cuban coast. Within thirty-six hours, the
President issued a call for 125,000 volunteers to swell the ranks of the
28,000-man regular army.[41]

The secretary notified Dewey at once of these developments, directing to him to prepare for action in the Philippines. Forewarned by Roosevelt, the commodore had recalled his ships to Hong Kong in late February. Now assembled in the harbor were his flagship *Olympia*, the
smaller protected cruisers *Raleigh* and *Boston*, and two gunboats, the
Concord and *Petrel*. The revenue cutter *McCulloch*, together with the
colliers *Nanshan* and *Zafira*, serving as train, would accompany the
squadron which was complete except for the *Baltimore*.

Realizing that British neutrality regulations might at any moment be
invoked by port authorities to compel his departure from Hong Kong,
Dewey awaited the appearance of the *Baltimore* with all the patience he
could muster. The cruiser would augment the squadron's firepower and
would also bring him the ammunition that might prove decisive in battle.

As the days wore on, the commodore's anxiety increased. In anticipation of a polite but firm British request to leave port, he had arranged
for a temporary base at Mirs Bay on the China coast, which lay about
thirty miles to the east of Hong Kong, well beyond the limit of British
jurisdiction. But the *Baltimore* would, he knew, require docking and
scraping at Hong Kong, in the absence of facilities at Mirs Bay. Otherwise, the cruiser would be unable to attain her top speed in combat
operations.

At last, on the afternoon of April 22, the *Baltimore* entered the harbor
channel. Not a minute was wasted in readying her for action. Seamen

---

41 Navy Dept., *Annual Report*, 1898; Leech, *McKinley*, 191; Chadwick, *Spanish
War*, I, 22–24. For the Army's statistics, see Bernardo and Bacon, *American
Military Policy*, 280.

transferred in record time the precious supply of ammunition to lighters for distribution to the other ships of the Asiatic Squadron. This done, the cruiser eased into drydock, where she was scraped, painted gray like her sisters, and provisioned. Just as the *Baltimore* emerged to take on coal, British officials boarded the *Olympia* to announce that a state of war existed between the United States and Spain. All American warships in port must clear Hong Kong within twenty-four hours, even though there had been no formal declaration, according to a dispatch received by Dewey that evening.

As soon as the American consul boarded his flagship the next morning, Commodore Dewey signaled the squadron to follow the *Olympia* out of the harbor. His ships steamed away from their anchorage amid loud cheering from the moored British vessels which they passed on course for the seaward channel.

British naval officers stationed at Hong Kong apparently believed the Americans were doomed to destruction. Courteous as they were while socializing with Dewey's officers at the Hong Kong Club's bar, they gave the Yankees little chance of victory over Montojo's squadron at Manila. As one Briton lamented, Dewey's men were "a fine set of fellows, but unhappily we shall never see them again." With such depressing thoughts to dwell upon, the Americans steamed on for Mirs Bay where they would stand by for orders from Washington.[42]

The orders were not long coming. The Sagasta ministry declared war on April 23, directly after it became known in Madrid that McKinley had signed the joint congressional resolution for Cuban independence. Congress responded on the following day—Monday—with a second joint resolution saying that a state of war had existed since April 21. The President used two pens in affixing his signature to the resolution, blotted it, and retired to his bedroom.[43] The war with Spain had begun.

42 Chadwick, *Spanish War*, I, 22–24. See *Senate Executive Documents*, 57th Cong., 1st Sess., No. 331; Long, *New Navy*, I, 181–82; Leech, *McKinley*, 199ff. Dates are reckoned by Manila time. Quotation from Dewey, *Autobiography*, 179.
43 Leech, *McKinley*, 193; J. Pratt, *Foreign Policy*, 381.

EPILOGUE

THE BULLY FIGHT

THE ONSET OF WAR IN APRIL, 1898, BROUGHT TO THE FORE A host of armchair strategists from the China coast to the River Tyne who aired their views and made book on the outcome. For the most part, western European observers favored the Spanish fleet over the unknown quantity across the Atlantic. The United States was characterized as an overconfident brute whose untrained gunners could never stand up to their disciplined adversaries.[1]

British naval officers felt concern for the Americans, though they predicted a protracted struggle in which Anglo-Saxon staying power would tell in the long run![2] Not all Britons agreed; no less an expert than the renowned naval annalist F. T. Jane warned America not to belittle Spanish sea power. If, as he believed, Cervera's squadron succeeded in lifting the blockade of Havana and securing a base for heavier units to follow, nothing could prevent them from bombarding coastal cities. In this case, declared Jane, "The patriotic citizens of the United States may . . . rue the day when the meddling finger of Uncle Sam was thrust into the hornet's nest of Cuba."[3]

The most accurate of the prophets proved to be Admiral Cervera, who foresaw a short war culminating in disaster for his country. Before he accepted command of the Cuba Squadron, which he knew was slated

1 F. Pratt, *Compact History of USN*, 180.
2 *Ibid.*, 181.
3 Frank Freidel, *The Splendid Little War* (Boston, 1958), 43. Jane was the editor and publisher of Britain's foremost naval annual.

for an offensive strike in the west, Cervera had weighed Spain's naval potential against the enemy's and found it wanting. The qualitative superiority of the American Navy, combined with its overwhelming logistical advantage, convinced him that the mission assigned his squadron was not only futile but suicidal.[4]

The admiral would have been astonished at the fear his ships inspired, especially along the east coast of the United States. By April, Long had detailed every unit of the Mosquito Fleet to local defense forces, but still a few "defenseless" communities were demanding protection. To silence such a demand, the department now was forced to send a tug with a Civil War monitor in tow to the harbor in question, whereupon "peace and joy descended" on the residents, though "one of the galleys of Alcibiades" would have afforded them greater security.[5]

Even American naval officers overestimated Spain's strength at sea. Captain Mahan, for one, ventured the opinion that the timely arrival of the *Oregon* alone stood between the North Atlantic Squadron and possible defeat.[6] Inadequate intelligence accounted in large measure for this and other inflated appraisals of the enemy's potential.

Cervera had on hand for his mission four armored cruisers, three new destroyers, and two old torpedo-boats. Three of the cruisers, the *Infanta Maria Teresa*, *Vizcaya*, and *Almirante Oquendo*, were of Spanish design, each displacing 6,890 tons. The *Cristobal Colón*, of Italian construction, had yet to receive her main guns; she was lighter and slower than the *Infantas*.[7] All four had less speed than the *Brooklyn* or *New York*,[8] but mounted heavier rifles. None of the Cervera's ships matched the *Texas*, let alone the *Oregons* and the *Iowa*. The admiral's Clyde-built destroyers *Pluton*, *Fury*, and *Terror* had been launched in 1896 and 1897, about six years later than his cruisers. These 400-tonners, which had no counterpart in the United States fleet, mounted two torpedo tubes apiece and could attain speeds of up to 30 knots.[9]

---

4 Wilson, *Battleships in Action*, II, 124–25. Cf. May, *Imperial Democracy*, 175; Mitchell, *Modern Navy*, 61.

5 Navy Dept., *Annual Report*, 1898. Quotation from Roosevelt, *Autobiography*, 236. See also, Chicago *Daily News*, June 18, 1898.

6 Mahan is quoted in Wilson, *Battleships in Action*, II, 129.

7 Navy Dept., *Annual Report*, 1898, 1899; Wilson, *Battleships in Action*, II, 123–25, 331–32.

8 The *New York* displaced 8,000 tons and the *Brooklyn* 9,215.

9 Wilson, *Battleships in Action*, II, 120; U.S. Navy Historical Division pamphlet, *Destroyers in the U.S. Navy* (Washington, 1963), *passim*. "Destroyer No. 1," the U.S.S. *Bainbridge*, entered service in 1901.

Of the older Spanish men-of-war, only two presented a possible threat to American forces—the 9,900-ton battleship *Pelayo* and the slightly lighter armored cruiser *Carlos V*. Like many of their obsolescent sisters, this pair had become paper tigers as a result of deficient maintenance. Neither was fit for sea duty when war broke out; the *Pelayo* was refitting at a yard in France, and the *Carlos V* lay rusting at her moorings.

Spain's collection of smaller vessels, which included protected cruisers, gunboats, destroyers, and torpedo-craft, had no strategic value. Inasmuch as it numbered more than one hundred ships, however, the armada's very existence added to the panic along America's eastern seaboard. By the same token, although the Ministry of Marine counted 25,000 officers, seamen, and marines against the Navy Department's total of 16,452, the decline of Spanish morale with the progressive deterioration of ships and equipment tended to nullify the disparity in manpower.[10]

When war came, therefore, Spain held a margin of numerical superiority in warships and precious little else of advantage. Assuming that the *Pelayo* and *Carlos V* could be activated in time, the Ministry of Marine would be able to deploy in the western Atlantic six armored vessels aggregating 47,000 tons and mounting thirteen heavy guns in broadside. The United States had ready for action seven armored warships—four first-rate battleships, two fast cruisers, and the hybrid *Texas*. Their combined displacement amounted to almost 65,000 tons, and their broadside armament consisted of forty-five heavy rifles. Even with the *Pelayo* and *Carlos V*, therefore, the odds against Cervera stood at three-to-two in tonnage and three-to-one in broadside firepower.[11]

Problems in logistics, complicated by sins of omission in Madrid, raised these odds. The Minister of Marine had drifted into war without preparing a detailed operations plan or even issuing charts of the enemy's east coast to Cervera's quartermasters. Nor had he arranged in advance to supply the squadron's needs in the Caribbean. Apart from Puerto Rico, which the Spanish commander avoided in anticipation of Sampson's move to intercept him on May 12, Cervera had to depend for coal and provisions on the chancy good will of neutral officials in the West Indies.[12]

The Navy Department, on the other hand, had the logistical situation well in hand by mid-April. Prodded by Roosevelt, Secretary Long had

10 Mitchell, *Modern Navy*, 53–54; Navy Dept., *Annual Report*, 1892, 1898. See also, Wilson, *Battleships in Action*, II, 122ff.
11 Chadwick, *Spanish War*, I, 44–46; Leech, *McKinley*, 176; Garraty, *Lodge*, 191; Philadelphia *Press*, March 13, 1898.
12 H. W. Wilson, *The Downfall of Spain* (London, 1900), 76–85.

requisitioned ample stocks of coal, food, and ammunition for Sampson as well as Dewey. Furthermore, the North Atlantic Squadron would operate from its Key West base, which offered complete facilities for repair, excepting a drydock capable of accomodating battleships.[13]

Despite his manifold advantages, Admiral Sampson faced one major drawback; half of his armored element lay in Hampton Roads. The absence of the *Brooklyn*, *Texas*, and *Massachusetts* forced him to give up his plan for attacking Havana, which he hoped would terminate the contest at the outset. The deprivation also caused unnecessary delays in establishing a legal blockade. When Admiral Sampson, yearning for action, decided to catch Cervera at San Juan, he was obliged to lift the blockade partly in order to gather sufficient strength for his abortive expedition. This had one unexpected result; Long sent the Flying Squadron south in haste to replace the *New York*, *Indiana*, and *Iowa* on the blockade line.[14]

Operations in the Far East were simpler. Here the question of armor did not arise; neither Dewey nor Montojo possessed a single armored ship. The latter's Manila-based squadron numbered five protected cruisers, one wooden cruiser, and three gunboats. His flagship *Reina Cristina*, the heaviest and best-armed of the lot, displaced only 3,500 tons and carried six 6.3 rifles. The fastest vessel of the Philippines Squadron, a gunboat, was capable of 16 knots at full speed.

Commodore Dewey's squadron totaled six men-of-war. But the superior characteristics of his ships, particularly the *Olympia* and *Baltimore* which outmatched the *Cristina* in all respects, gave him a distinct advantage over his foe. Only one of his units was slower than the fastest Spaniard.[15]

The Asiatic Squadron rounded Corregidor shortly after midnight on May 1 and headed northeast in column for Manila. The flagship *Olympia* led the way, followed in order by the *Baltimore*, *Raleigh*, *Concord*, *Petrel*, and *Boston*. Having detached the revenue cutter *McCulloch* and two colliers with instructions to keep clear of shore guns, Dewey reduced speed for the twenty-seven-mile run ahead. At daybreak, just as Manila's batteries opened fire, the *Olympia's* lookouts sighted the Spanish squadron lying motionless off Sangley Point, some six miles to the south of the flagship.

13 Navy Dept., *Annual Report*, 1898, 1899. The nearest drydock capable of taking battleships was located at Port Royal, S. C.
14 Chadwick, *The Spanish War*, I, Chaps. 1 and 7, *passim*.
15 *Ibid.*, Chap. 2, *passim*. Cf. Mitchell, *Modern Navy*, 54; Wilson, *Battleships in Action*, II, 333; Navy Dept., *Annual Report*, 1898.

Closing the enemy to a range of 5,500 yards, the invading column swung smartly to port, picked up speed, and executed five marches and countermarches—east and west—blasting the hapless Spaniards with salvo after salvo. Montojo's crews stubbornly returned the fire until the constant battering compelled them to flee or strike their colors. By noon, it was over. Dewey hauled off to the north for an anchorage midway between Sangley Point and Manila.

The Spanish warships had, before the battle ended, caught fire, sunk, or run aground; their casualties came to 381 men wounded or killed. In the American force, whose ships suffered no appreciable damage, not one man died and only seven were injured.[16]

Dewey's victory did not materially affect developments in the crucial war zone, for even if Montojo had won he lacked the power and opportunity to challenge the main American fleet in the Atlantic. In view of the battle's immediate and long-range consequences, however, it became one of the most decisive engagements in the nation's history. By destroying the enemy force under the protection of Cavite's batteries, Dewey eliminated Spain's naval control of Luzon, thereby making it impossible for Madrid to reinforce the island's defenses with fresh troops.[17]

The commodore's mastery of Manila Bay, which a German squadron tried unsuccessfully to undermine through pressure tactics short of fighting, strengthened the imperialists' stand for annexing all or part of the Philippines. And, over the protest of isolationists and reformers, businessmen began to favor annexation as a means of sustaining American trade in the Far East when the partition of China was all but complete. Consequently, the administration responded to Dewey's request for five thousand occupation troops by embarking on May 28 at San Francisco a contingent of twice that size, under the command of Major-General Wesley Merritt. Ten weeks later, Manila fell to Merritt's force.[18]

At Key West, meanwhile, Commodore Schley's armored ships were

16 The most detailed narration of the battle is in Chadwick, *Spanish War*, I, Chap. 6, *passim*. Other reliable, but more general, accounts appear in New York *Herald*, May 2, 1898; Chicago *Times-Herald*, May 3, 1898; Potter and Nimitz (eds.), *Sea Power*, 368ff.; Freidel, *Splendid Little War*, 176; F. Pratt, *Compact History of USN*, 184. A thorough compilation of notes may be found in C. G. Calkins, "Historical and Professional Notes on the Naval Campaign of Manila Bay," *NIP* (June, 1899), 274ff.
17 Potter and Nimitz (eds.), *Sea Power*, 368ff.; Sprout, *Naval Power*, 231; Bemis, *Diplomatic History of the United States*, 464–66.
18 Chadwick, *Spanish War*, I, 213. For evaluations of the battle's effects on subsequent events, see Moore, *Principles of American Diplomacy*, 354; Sprout, *Naval Power*, 230–36. See also, New York *Herald*, August 15, 1898; Chicago *Times-Herald*, August 15, 1898; Cleveland *Plain Dealer*, August 16, 1898.

coaling as the Puerto Rican expedition returned empty-handed on May 18. While en route from San Juan, Admiral Sampson received a report indicating that Cervera's squadron had entered the Caribbean and was heading for Cuba with arms and ammunition for the defense of Havana.[19] Mindful of the second portion of this message—which turned out to be false—Sampson decided to reinforce the blockade of Havana and Cienfuegos. As he explained to Schley, Cervera would undoubtedly choose to land his cargo at the latter port, which had rail connections with Havana and would presumably be less closely guarded than the capital.

Probably to propitiate the commodore, who did not conceal his chagrin upon finding himself subordinate to his former junior, Admiral Sampson offered him not only the first chance to engage the enemy at Cienfuegos, but also the services of the North Atlantic Squadron's best ship, the *Iowa*, in support of the operation. When fully coaled, the latter would follow the Flying Squadron to the southeast coast of Cuba.

Schley's orders were clear. He was to steam without delay to Cienfuegos and, if he found the enemy there, to establish a close blockade of the harbor. Otherwise, he was expected to proceed at top speed to Santiago and follow the same procedure.

For ten days after his departure on May 19, the commodore's conduct dismayed his superiors in Key West and Washington. He wasted three days on the 520-mile run to Cienfuegos, where he waited for sixty hours more before attempting to find out if Cervera was in port. Learning that the Spanish were elsewhere—probably at Santiago—Schley moved on to the provincial capital at a speed of seven knots! Reaching the approaches to Santiago Bay on the evening of May 26, the commodore reported to Secretary Long that coal shortages compelled him to return to Key West.[20]

This behavior shocked Long, who had received confirmation of reports indicating Cervera's presence at Santiago. Fearing that the enemy

---

19 Mayo (ed.), *Journal of Long*, 183ff.; Leech, *McKinley*, 197–98; Chadwick, *Spanish War*, I, 244–49. Sampson's arrival coincided with that of the Spanish squadron at Santiago and that of the *Oregon* at Barbados.

20 The texts of dispatches exchanged between Schley and Sampson and Schley and Long during the Commodore's ten-day aberration are reproduced in Chadwick, *Spanish War*, I, 286–307. For analyses of Schley's strange behavior in this period, see Leech, *McKinley*, 220–23; Mitchell, *Modern Navy*, 95–97, 144–46; Long, *New Navy*, I, 275, II, 189–94; Mayo (ed.), *Journal of Long*, 232–33; Cummings, *Wainwright*, Chap. 18, *passim*. Schley's version of the case appears in his book, *Forty-Five Years under the Flag*, which was published about three years after his censure by a court of inquiry.

squadron might escape in Schley's absence, he ordered Sampson to make all possible speed for Santiago with the *New York* and *Oregon*.[21] But Commodore Schley had in the meantime managed to coal at sea. This accomplished, he headed back for Santiago, arriving at dusk on May 28. The next morning his lookouts discovered the *Colón* lying at anchor near the harbor entrance. The Flying Squadron and the *Iowa* maintained a blockade for three days thereafter, without making a serious move against the enemy.[22]

On June 1 the *New York* and the *Oregon*, in company with the armed yacht *Mayflower* and the torpedo-boat *Porter*, joined the blockade line off Santiago. Thereupon, Admiral Sampson assumed command of the operation, deploying his ships at intervals on the perimeter of a semi-circle whose center lay opposite the Morro Castle battery and whose ends ranged from four to six miles off the coast. Thus began the siege of Santiago, in which a total of eighteen men-of-war took part, including the protected cruiser *Marblehead*; the auxiliaries *Harvard, Yankee, Suwanee, New Orleans,* and *St. Louis;* the armed yachts *Vixen* and *Gloucester;* the dynamite crusier *Vesuvius;* and the aged dispatch-boat *Dolphin*.[23] The Navy Department was taking no chances; as a cartoonist depicting Uncle Sam holding Santiago in a nutcracker suggested, "This one's tougher than Manila, but I'll crack it all right, all right!" [24]

Further to seal off the enemy's escape route, Admiral Sampson detailed Lieutenant R. P. Hobson of the *New York* to sink the collier *Merrimac* in mid-channel just inside the harbor mouth. Hobson attempted this feat on the night of June 3 but, though hailed as a hero in the press, he failed when the *Merrimac* sank short of the mark.[25] For a month following this attempt, the blockaders subjected the shore batteries to continuous bombardment.

During this period, in compliance with the department's decision to acquire a base closer than Key West to the scene of action, the *Marblehead* and *Yankee* took aboard 100 marines from the *New York* and *Oregon* and departed for Guantanamo. The marines landed on June 7

21 Chadwick, *Spanish War,* I, 322–25.
22 *Ibid.,* 324–26.
23 Wilson, *The Downfall of Spain,* 254-58; Potter and Nimitz (eds.), *Sea Power,* 372–73; Navy Dept., *Annual Report,* 1898; Mitchell, *Modern Navy,* 99.
24 This cartoon appeared in Chicago *Times-Herald,* June 13, 1898.
25 Chadwick, *Spanish War,* I, 335–46. Hobson was taken prisoner by an armed launch after the attempt to block the channel failed. Cervera treated him well while he was held at Morro Castle. For press accounts, see: New York *Tribune,* and Norwich (Conn.) *Weekly Courier,* June 5, 1898.

and, within three days, received 647 reinforcements brought by the *Panther* from Key West. After taking heavy casualties, the Americans ultimately secured Guantanamo.[26]

These landings served as the prelude to the more complex amphibious operation undertaken by Major-General William Shafter's 5th Army Corps in late June at Daiquiri, some fifteen nautical miles east of Santiago. This expedition, which involved 20,000 men, 37 chartered transports, and a naval escort of 16 warships led by the *Indiana*, was held up for a week at the embarkation port of Tampa in deference to a false report of enemy warships in the Florida Straits.[27]

As conceived by the War and Navy Departments, the Army's mission was to cooperate with Admiral Sampson in his effort to destroy the Spanish fleet in Santiago Bay. Sampson interpreted this as a measure to silence the batteries ringing the bay in order to allow him time to clear the channel of live mines before forcing the entrance and attacking Cervera's warships. Unknown to the admiral, however, General Shafter construed his orders as a carte blanche for whatever line of action he chose to pursue. Disdaining a subordinate role, he selected as his primary objective the city of Santiago instead of the harbor batteries. With this in mind, the general halted the convoy on June 20 at a point fifteen miles off Daiquiri's coral strand, though smoother beaches lay nearer the entrance to Santiago Bay.[28]

Since the War Department had not provided lighters for the landing at Daiquiri, the North Atlantic Squadron, most of whose small boats had on Long's orders been laid up at Key West, was obliged to furnish fifty launches, cutters, and whaleboats, with crews, to ferry the troops to shore.[29]

The naval crews landed their charges on schedule and without mishap. Once ashore, the soldiers moved rapidly inland on the twenty-two-mile

26 A good description of the fighting at Guantanamo was published in the New York *Tribune*, June 13, 1898. See also, Chadwick, *Spanish War*, II, 355–56; Navy Dept., *Annual Report*, 1898; Chicago *Times-Herald*, New York *Herald*, June 13, 1898.

27 T. Roosevelt, *The Rough Riders* (New York, 1904), 54–62; Chadwick, *Spanish War*, II, 3–19. Briefer descriptions of the embarkation at Tampa appear in Leech, *McKinley*, 225–27.

28 Long, *New Navy*, II, 23–26; Mayo (ed.), *Journal of Long*, 203–204; Chadwick, *Spanish War*, II, 6, 191–204. Despite Chadwick's loyalty to Sampson and Shafter's loose interpretation of the War Department's orders, the captain developed a liking for the general. For a critical view of the Daiquiri operation, see New York *Herald*, July 7, 1898.

29 Chadwick, *Spanish War*, II, 30.

march toward their goal. But Spanish resistance stiffened along the route, especially at El Caney and San Juan, where the American drive was checked with heavy losses. On July 2, despairing of his hope to capture Santiago, Shafter dispatched a message to Sampson requesting him to force the harbor entrance at once for the purpose of relieving the pressure on the Army. To this, Sampson replied that he would comply if the general insisted, but that he preferred to countermine the harbor first lest he jeopardize further the positions of both services.[30]

The admiral's patience never failed him during this remarkable exchange, despite his private exasperation at Shafter's patent desire to reverse their missions. As Sampson knew, the Army was expected to serve as an adjunct to the fleet, but the general's message of July 2 put the shoe on the other foot.

In any event, before the admiral had a chance to discuss the matter with Shafter in person on the morning of July 3, Cervera called the tune. Less than forty minutes after the New York left station to carry Sampson eastward to the Army's field headquarters, the Cuba Squadron weighed anchor and made for the open sea.

The Spanish commander's sortie that eventful morning followed weeks of agonizing evaluations of his position. He had arrived on May 19 with one ship missing and two others in deplorable condition. The Terror had broken down at sea and, after the rest of the squadron had fueled at Martinique, had remained in port to make repairs. The Vizcaya's bottom was foul and unless she could be scraped beforehand, her speed in combat would be drastically reduced. Worst of all, the Colón's main guns, which had not been ready prior to the departure from Cape Verde, were still in Spain.

Contrary to American intelligence reports, Cervera had neither guns nor extra provisions aboard his ships when he arrived at Santiago in mid-May. Both coal and food were scarce in the city, which meant that fires must be banked and meals rationed. The city's defenses needed men, and Cervera reluctantly supplied seamen to reinforce them. With his ships in dubious repair, fires banked, and two thirds of his sailors ashore, the commander felt constrained to reject Governor Blanco's repeated pleas for a surprise sortie.

As time passed with no solution in sight, Blanco's pleas became more insistent. Finally, declaring that Spain must not suffer the shame of losing the fleet in port, he ordered Cervera to prepare for departure

30 *Ibid.*, 33.

before the city fell. The admiral answered that he would leave port as soon as steam could be built up and his men re-embarked.

On July 2, Captain Victor Concas, Cervera's chief of staff, reported the current disposition of enemy ships. "His ships resting against Daiquiri in the east . . . formed a great arc; on the east was the *Indiana*, and thence toward the west, the *New York*, *Oregon*, *Iowa*, *Massachusetts*, and *Texas*, which latter was . . . about south of the entrance. Near the shore to the west was the yacht *Vixen* . . . , and supporting the yacht was the *Brooklyn* in the middle of this interval and far away from the other ships; leaving always a large space open to the southwest, between the *Texas* and the shore." [31]

Using Concas' report as a base, the Spanish staff plotted the order of steaming for the next morning. The *Vizcaya*, *Colón*, and *Oquendo* in that order would form a column astern of the flagship *Maria Teresa* and stand out the harbor at six hundred-yard intervals, followed at one thousand yards by the *Pluton* and finally the *Fury*. Once clear of the harbor, the column was to head due west for Cienfuegos or Havana at flank speed. The flagship would then, in hopes of distracting the Americans and eliminating their fastest ship, close the *Brooklyn* to ram, while the column, now led by the *Vizcaya*, would continue westward, between the *Brooklyn* and the coast, without going to the aid of the *Teresa*. Excepting the latter, Cervera's men-of-war were not to engage the enemy "unless a good chance should offer." [32]

Reconnoitering again on the morning of July 3, Captain Concas observed the absence of the *Massachusetts*, which had left the line to refuel at Guantanamo, and noted that the *Indiana* stood closer to the shore than usual. The *Brooklyn*, "perhaps because it was Sunday and she could not communicate with the land," had moved nearer the *Texas* and thus opened wider the gap to the southwest, with only the *Vixen* between her and the shore. Concas did not realize of course that the *New York* would leave her station before nine o'clock and be replaced by the slower *Indiana*. Nor did he know that none of the remaining blockaders, excepting the *Oregon* and *Texas*, were capable of instantaneous operation at full power; they had secured some of their boilers to save coal.[33]

31 *Ibid.*, 107–108, 129. See also, Mitchell, *Modern Navy*, 100–101.
32 Chadwick has reproduced in his *Spanish War*, II, Chap. 6, the texts of messages exchanged between Cervera and his superiors, especially Governor Blanco, citing Cervera, *Collection of Documents*, 106.
33 Chadwick, *Spanish War*, II, Chap. 6, *passim*.

At 9:35 A.M. Cervera's black hulls emerged in single file from the bay, with red and gold ensigns flying at the peak and figureheads glistening in the morning sun. They came out, according to Captain John Philip of the *Texas*, "as gaily as brides to the altar." The simile did not apply for long; soon the "brides" were belching fire and smoke, while the Americans returned the fire and struggled to execute Sampson's standing order to close and engage the enemy on sight.[34]

Schley, who had received no official word of the admiral's departure, was happy to find himself senior officer present. With only half of his boilers lit off, he headed for the Spanish column, signaling the squadron to follow the *Brooklyn's* movements and opening fire with his port forward guns. Then, seeing the *Teresa* closing rapidly, the commodore swung his flagship sharply to starboard, away from the oncoming enemy cruiser and directly into the path of the *Texas*. Backing down hard, the latter barely escaped a collision with the *Brooklyn*, which continued her loop until both the Texas and Iowa stood between her and the *Teresa*.

Her turn completed, the *Brooklyn* picked up speed and joined the *Iowa*, *Texas*, *Oregon*, and *Indiana* in hot pursuit of the fleeing Spanish cruisers, while the *Gloucester* and *Vixen* harried the destroyers. Having heard the gunfire, Admiral Sampson ordered the *New York's* course reversed and her engines brought up to flank speed to overtake the pursuers as rapidly as possible.

Before the chase was fairly underway, with the *Brooklyn* and the battleships paralleling the enemy's westerly heading, the Americans' heavy guns began to take effect. Devastated by the punishing fire, Cervera's ships fought on until, one by one, they were sunk or forced to run aground and surrender. By noon, only the *Colón* remained in action, with a six-mile lead over the *Brooklyn* and *Oregon*. Taking hits at long range, the *Colón* seemed on the verge of escape when the *Oregon*, with an unexpected burst of speed, reduced the interval between them. At 1:20

---

34 Captain Philip is quoted in Leech, *McKinley*, 255. See also: "The Story of the Captains," *Century Magazine* (May, 1899). This describes the blockading fleet as it was on the morning of July 3, prior to the Spanish sortie. Schley claimed that his suspicions were aroused on the preceding evening when rumors reached the *Brooklyn* that Cervera was getting up steam. See Schley, *Forty-Five Years*, 296–97; *Record of Proceedings of a Court of Inquiry in the Case of Rear-Admiral W. S. Schley* (Washington, 1902), II, 1384; hereinafter cited as *Case of Schley*. If so, it seems curious that the commodore neither alerted Sampson nor lit off his own boilers on the *Brooklyn*.

P.M. the *Colón's* commander gave up the race, struck his colors and opened the ship's sea cocks.[35] The battle of Santiago was over; Spanish losses included Cervera's six ships and some six hundred men, killed or wounded. The North Atlantic Squadron suffered slight damage to its ships and the loss of only one life. The destruction of the Cuba Squadron enabled General Shafter to start advancing again on Santiago; he received the city's surrender within two weeks of the naval engagement.[36]

The Navy's victory off Santiago, which virtually ended the war, evoked thunderous applause across the nation. Sampson and Schley became heroes overnight, though their reputations never reached the rarefied air surrounding Dewey's image.[37] Despite the apparent ease with which the American commanders destroyed the enemy forces at Manila and Santiago, they took unnecessary chances and made numerous mistakes in the process. Dewey risked his entire squadron by attacking Montojo's position within range of Cavite's batteries. If the Spanish gunners had been more accurate, the commodore might well have found himself with several disabled ships some seven thousand miles from the nearest American shipyard.

Sampson left himself open to criticism when, to form his Puerto Rican expedition in May, he weakened the blockade of Cuba. Captain Mahan condemned this move on the grounds that Sampson abandoned the island—his primary responsibility as long as Cervera's squadron remained at large and intact—to chase a will-of-the-wisp at San Juan. In the opinion of experts, Sampson erred again on two occasions at Santiago: first, by removing the *New York* from the line despite the absence of the *Massa-*

---

35 For the official account of the battle, written by Admiral Sampson, see Navy Dept., *Annual Report*, 1898. He narrates his actions during the chase in an article, "The Atlantic Fleet in the Spanish War," *Century Magazine* (April, 1899). Of the many accounts of the battle of Santiago, perhaps the most reliable besides the official one appears in Chadwick, *Spanish War*, II, Chap. 7, *passim*. Other accounts by naval authors include Schley, *Forty-Five Years*, 310–11; Robley Evans, *Sailor's Log*, 448. Evans was commanding officer of the *Brooklyn*, Schley's flagship. For newspaper reports of the naval action, see Chicago *Daily News*, July 5, 1898; New York *Times*, July 5, 1898; Philadelphia *Press*, July 6, 1898.

36 Navy Dept., *Annual Report*, 1898.

37 Throughout the war, however, Schley enjoyed great familiarity with correspondents who depicted him as a gruff sea-dog; they had less liking for the taciturn Sampson. The differences between these two men, and the complicated preliminaries to the destruction of the enemy squadron, undoubtedly cast them in Dewey's shadow. His campaign was characterized by direct action and singleness of purpose. Far more remote than Sampson's force, the Asiatic Squadron achieved a success unmarred by disputes over command, movements, and the like.

chusetts and by allowing his ship captains to shut down their boilers at will—in the face of the Spanish force.[38]

Commodore Schley's conduct during the passage to Cienfuegos and Santiago in late May and his turn away from the *Maria Teresa* on July 3 became the subjects of a court of inquiry convened at his request in 1901. The court found that his behavior in the first instance was "characterized by vacillation, dilatoriness, and a lack of enterprise," and that his reports of coal consumption by the Flying Squadron "were inaccurate and misleading." In the second instance, the court berated Schley for turning into the path of the *Texas* and thus causing her to back down and lose time, but judged him "self-possessed" in battle and praised him for encouraging, "in his own person, his subordinate officers and men to fight courageously." The court then recommended that the case be dropped; the secretary of the navy concurred.[39]

According to that son of old Ireland, Mr. Dooley, the United States carried on the war in a dream, while Spain fought in a trance. Although the Navy performed well in contrast with the enemy and the Army, it was by no means free of defects. American gunnery, though more accurate than the enemy's, left much to be desired. Long-range bombardments of shore batteries, such as those undertaken at San Juan and Santiago, proved worthless. Squadron commanders assigned torpedoboats to every conceivable mission except that for which they were designed. Security at sea was lax; correspondents on press boats followed warships and reported their movements freely, no matter how urgent the need for secrecy. Even graver was the absence of a general board to oversee naval operations and insure proper liaison with the Army.

The Spanish naval efforts suffered from even more serious ills. From the outset, a conspicuous lack of planning marked the enemy's operations. Cervera's hasty departure from the Cape Verde Islands provided a case in point. If the ministry had delayed him long enough to allow for the installation of the *Colón's* heavy guns, he might have been able to count on the services of the *Pelayo* and *Carlos V*. Cervera himself overestimated the strength of the blockade before the Flying Squadron returned to Santiago and thus failed to avail himself of the opportunity to escape presented by Schley's inept—or insubordinate—actions. Indeed, Governor

38 Potter and Nimitz (eds.), *Sea Power*, 371; Mitchell, *Modern Navy*, 102, 107. A. T. Mahan, *Lessons of the War with Spain and Other Articles* (Boston, 1899), 43–48.
39 *Case of Schley*, II, 2290ff.

Blanco might well have accused him of "dilatoriness" for refusing to consider a sortie at the time.[40]

After the victory at Santiago, there remained certain unfinished business of concern to the Navy. A Spanish fleet under the command of Admiral Camara, consisting of the *Pelayo, Carlos V,* and six lighter warships, had left Cadiz on June 16 with four troop transports under escort. When this force entered the Suez Canal in July, the Navy Department decided to reinforce Dewey, lest Camara attack him, and to organize an Eastern Squadron for the purpose of raiding the coast of Spain. The war board need not have worried; Camara was heading for the Philippines, not to attack Dewey's squadron but to sustain Spanish claims to the islands by his presence when peace negotiations began, as they did on June 30. When word of the plan to raid the coast reached Madrid, the ministry, on July 5, recalled Camara's fleet to Cadíz.[41]

Dewey's reinforcements included the *Charleston,* which arrived at Manila on June 30, having seized Guam and Wake while escorting Merritt's first division from California. By mid-August, when hostilities ceased, the *Monterey* and *Monadnock* had also joined the Asiatic Squadron. Thus enlarged, Dewey's force supported the campaign of General Merritt in uneasy alliance with Filipino rebel leader Emilio Aguinaldo, whom the commodore had imported from Hong Kong in May to harass the Spanish. Manila fell on August 14, about a month after the *Philadelphia* and *Mohican* had arrived at Honolulu to participate in ceremonies marking the annexation of Hawaii.[42] Before the war ended, General Nelson Mile's 1st Army Group had, with the assistance of the North Atlantic Squadron, landed in Puerto Rico, where he proceeded against token Spanish resistance to take possession and to establish military governments in the principal towns.[43]

Preliminary peace negotiations were underway when Cervera made

40 Mitchell, *Modern Navy,* 107; Chadwick, *Spanish War,* Chap. 6, *passim.* For mistakes on both sides, see Sprout, *Naval Power,* 230–40; Mahan, *Lessons of the War with Spain, passim.*
41 Chadwick, *Spanish War,* II, Chap. 17, *passim;* Mitchell, *Modern Navy,* 75–76, 92, 106.
42 Potter and Nimitz (eds.), *Sea Power,* 370ff. See also, Navy Dept., *Annual Report,* 1898. For the jubilant press reaction to the surrender of Manila, see for example, Chicago *Times-Herald,* August 18, 1898; New York *Herald,* August 18, 1898; Baltimore *American,* August 19, 1898. The press hailed also the annexation of Hawaii; see Chicago *Times-Herald,* July 28, 1898; New York *Times,* July 28, 1898.
43 Navy Dept., *Annual Report,* 1898; Chadwick, *Spanish War,* II, Chap. 13, *passim.* See New York *Herald,* July 28, 1898; Chicago *Times-Herald,* July 28, 1898.

his final sortie, with French Ambassador Jules Cambon acting as Spain's envoy extraordinary with full authority to arrange an armistice. McKinley signed this agreement on August 12 and ordered his commanders to cease hostilities in all zones. By the terms of the preliminary protocol, Spain relinquished its sovereignty over Cuba and Puerto Rico, recognized America's control of Manila Bay, and promised to evacuate these areas as quickly as possible. The fate of the entire Philippine chain was to be left to a formal peace conference to convene at Paris by October 1. [44]

Thus, in one hundred days, the United States rose from continental to world power, with a Navy ranking sixth among the fleets of the world. Despite their shortcomings, American naval operations vindicated the theories of Mahan as applied in Tracy's policy revolution of 1890 and more than justified the general's preservation of the War College, whose graduates in many cases handled the warships engaged. Teddy Roosevelt had his war; it was indeed a bully fight. [45]

44 For the final peace negotiations by the commissioners in Paris, see Bemis, *Diplomatic History of the United States*, 469–75; J. Pratt, *Foreign Policy*, 384–94. Reflections of newspaper editorial reaction to the armistice signed in August appear in New York *Commercial Advertiser*, August 13, 1898; New York *Tribune*, August 13, 1898; Boston *Transcript*, August 13, 1898; London *Daily Mail*, August 15, 1898; New York *Sun*, August 15, 1898. By virtue of the Teller Amendment to the congressional resolutions for intervention, Cuba would gain independence as an American protectorate.

45 Roosevelt is said to have responded to John Hay's observation that the contest with Spain had been a "splendid little war" with the remark that it had indeed been a "bully fight."

BIBLIOGRAPHY

Official Papers

U.S. Navy Department. Bureau of Construction and Repair Memorandum October 18, 1915. Southern Historical Collection, University of North Carolina Library, Chapel Hill.

————. Bureau of Navigation Cipher Records, 1889–97. National Archives, Washington, D. C.

————. Bureau of Navigation Dispatch Files, 1889–97. National Archives.

————. Bureau of Navigation Executive Books, No. I, II, 1889–93. National Archives.

————. Bureau of Navigation General Letters Books, Sent and Received, 1889–98. National Archives.

————. Memoranda to the Secretary, 1892–98. National Archives.

————. Naval War College. Letters of the Presidents of the War College, 1889–1914. Naval War College Library, Newport, R. I.

U. S. State Department. Dispatches: Chile, 1889–92. National Archives.

————. Dispatches: Haiti, 1886–92. National Archives.

————. Dispatches: Santo Domingo, 1889–93. National Archives.

————. Instructions: Chile, 1889–92. National Archives.

————. Instructions: Haiti, 1886–92. National Archives.

————. Instructions: Santo Domingo, 1889–93. National Archives.

————. Miscellaneous Letters, 1889–95. National Archives.

Private Papers

William E. Chandler Papers. Manuscript Division, Library of Congress, Washington, D. C.
Stephen B. Elkins Papers. West Virginia University Library, Morgantown, W. Va.
Eugene Hale Letters. Manuscript Division, Library of Congress.
Benjamin Harrison Papers. Manuscript Division, Library of Congress.
Hilary A. Herbert Papers. Southern Historical Collection, University of North Carolina Library.
Stephen B. Luce Papers. Naval Historical Foundation Collection, Manuscript Division, Library of Congress.
Alfred T. Mahan Papers. Puleston Collection, Manuscript Division, Library of Congress.
Alfred T. Mahan Miscellaneous Letters and Papers. Naval War College Library.
Lewis T. Michener Papers. Manuscript Division, Library of Congress.
Division, Library of Congress.
Whitelaw Reid Papers. Manuscript Division, Library of Congress.
Benjamin F. Tracy Papers. Manuscript Division, Library of Congress.
David D. Porter Papers. Naval Historical Foundation Collection, Manuscript

Government Documents

Bureau of the Census. *Historical Statistics of the United States*, 1789–1945. Washington, D. C., 1946.
Congressional Record, 39th Congress, 1st Session, through 55th Congress, 2nd Session. Washington, D. C., 1865–1911.
House Executives Documents. 39th Congress, 1st Session, to 55th Congress, 2nd Session. Washington, D. C., 1865–1909.
Official Records of the Union and Confederate Navies in the War of the Rebellion. 31 vols. Washington, D. C., 1880–1912.
The Printed Argument on Behalf of the United States of Venezuela before the Tribunal of Arbitration. London, 1899.
Richardson, James D. (comp.), *A Compilation of the Messages and Papers of the Presidents*. 11 vols. Washington, D. C., 1890–1912.
Senate Executive Documents. 39th Congress, 1st Session, through 55th Congress, 2nd Session. Washington, D. C., 1865–1911.
U. S. Navy Department. *Annual Reports of the Secretary of the Navy*. Washington, D. C., 1865–99.
————. *Navy Register*. Washington, D. C., 1886–98.
————. *Navy Yearbook*. Washington, D. C., 1911, 1917.
————. Office of Naval Intelligence. *War Series, IV*. Washington, D. C., 1892.
————. *Record of Proceedings of a Court of Inquiry in the Case of Rear Admiral W. S. Schley*. Washington, D. C., 1902.
————. *Regulations for the Government of the Navy*. Washington, D. C., 1880, 1893.
U. S. Navy Historical Division. *Destroyers in the U. S. Navy*. Washington, D. C., 1963.

The War of the Rebellion: A Compilation of the Official Records of the Union and Confederate Armies. 70 vols., 128 parts. Washington, D. C., 1880–1901.

Writings of Contemporaries

Alexander, D. S. *A Political History of the State of New York.* 3 vols. New York, 1909–21.

————. *Four Famous New Yorkers.* New York, 1923.

American Iron and Steel Association. *History of the Manufacture of Armor Plate for the United States Navy.* Philadelphia, 1899.

Ammen, David. *The Atlantic Coast.* New York, 1883.

————. *The Old Navy and the New.* Philadelphia, 1891.

Baird, G. W. "The U.S. Ship Trenton," U. S. Naval Institute *Proceedings*, IV, Pt. I (1878), 5–20.

Bennett, F. M. *The Monitor and the Navy under Steam.* Cambridge, Mass., 1900.

————. *The Steam Navy of the United States.* Pittsburgh, 1896.

Boutwell, G. S. *Reminiscences of Sixty Years in Public Affairs,* 2 vols. New York, 1902.

Bowles, F. T. "Our New Cruisers," U. S. Naval Institute *Proceedings*, IX (1883), 596ff.

Breen, M. P. *Thirty Years of New York Politics.* New York, 1899.

Calkins, G. G. "Historical and Professional Notes on the Naval Campaign of Manila Bay," U. S. Naval Institute *Proceedings*, XXVI (1899), 274ff.

Campbell-Copeland, Thomas. *Harrison and Reid: Their Lives and Records.* New York, 1892.

Carnegie, Andrew. *The Autobiography of Andrew Carnegie.* New York, 1905.

Chadwick, F. E. "Navy Department Organization," U. S. Naval Institute *Proceedings*, XX (1894), 493ff.

————. *The New American Navy.* New York, 1915.

————. *The Relations of the United States and Spain: Diplomacy.* New York, 1910.

————. *The Relations of the United States and Spain: The Spanish War.* 2 vols. New York, 1911.

Clark, N. B. "Petroleum for Warships," U. S. Naval Institute *Proceedings*, IX (1883), 798ff.

Collins, Frederick. "Naval Affairs," U. S. Naval Institute *Proceedings*, V (1879), 166ff.

Curtis, W. E. *From the Andes to the Ocean.* Chicago, 1900.

Dewey, George. *Autobiography of George Dewey, Admiral of the Navy.* New York, 1913.

Douglass, Frederick. "Haiti and the United States," *North American Review*, CLIII (1891), 342ff.

Dunnell, E. G. "Secretary of the Navy Benjamin F. Tracy," *The Epoch* (June 7, 1889).

Evans, R. D. *A Sailor's Log: Recollections of Forty Years of Naval Life.* New York, 1903.

Fiske, B. A. *From Midshipman to Rear Admiral.* New York, 1919.

Foster, John W. *Diplomatic Memoirs.* 2 vols. Boston, 1909.

Fox, Gustavus Vasa. *The Confidential Correspondence of Gustavus Vasa Fox,*
   ed. Robert M. Thompson. 2 vols. New York, 1918.
Fullam, W. F. "The Organization of Naval Personnel," U. S. Naval Institute
   Proceedings, XX (1896), 83ff.
Gay, W. B. (comp.) *Historical Gazetteer of Tioga County, New York,*
   1785-1888. Syracuse, 1888.
Gwynne, Stephen. *The Letters and Friendships of Sir Cecil Spring-Rice.*
   2 vols. Boston, 1929.
Hall, Henry. "American Shipping," *Atlantic Monthly* (February, 1881), 162ff.
Hancock, A. U. *History of Chile.* Chicago, 1893.
Hart, A. B. *Practical Essays on American Government.* New York, 1893.
————. "The Monroe Doctrine in Its Territorial Extent and Application,"
   U. S. Naval Institute *Proceedings,* XXXII (1906), 788ff.
Hoff, W. B. "A View of Our Naval Policy," U. S. Naval Institute *Proceed-*
   ings, XII (1886), 126ff.
Jeffers, W. N. "The Armament of Our Ships of War," U. S. Naval Institute
   Proceedings, I (1874), 119-20.
Lodge, H. C. *Selections from the Correspondence of Theodore Roosevelt*
   and Henry Cabot Lodge. 2 vols. New York, 1925.
Long, J. D. *The New American Navy.* 2 vols. New York, 1903.
Luce, S. B. "As to Navy Yards and Their Defense," U. S. Naval Institute
   Proceedings, XXI (1895), 638ff.
————. "Benefits of War," *Literary Digest,* IV (1891), 6ff.
————. "Fleets of the World," U. S. Naval Institute *Proceedings,* III
   (1877), 20ff.
————. "The Naval War College," U. S. Naval Institute *Proceedings,*
   XXXVI (1911), 571ff.
————. "War Schools," U. S. Naval Institute *Proceedings,* IX (1883), 658ff.
McAdoo, W. G. "The Navy and the Nation," U. S. Naval Institute *Proceed-*
   ings, XX (1894). 399ff.
Mahan, A. T. *From Sail to Steam: Recollections of Naval Life.* 2 vols. New
   York, 1908.
————. "The Future in Relation to American Naval Power," *Harper's*
   Magazine, XLI (October, 1895), 773ff.
————. *The Gulf and Inland Waters.* New York, 1883.
————. "Hawaii and Our Future Sea Power," *The Forum,* XV (March,
   1893).
————. *The Influence of Sea Power upon History.* Boston, 1890.
————. *The Interest of America in Sea Power: Present and Future.* New
   York, 1898.
————. "The Isthmus and Sea Power," *Atlantic Monthly,* LXXII (October,
   1893), 471ff.
————. *Lessons of the War with Spain and Other Articles.* Boston, 1899.
————. *Life of Nelson: The Embodiment of the Sea Power of Great*
   Britain. Boston, 1899.
————. *Sea Power in Its Relations to the War of 1812.* 2 vols. Boston, 1905.
————. "The Strategic Future of the Gulf of Mexico and the Caribbean
   Sea," *Harper's Magazine,* XCV (October, 1897), 680ff.

————. "A Twentieth-Century Outlook," *Harper's Magazine*, XCV (September, 1897).

————. "The United States Looking Outward," *Atlantic Monthly*, LXVI (December, 1890).

Mayo, L. S. (ed.). *American of Yesterday, As Reflected in the Journal of John Davis Long*. Boston, 1923.

Moore, J. B. *Principles of American Diplomacy*. New York, 1918.

————. "The Late Chilean Controversy," *Political Science Quarterly*, III (September, 1893), 467ff.

————. *The United States*. Vol. VII of *The Cambridge Modern History*, eds. Ward, A. A., and others. 13 vols. London, 1902–12.

Parker, F. A. "Our Fleet Maneuvers in the Bay of Florida and the Navy of the Future," U. S. Naval Institute *Proceedings*, I, (1874), 163ff.

Peck, H. T. "Twenty Years of the Republic," *The Bookman*, XXI, (April, 1905), Pt. IV.

Platt, F. H. *Memorial to Benjamin Franklin Tracy*, privately printed by the New York Bar Association. New York, 1916.

Platt, T. C. *The Autobiography of Thomas Collier Platt*. New York, 1910.

Porter, D. D., *Naval History of the Civil War*. New York, 1886.

Robie, E. D. "Discussion of Iron and Steel in the Construction of Vessels of War," U. S. Naval Institute *Proceedings*, VIII (1882), 168ff.

Rodgers, W. L. "Examination of the Testimony Taken by the Joint Committees of the House and Senate in regard to the reorganization of the Navy," U. S. Naval Institute *Proceedings*, XX (1894), 747ff.

Roosevelt, Theodore. *An Autobiography*. New York, 1913.

————. "The Foreign Policy of Benjamin Harrison," *The Independence* (New York), August 11, 1892, 1ff.

————. *The Naval War of 1812*. New York, 1903.

————. *The Rough Riders*. New York, 1904.

Sampson, W. T. "The Atlantic Fleet in the Spanish War," *Century Magazine* (April, 1899), 3ff.

Schley, W. S. *Forty-Five Years under the Flag*. New York, 1904.

Schurz, Carl. "Manifest Destiny," *Harper's Magazine*, LXXXVIII (March, 1893), 753ff.

Simpson, Edward. "The Navy and Its Prospects of Rehabilitation," U. S. Naval Institute *Proceedings*, XII (1886), 1ff.

————. "The United States Navy in Transition," *Harper's Magazine*, LXXIII (June, 1886), 4ff.

Smith, R. C. "Disposition of the Fleet," U. S. Naval Institute *Proceedings*, XVII (1891), 123ff.

Soley, J. C. "On a Proposed Type of Cruiser," U. S. Naval Institute *Proceedings*, VI, Pt. II (1878), 126ff.

Soley, J. R. *Admiral Porter*. New York, 1913.

————. *Report on Foreign Systems of Naval Education*. Washington, D. C., 1880.

————. *The Blockade and the Cruisers*. New York, 1883.

Spears, John. "The American Navy," *The Chatauquan* (May, 1890) 11ff.

Stebbins, N. L. *The New Navy of the United States*. New York, 1912.

Storer, M. L. "How Theodore Roosevelt was Appointed Assistant Secretary of the Navy," *Harper's Weekly*, LVI (June 11, 1912), 9ff.

"The Story of the Captains," *Century Magazine* (May 1899), 8ff.

Taylor, H. C. "Extracts from Captain Taylor's Address," U. S. Naval Institute *Proceedings*, XX (1894), 796ff.

Tracy, B. F. "Our New Warships," *North American Review*, CLII (June, 1891), 641ff.

————. "The Behring Sea Question," *North American Review*, CLVI (May, 1893), 513ff.

Very, E. W. "Prize Essay Discussion," U. S. Naval Institute *Proceedings*, VIII (1882), 454ff.

————. "Development of Armor for Naval Use," U. S. Naval Institute *Proceedings*, IX (1883), 421ff.

Welles, Gideon. *The Diary of Gideon Welles, Secretary of the Navy under Lincoln and Johnson*, ed. J. T. Morse. 3 vols. Boston, 1911.

Recent Books

Alden, C. S., and Allan Westcott. *The United States Navy: A History.* Chicago, 1943.

Ambrose, S. E. *Upton and the Army.* Baton Rouge, 1964.

Ballard, R. N. *The Influence of the Sea on the Political History of Japan.* New York, 1921.

Baxter, J. P. *Introduction of the Ironclad Warship.* Cambridge, Mass., 1933.

Beale, H. K. *Theodore Roosevelt and the Rise of America to World Power.* Baltimore, 1956.

Bemis, S. F. *A Diplomatic History of the United States.* New York, 1965.

————. (ed.). *American Secretaries of State and Their Diplomacy.* 10 vols. New York, 1927–29.

Bernardo, C. J., and E. H. Bacon. *American Military Policy: Its Development since 1775.* Harrisburg, Pa., 1957.

Chapelle, H. I. *The History of the American Sailing Navy.* New York, 1949.

Cortissoz, Royal. *The Life of Whitelaw Reid.* 2 vols. New York, 1921.

Craven, Avery (ed.). *Essays in Honor of William E. Dodd.* Chicago, 1935.

Cummings, D. E. *Admiral Richard Wainwright and the U. S. Fleet.* Washington, D. C., 1962.

Davis, G. T. *A Navy Second to None.* New York, 1940.

Dennett, Tyler, *John Hay: From Poetry to Politics.* New York, 1933.

Dulles, F. R. *America's Rise to World Power.* New York, 1954.

Durkin, J. T. *Stephen R. Mallory, Confederate Navy Chief.* Chapel Hill, N. C., 1954.

Evans, H. C. *Chile and Its Relations with the United States.* Durham, N. C., 1927.

Falk, E. A. *Fighting Bob Evans.* New York, 1931.

————. *Togo and the Rise of Japanese Sea Power.* New York, 1936.

Forester, C. S. *The Age of Fighting Sail.* Garden City, N. Y., 1956.

Freidel, Frank. *The Splendid Little War.* Boston, 1958.

Galdames, Luis. *Estudio de la Historica de Chile.* Santiago de Chile, 1911.

Garraty, J. A. *Henry Cabot Lodge: A Biography.* New York, 1953.

Gleaves, Albert. *The Life and Letters of Rear Admiral Stephen B. Luce.* New York, 1925.

Gosnell, H. F. *Boss Platt and His New York Machine.* New York, 1924.

Green, T. P. *American Imperialism in 1898.* Boston, 1955.

Hendrick, B. J. *Andrew Carnegie.* 2 vols. New York, 1932.

Hill, L. F. *Diplomatic Relations Between the United States and Brazil.* New York, 1937.

Hirsch, M. D. *William C. Whitney: Modern Warwick.* New York, 1938.

Hough, Richard. *Admirals in Collision.* New York, 1960.

Howe, G. P. *Chester A. Arthur.* New York, 1934.

Hunt, Thomas. *The Life of William H. Hunt.* Brattleboro, Vt., 1922.

Huntington, S. P. *The Soldier and the State.* New York, 1964.

Kirkland, E. C. *Industry Comes of Age.* New York, 1961.

Knox, D. W. *A History of the United States Navy.* New York, 1936.

Kraft, H. F., and W. B. Norris. *Sea Power in American History.* New York, 1920.

La Feber, Walter. *The New Empire: An Interpretation of American Expansion.* Ithaca, N. Y., 1963.

Leech, Margaret. *In the Days of McKinley.* New York, 1959.

Lewis, Michael. *The History of the British Navy.* Harmondsworth, Essex, 1957.

Livezey, W. E. *Mahan on Sea Power.* Norman, Okla., 1947.

Lovette, L. P. *Naval Customs, Traditions and Usage.* Annapolis, 1934.

Low, R. C. *Seth Low.* New York, 1925.

Macartney, C. E. *Mr. Lincoln's Admirals.* New York, 1956.

May, E. R. *Imperial Democracy.* New York, 1961.

Millis, Walter. *Arms and Men.* New York, 1956.

————. *The Martial Spirit.* Cambridge, Mass., 1931.

Mitchell, D. W. *History of the Modern American Navy from 1883 through Pearl Harbor.* New York, 1946.

Montague, L. L. *Haiti and the United States: 1714–1948.* Durham, N. C., 1948.

Moos, Malsolm. *The Republicans: A History of Their Party.* New York, 1956.

Morgan, H. W. *William McKinley and His America.* Syracuse, N. Y., 1963.

Morison, E. E., and J. H. Blum (eds.). *The Letters of Theodore Roosevelt.* 8 vols. Cambridge, Mass., 1951–54.

Mowat, R. D. *The Life of Lord Pauncefote.* Boston, 1929.

Muzzey, D. S. *James Gillespie Blaine.* New York, 1934.

Nevins, Allan. *Grover Cleveland: A Study in Courage.* New York, 1941.

————. *Henry White.* New York, 1930.

Oberholtzer, E. P. *History of the United States since the Civil War.* 4 vols. New York, 1917–37.

Perkins, Dexter. *A History of the Monroe Doctrine.* Boston, 1955.

Pike, F. B. *Chile and the United States: 1880–1962.* South Bend, Ind., 1963.

Poter, E. B. (ed.). *The United States and World Sea Power.* Englewood Cliffs, N. J., 1955.

————, and C. W. Nimitz, (eds.). *Sea Power: A Naval History.* Englewood Cliffs, N. J., 1961.

Pratt, Fletcher. *The Compact History of the United States Navy.* New York, 1951.
Pratt, J. W. *A History of United States Foreign Policy.* Englewood Cliffs, N. J., 1955.
————. *Expansionists of 1898.* New York, 1951.
Pringle, Henry. *Theodore Roosevelt.* New York, 1956.
Puleston, W. D. *The Life and Works of Captain Alfred Thayer Mahan.* New Haven, Conn., 1939.
Remey, C. M. *The Life and Letters of Captain George C. Remey.* Washington, D. C., 1937.
Richardson, L. B. *William E. Chandler, Republican.* New York, 1940.
Roll, Charles. *Colonel Dick Thompson.* Indianapolis, 1948.
Sievers, H. J. *Benjamin Harrison.* 2 vols. Chicago, 1952–54.
Sprout, Harold, and Margaret. *The Rise of American Naval Power: 1776–1918.* Princeton, N. J., 1946.
Tansill, C. C. *The Purchase of the Danish West Indies.* Baltimore, 1932.
Taylor, C. C. *Mahan, Alfred Thayer: 1840–1914.* New York, 1920.
Tyler, A. F. *The Foreign Policy of James G. Blaine.* Minneapolis, 1927.
Volwiler, Albert T. (ed.). *The Correspondence between Benjamin Harrison and James G. Blaine.* Philadelphia, 1940.
Weems, J. E. *The Fate of the Maine.* New York, 1948.
Weinberg, A. K. *Manifest Destiny: A Study of National Expansion.* Baltimore, 1935.
Welles, Sumner. *Naboth's Vineyard.* 2 vols. New York, 1928.
West, R. S., Jr. *Admirals of American Empire.* Indianapolis, 1948.
————. *Mr. Lincoln's Navy.* New York, 1957.
————. *Gideon Welles: Lincoln's Navy Department.* Indianapolis, 1943.
White, Leonard. *The Republican Era: 1869–1901.* New York, 1958.
Wilson, H. W. *Battleships in Action.* 2 vols. New York, 1928.
————. *The Downfall of Spain.* London, 1900.
Wisan, J. E. *The Cuban Crisis as Reflected in the New York Press.* New York, 1934.
Younger, Edward. *John A. Kasson.* Iowa City, 1955.

Recent Articles

Bailey, T. A. "America's Emergence as a World Power: The Myth and the Verity," *Pacific Historical Review,* XXX (February, 1961), 8ff.
Blake, N. M. "Background of Cleveland's Venezuelan Policy," *American Historical Review.* XLVII (1942), 259ff.
Butler, John. "General Board of the Navy," U. S. Naval Institute *Proceedings,* LXVI (1930), 18ff.
Campbell, C. S. "The Anglo–American Crisis in the Bering Sea," *Mississippi Valley Historical Review,* XLVII (1961), 393ff.
Hardy, Osgood. "The Itata Incident," *Hispanic–American Historical Review,* V (May, 1922), 195ff.
————. "Was Patrick Egan a Blundering Minister?" *Hispanic–American Historical Review,* VIII (February, 1928), 65ff.
Hunt, Livingston. "Founder of the New Navy," U. S. Naval Institute *Proceedings,* XXXI (1905), 33ff.

Mahon, J. K. "Benjamin Franklin Tracy, Secretary of the Navy," New York Historical Society *Quarterly*, XLIV (April, 1960), 179ff.

Meadows, Martin. "Eugene Hale and the American Navy," *American Neptune* (July, 1962), 187ff.

Paullin, C. O. "A Half-Century of Naval Administration in America," U. S. Naval Institute *Proceedings*, XL (1914), 21ff.

Pratt, J. W. "American Business and the Spanish–American War," *Hispanic-American Historical Review*, XIV (May, 1934), 163ff.

Seager, Robert. "Ten Years before Mahan: The Unofficial Case for the New Navy, 1880–1890," *Mississippi Valley Historical Review*, XL (December, 1935), 497ff.

Vevier, Charles. "American Continentalism: An Idea of Expansion," *American Historical Review*, LXV (January, 1960), 323ff.

Volwiler, A. T. "Harrison, Blaine and American Foreign Policy," American Philosophical Society *Proceedings*, LXXIX (1938), 637ff.

Worcester, D. E. "Naval Strategy in the War of the Pacific," *Journal of Inter-American Studies*, V (January, 1963), 37ff.

Reference works

Fitch, C. E. *Encyclopedia of Biography of New York.* New York, 1916.

Malone, Dumas, and Allen Johnson, (eds.). *Dictionary of American Biography.* 20 vols. New York, 1946.

Moore, John B. *A Digest of International Law.* 2 vols. New York, 1906.

New York County Lawyers' Association. *Year Book.* New York, 1916.

White, J. T. (ed.). *National Cyclopaedia of American Biography.* 6 vols. New York, 1888–93.

Unpublished Material

Allard, Dean. "The Influence of the U. S. Navy upon the American Steel Industry, 1880–1900." M.A. thesis, Georgetown University, 1959.

Bastert, R. H. "James G. Blaine and the Origins of the First International Conference of American States." Ph.D. dissertation, Yale University, 1952.

Eure, L. T. "History of Military Colleges." Unpublished article, Naval War College Library.

Herrick, W. R. "General Tracy's Navy." Ph.D. dissertation, University of Virginia, 1962.

————. "The Naval Policy of Theodore Roosevelt." M.A. thesis, Columbia University, 1959.

Luce, Stephen B. Unpublished address delivered at the opening of the Naval War College, 1886. Naval War College Library.

Mahan, Alfred T. "Reminiscences of the War College," unpublished typescript, undated, Naval War College Library.

Smith, Russell. "Robert W. Schufeldt." M.A. thesis, University of Virginia, 1956.

Periodicals

American Historical Review, 1939–65.
The American Neptune, 1962.
Army and Navy Journal, 1886–98.

Army and Navy Register, 1889–92.
Atlantic Monthly, 1889–97.
The Bookman, 1889–90.
Century Magazine, 1889–99.
The Chatauquan, 1890
The Epoch, 1889–91.
The Forum, 1889–98.
Harper's Magazine, 1889–99.
Harper's Weekly, 1890.
Hispanic–American Historical Review, 1922, 1928.
The Independent, 1892–93.
Journal of Inter-American Studies, 1963.
Journal of the Iron and Steel Institute, 1881.
Literary Digest, 1884–98.
Mississippi Valley Historical Review, 1958–64.
The Nation, 1885, 1887, 1889–98.
New York Historical Society Quarterly, 1960.
North American Review, 1888–97.
Pacific Historical Review, 1961.
Political Science Quarterly, 1893.
Review of Reviews, 1893–96.
U. S. Naval Institute *Proceedings*, 1874–1930.

Newspapers

Baltimore *American*, 1891.
———— *Morning Herald*, 1890.
———— *Sun*, 1890, 1898.
Binghamton (N. Y.) *Call*, 1892.
———— *Republican*, 1889–93.
Birmingham *Age-Herald*, 1893.
Boston *Herald*, 1890–95.
———— *Journal*, 1892.
———— *Transcript*, 1890–92, 1895–98.
Brooklyn *Daily Eagle*, 1889–97, 1908.
———— *Daily Standard-Union*, 1892.
———— *Daily Times*, 1889–94.
Chicago *Daily News*, 1898.
———— *Inter-Ocean*, 1891.
———— *Times-Herald*, 1898.
———— *Tribune*, 1890.
Cleveland *Plain Dealer*, 1898.
Indianapolis *Journal*, 1890–91.
London *Daily Mail*, 1898.
———— *Times*, 1891.
Los Angeles *Times*, 1891.
Louisville *Courier-Journal*, 1889.
New York *Commercial Advertiser*, 1893, 1897–98.
———— *Daily Mercury*, 1898.

————— *Evening Post*, 1889-98.
————— *Evening Telegraph*, 1892.
————— *Frank Leslie's Illustrated Newspaper*, 1890.
————— *Herald*, 1875, 1889–99.
————— *Journal*, 1897–98.
————— *Journal of Commerce*, 1897–98.
————— *Mail and Express*, 1889.
————— *Morning Advertiser*, 1892.
————— *Recorder*, 1891–93.
————— *The Seaboard*, 1889–90.
————— *Sun*, 1889–98, 1908.
————— *Times*, 1889–98, 1904.
————— *Tribune*, 1889–98.
————— *World*, 1890–92, 1897–98.
Norfolk (Va.) *The Landmark*, 1890.
Norwich (Conn.) *Weekly Courier*, 1898.
Pensacola (Fla.) *Daily News*, 1893.
Philadelphia *Bulletin*, 1889.
————— *Evening Telegram*, 1893.
————— *Inquirer*, 1892–93.
————— *Press*, 1889–93.
————— *Public Ledger and Daily Trinscript*, 1892.
Pittsburgh *Press*, 1898.
Portland (Ore.) *Oregonian*, 1893.
Portsmouth (N. H.) *Daily Chronicle*, 1892.
Rochester (N. Y.) *Post-Express*, 1893.
St. Louis *Globe-Democrat*, 1890.
————— *Post-Dispatch*, 1893.
————— *Republic*, 1889–97.
San Francisco *Call*, 1891–92, 1898.
————— *Daily Evening Bulletin*, 1889–94.
Toronto *Globe*, 1892.
Trenton (N. J.) *Daily State Gazette*, 1890.
Troy (N. Y.) *Daily Press*, 1893–96.
————— *Daily Times*, 1893.
Utica (N. Y.) *Press*, 1892.
Washington *Evening Star*, 1891–93, 1898.
————— *Post*, 1891.
————— *Sentinel*, 1893-95, 1898.

Oral Interviews

Mrs. Frederic C. Condert, granddaughter of Benjamin F. Tracy, at her residence, 37 East 64th Street, New York City, April 14, 1960.

INDEX